The Ripper Inside Us

ALSO BY REBECCA FROST

Surviving Stephen King: Reactions to the Supernatural in Works by the Master of Horror (McFarland, 2021)

Media and the Murderer: Jack the Ripper, Steven Avery and an Enduring Formula for Notoriety (Exposit, 2020)

Words of a Monster: Analyzing the Writings of H.H. Holmes, America's First Serial Killer (Exposit, 2019)

The Ripper's Victims in Print: The Rhetoric of Portrayals Since 1929 (McFarland, 2018)

The Ripper Inside Us
What Interpretations of Jack Reveal About Ourselves

REBECCA FROST

McFarland & Company, Inc., Publishers
Jefferson, North Carolina

LIBRARY OF CONGRESS CATALOGUING-IN-PUBLICATION DATA

Names: Frost, Rebecca, 1985– author.
Title: The Ripper inside us : what interpretations of Jack reveal about ourselves / Rebecca Frost.
Description: Jefferson, North Carolina : McFarland & Company, Inc., Publishers, 2024 | Includes bibliographical references and index.
Identifiers: LCCN 2024008778 | ISBN 9781476692722 (paperback : acid free paper) ∞
ISBN 9781476652566 (ebook)
Subjects: LCSH: Jack, the Ripper. | Jack, the Ripper—In mass media. | Serial murderers—England—London—History—19th century. | Criminal psychology.
Classification: LCC HV6535.G6 L63648 2024 | DDC 364.152/32—dc23/eng/20240317
LC record available at https://lccn.loc.gov/2024008778

BRITISH LIBRARY CATALOGUING DATA ARE AVAILABLE

ISBN (print) 978-1-4766-9272-2
ISBN (ebook) 978-1-4766-5256-6

© 2024 Rebecca Frost. All rights reserved

No part of this book may be reproduced or transmitted in any form or by any means, electronic or mechanical, including photocopying or recording, or by any information storage and retrieval system, without permission in writing from the publisher.

Front cover images: © Spectr Design/guidopiano/Shutterstock

Printed in the United States of America

McFarland & Company, Inc., Publishers
  Box 611, Jefferson, North Carolina 28640
    www.mcfarlandpub.com

To everyone who knows about the mystery shoe.
We've been through a lot together.

Acknowledgments

I would like to thank Hallie Rubenhold for our conversations about the Ripper (and zombies); Katrina Jan for our discussions of all things bloody, Gothic, and darkly romantic; and my new colleagues and students for the support, questions, and energy that remind me why this work matters.

Thank you to my ever-encouraging constant supporters: Angela Badke, Tom Blessing, Zach Blessing, Isaac Flint, Stephanie Flint, Colleen Hix, Rae Hix, Jesse Koenig, Angela Musser, and Michelle Wright-Blessing.

And, of course, thank you to my parents, who have resigned themselves to telling people their daughter knows far too much about serial killers, and Eric, who smiles and nods his way through many of my monologues and always gives me a thumbs-up at the end.

Table of Contents

Acknowledgments vi
Introduction: The Fact of a Crime 1

1. Sketching the Ripper, 1888   21
2. The Changing of the Guard   42
3. Fit to Print   57
4. The New Experts   77
5. Lights, Camera ... Murder   91
6. Once Upon a Time   101
7. Reach Out and Touch Someone   119
8. Raised Voices   135
9. I'm No Expert, But...   143

Conclusion: Connect the Dots 161
Chapter Notes 181
Bibliography 189
Index 195

Introduction:
The Fact of a Crime

This is not a book to increase your knowledge about the historical figure known as Jack the Ripper. There will be no answer to the mystery of his identity, and no new facts—or "facts"—revealed. This is not a book about him at all, but, rather, a book about us.

People the world over like telling stories. We use narratives not only to pass the time, but also to tell about time. When something interesting happens, we want to share it, and the only way we can relate a series of events is through a narrative. By telling events, we turn them from individual actions into a story, with connections, causations, and even endings. We like our stories to be neatly packaged and contained so that they make sense and leave us feeling as though a resolution has occurred.

This applies even in the genre now commonly known as true crime. Although news media might publish daily updates in unfolding cases, true crime books are largely not published until after a trial and a verdict. The Ripper murders are a rare exception.

More than 100 books have been published about the murderer known most concretely as "Jack the Ripper." He—or she, or they—has been given numerous other names in the more than 130 years since the Autumn of Terror in the fall of 1888 as various people have proposed their theories of the identity of the person who killed five—or fewer, or maybe more—women in London's East End.

The continuing mystery is in large part responsible for the Ripper's popularity. As information is (claimed to be) uncovered, authors can put forth a case for a new suspect, or a new, apparently more solid case for a previously-named suspect. Arguments are made over whether the Ripper did indeed kill all five "Canonical" victims, or if others should be added before or after them. Witness testimony is likewise up for interpretation as authors choose to include, ignore, or temper it. When the sealed files were opened almost a century after the murders, much of the documentation was discovered to be missing, leading to continued reliance on newspaper reports of the events. The only certainty of the case is that, in the twenty-first century, the murderer is dead and authors will not be making accusations against the living.

This is another aspect of the Ripper case that allows it to hold such fascination without forcing readers to confront uncertainty while engaging with it: the killer cannot harm them. This is not a case unfolding right now, where he might be lurking outside a reader's house in the bushes and waiting to strike. These murders happened in the long-ago Victorian era, which none of us has experienced firsthand. Even current tours of the murder sites direct visitors to gaze upon places where buildings used to stand, since progress has reshaped the landscape.

Rather than fade into history, however, the Ripper continues to maintain a hold over public fascination. What began in Victorian newspapers has expanded not just to books, but also to movies, documentaries, television shows, graphic novels, and souvenirs. The Ripper Museum and myriad Ripper tours invite tourists to learn about the murders, but to have fun doing it. *They*, of course, are safe, but the mystery still remains: who was Jack the Ripper?

The East End

Although panic during the Autumn of Terror spread to all of London and beyond, the murders themselves were confined to a small geographical area. Of the Canonical Five Ripper victims, four were murdered in Whitechapel while one, Catherine Eddowes, was murdered within the square mile of the City of London itself. They are in fact close enough together that walking tours of the murder sites abound (see Chapter 7). The Ripper murders are not just bounded by a short timeline—ten weeks for the Canonical Five—but by such a small physical area. The Ripper is nearly (see Chapter 5) inextricable from London's East End.

Even in 1888, newspapers had to educate their readers about conditions in the East End, a tradition carried on by many more recent narratives. Therefore we learn that the "East End is the last refuge of human wrecks,"[1] "a human cauldron of the marginalised,"[2] and "a distant land, an alien planet, a world apart."[3] Although outsiders may have ventured in to assist with social services or for adventurous "slumming" (see Chapter 1), these interactions between the East Enders and outsiders and the reports made by these outsiders often failed to truly bridge the gap. It was difficult for other Victorians to understand life in Whitechapel, and today we are even further removed.

Although Whitechapel is home to the London Hospital, its location by the Thames also meant that it housed some of the more polluting trades such as tanneries, slaughterhouses, and cloth work including weaving and dying. By the end of the nineteenth century, it was also known for poverty. Charles Booth's 1889 map of the area[4] included some sections labeled "middle class," but others marked as "chronic poor" and, the lowest rating, "semi-criminal." William Booth's charitable work in the area led to the founding of the Salvation Army in 1878 and other volunteers, many associated with the church, worked to provide services to the poor. Much of this work focused on presumed moral failings, such as alcoholism, and strove to teach East Enders the ways of proper Christian living. A good number of these attempts were foiled by the extreme poverty and dismal living conditions of the area. For example, many families shared a single room for all of them, or shared it with another family, and "on almost every corner a public house offered a respite from reality"[5] that countless people desperately needed. A lack of private space and a lack of steady labor went hand in hand, as did a lack of access to clean water, and daily survival took precedence over following the word of the Lord.

The Victorian East End was also home to a number of immigrants, many of them Irish and Jewish. On top of this, in early 1888 the police estimated it was also home to 1,200 sex workers and sixty-two brothels,[6] although others have argued that they lowballed their estimate by a factor of ten or even one hundred. In short, "[t]he East End embodied the fears of the late-nineteenth-century Londoner as no other place on earth could,"[7] and this was even before the murders began. Then again, the Ripper murders only made such headlines because of their brutality—murder was common in the East End and so unremarkable that citizens would ignore it if anyone shouted the word in the street.

Many living in the East End were unhoused. They had three choices: sleeping in the streets, queuing up with hopes of getting into a workhouse, or paying for a bed in a doss house. Workhouses carefully screened inmates to ensure they had no money—and no alcohol—in their possession before passing them on to a medical screening and then separating inmates, even families, by gender. They were usually forced to surrender their personal possessions for the length of their stay, bathe in a tub that others had used before them, and wear items provided by the workhouse. Inmates slept on cots in large rooms and spent their days doing assigned work according to their gender. Generally women's assigned work was easier and less physical than men's, a consideration undertaken by at least one of the Canonical Five: Catherine Eddowes and her boyfriend John Kelly slept separately prior to her murder since they only had enough money to pay for a single bed, so Eddowes chose the workhouse and gave Kelly the money.

A doss house was frequently owned by someone who had never set foot in it, much less in the East End, and run by a deputy whose job it was to oust those who could not pay for the night. Some doss houses only allowed a single gender, while others had double beds and allowed men and women to share them. A single bed generally ran the rate of four pence a night, to be paid daily by the deadline after which anyone who could not pay was turned out onto the street—an event that took place with three of the Canonical Five victims. Unlike workhouses, which did feed their inmates, doss houses held kitchens where residents could warm themselves and cook food they brought, but did not offer any food for sale. Those who did not have four pence for a single bed might, if they were lucky, pay two pence instead for a "line": a rope strung across the room against which they could lean, often on a bench packed between strangers. As uncomfortable or unsanitary as doss houses were, they at least kept people off the street at night, a growing concern as the Autumn of Terror wore on.

Many residents of the East End did not have reliable work and would rise early to queue at places where day labor was offered, such as the docks. Women, it was assumed, resorted to "casual" sex work to make ends meet, diminishing the act of being forced to sell sex in order to stay alive. In general, sex workers were considered to be "oversexed" women who craved the act far more than was natural and, once having engaged in sex outside of marriage, were "fallen" women with no hope of redemption. This did, however, allow a Victorian husband to find a loophole: although he was expected to still be monetarily responsible for an estranged wife, if he could argue that she was a sex worker or living with another man, then his responsibility—if not the marriage itself—ceased. Otherwise the state could be called in to deal with husbands who did not support their wives and forced those wives to rely on other, state-provided handouts.

These conditions of overpopulation and want "resulted in intense public scrutiny and an ever-expanding network of public and private reform organizations which battled to control and domesticate the influx of this massive immigration"[8] even before the Autumn of Terror, but the Ripper murders and resulting media expanded the circle of those engaging in social critique and suggestions for reform. In fact, at times the Ripper is presented as a social reformer himself and almost praised for increasing the scrutiny of such an impoverished area and its people. This is a rather naïve approach to a figure who killed "at least four, probably six, [and] just possibly eight"[9] people in such a way as to capture newspaper headlines then and our imaginations ever since. Indeed, when Patricia Cornwell writes in 2017 that the Ripper's "butcheries no longer inspire fright, rage or even pity,"[10] it seems she hardly needs the modifier "no longer." Although the killer himself remains an object of fascination, "his victims are usually just referred to as prostitutes,"[11] demoted from human beings to corpses with evidence that can point to the killer. (Note that while "prostitute" is the contemporary term and the one most frequently used to refer to the presumed profession of these murdered women, it is now outdated. "Sex worker" is the preferred language at the time of this writing.)

It is within these geographical, social, cultural, and narrative bounds that we encounter the women murdered by Jack the Ripper. Although the narrative has continued on long after their deaths, their names are still mentioned and still known, even if very little about them can be conclusively stated as truth. It is that lack of solid biography that has allowed so many to speculate about the identity of the man who killed them, because their lives, along with the chosen killer's, can be molded to fit most any theory.

The Canonical Five

Because the Whitechapel Murderer was never caught, it has never been confirmed exactly how many people he—or she, or they—killed. Even the newspapers at the time started connecting current murders with previously-reported ones, even if those previous reports were in fact not true. In order to tackle this uncertainty, we refer to the most likely victims of the Ripper as "the Canonical Five," a group that includes Mary Ann "Polly" Nichols, Annie Chapman, Elizabeth Stride, Catherine Eddowes, and Mary Jane Kelly. Given these restrictions, the Ripper murders began on August 31, 1888, and ended on November 9 of that same year.

Most of the known facts about the Canonical Five women murdered by Jack the Ripper center on the discoveries of the murdered women's bodies, but not on the women themselves. Some of them had living husbands, boyfriends, or family members who could recall their histories, but many of them have also been accused of improving their backstories or making them up wholesale. Because these women were living in the poor East End and only one had a fixed address, they were generally overlooked during this period of their lives or looked down upon if anyone chose to notice them. Otherwise they were just part of the masses, dismissed as sex workers who had left their husbands, children, and the only stability the Victorian era offered women: their roles as wives and mothers.

Because these women only caught media attention after their murders, everything written about them had to come from the survivors who knew, or claimed to know, them. The information that has been passed down and repeated in various narratives comes from coroners' reports and the newspapers. Much of it has been accepted as truth whether or not the information was corroborated by other people or other sources. After all, why would surviving family members willingly speak ill of the dead?

Mary Ann "Polly" Nichols, the first of the Canonical Five, was found early in the morning of August 31, 1888, in front of a gate on Buck's Row. The man who found her, Charles Allen Cross, was on his way to work. He called over another man who was also heading to work and the two of them disagreed over whether Nichols was dead or in a drunken stupor. They were both afraid of being late for work and left to inform the first policeman they saw, although another reached Nichols' body first and, with the aid of his lantern, saw that her throat had been cut. They sent for a doctor who gave Nichols a cursory inspection and declared she was dead and should be moved to the mortuary. It was only there, after workers started undressing Nichols' body, that they realized she had more wounds than just to her throat.

Although a murdered woman, like a woman so drunk as to be passed out on the street at all hours, was not out of the ordinary for the East End, these further mutilations were part of what made the Autumn of Terror. There were no organs missing from Nichols' body—a fact that took on more importance as the season wore on—but her abdomen and genitals had been attacked with a knife in such a way that it was embarrassing for Dr. Llewellyn not to have noticed during his initial cursory inspection. Her wounds as well as her belongings were documented, and it was a laundry mark in her petticoats that pointed them toward Lambeth Workhouse.[12] Although the matron could not identify her, another inmate indicated that the deceased was Polly Nichols.

In one of the most oft-repeated quotes of these murders, Polly's estranged husband, William, came to identify his wife's body and said, "I forgive you, as you are, for what you have been to me."[13] This newspaper-worthy lament has been frequently interpreted to mean that he forgave his estranged wife for leaving the family and becoming a sex worker since she had, at one point, been a loving wife and mother. During the inquest, however, William Nichols reported that his wife left because of her alcoholism. Polly Nichols was therefore branded not only a sex worker but also an alcoholic, both considered dire moral failings in the Victorian era. William Nichols had earlier testified that his wife was living with another man, and his testimony was taken as further support of his estranged wife's new occupation. Only recently has it been emphasized that a man in his position would tell such a lie in order to legally end his responsibility to his wife and be able to stop maintenance payments for her upkeep.[14] It is important to note that this additional insight into social and legal norms of the late nineteenth century have only recently been highlighted, and that Polly Nichols has spent more than a century after her death being an alcoholic sex worker who stumbled heedlessly into her own violent death.

This was a story that took hold and became quickly repeated with the discovery of another murdered woman. Annie Chapman's body was discovered in the backyard of 29 Hanbury Street, also in the early morning. A resident of the house noticed an open door and went to investigate. This was the first sign that anything was wrong since, although the house was occupied by multiple residents on various floors, no one heard a struggle. Chapman's abdominal mutilations were clearly visible since the murderer took the time to remove various organs, strewing some over her body and taking parts of her uterus and bladder with him. A wet leather apron was also found in the yard, sparking a frenzy because a man with the nickname Leather Apron had already been identified as a possible suspect in Nichols' murder. That man—real name John Pizer—was cleared of suspicion, as further discussed in Chapter 1, because he had an alibi for both murders, which were quickly connected. Whoever murdered and mutilated Polly Nichols was immediately determined to be the same man who murdered Annie Chapman.

Out of the Canonical Five, Chapman is the woman to historically receive the most sympathy. Although she, too, left her husband and children, it was a mutual separation due to the death of one of their children, and her husband kept up maintenance payments until his death in 1886. Unlike William Nichols, John Chapman did not resist supporting his wife, even though it was reported that Annie lived with another man at the time. That man seems to have left her once the payments stopped, once again forcing her to strike out on her own.

Unlike the other women, Chapman's sex work is frequently framed as a move out of desperation rather than an apparent "easy" answer. Narratives emphasize that she engaged in selling handicrafts and flowers in order to pay for her bed. Further, it seems that Chapman engaged in serial monogamy—or might she have had two men paying for her bed at the same time?—and attempted in some ways to uphold Victorian morals despite her situation. While she told others that her husband used to work for a nobleman, however, many of these same narratives sadly lament her pretensions and attempt to make herself look more presentable than she really was. It is one of Rubenhold's contentions that John Chapman really did hold such a position.[15]

Like Polly Nichols, Annie Chapman was said to have been an alcoholic. Unlike Nichols, Chapman is frequently given a pass for this apparent weakness because of the physical disability of one of her children and the early death of another. Her married life fell apart through no fault of her own and it is understandable that a mother might turn to drink in the wake of such tragedy, and that both parents might agree to part but stay on good terms. The marriage of John and Annie Chapman, unlike that of William and Polly Nichols, dissolved mutually and without one-sided blame, leaving Annie on the street. On the night of her murder something seemed off about her, and although early reports indicated that she was drunk when she crossed paths with the Ripper, others quickly pointed out that she had spent time recently in the hospital and was likely ill. Chapman had no money for a bed because she had been in the hospital and unable to work and not because she drank it all away. During her autopsy, Dr. George Bagster Phillips discovered evidence that Chapman was very ill indeed and would likely have died soon from advanced lung disease if she had not been murdered.[16]

The next two of the Canonical Five victims, Elizabeth Stride and Catherine Eddowes, both died on September 30. Liz Stride was the only one of the Five to be a foreigner, born and raised in Sweden. While still in her home country she was officially registered as a sex worker, providing documentation through arrest records and hospital records to support that, at least during her youth, she did indeed engage in sex work. Stride came to England in 1866 and married John Thomas Stride in 1869. However, records show she was admitted to a workhouse in 1877, suggesting that their marriage had dissolved by that time. Stride herself was not considered a viable source for information about her past, since she told friends that she lost her husband and two of their nine children during the sinking of the pleasure craft the *Princess Alice* in 1878. However, John Thomas Stride had died in 1884 and there was no record that the couple had any children.

At the time of her death, Stride worked as a charwoman and had a volatile on-again, off-again relationship with a dock laborer named Michael Kidney. That relationship was off-again at the end of September, although witnesses who say they saw Stride shortly before her death reported seeing her in a conversation with, in a fight with, or accosted by a man who may or may not have been Kidney. What sets Stride apart from the other four Canonical victims, aside from being Swedish, is the fact that only her throat was cut and no other mutilations were performed. One argument is that, since Kidney was the murderer, he would not have undertaken any further mutilations even if given the time. The other is that the Ripper was interrupted in Dutfield's Yard after he had cut Stride's throat, but before he could continue with the rest of his process. A man returning to the nearby International Working Men's Educational Club noticed his horse shying away from something and discovered it was Stride's body, still warm, with the blood flowing from her neck.

If this was the work of the Ripper, he was not satisfied, because it was less than an hour later that Catherine Eddowes was found murdered in nearby Mitre Square. While Stride died from a cut throat and had no other injuries, Eddowes' body was the most mutilated so far, despite the fact that a policeman's steady beat took him past the square every fourteen minutes. The Ripper either planned the crime well or was once again lucky since PC Edward Watkins passed an empty square and then, upon his return, found Eddowes' mutilated body. Her injuries were not confined to her throat and her abdomen, but also covered her face, and she was missing a kidney. Eddowes' long-term boyfriend, John Kelly, was part of the crowd visiting Mitre Square the following day to see the location and attempt to catch sight of any remaining blood, because he was told that Eddowes had been locked up for being drunk and disorderly. While this was true—although it has never been explained how Eddowes and Kelly could have parted on the morning of the 29th penniless, but she managed to buy enough alcohol to be falling-down drunk that evening—Eddowes was released from police custody at 1 a.m. only to be found dead forty-four minutes later.

Of the Canonical Five, Eddowes had the most possessions on her at the time of her death, indicating that she had no permanent address and nowhere to keep her belongings. Reports at the inquest indicated that she and Kelly were living hand to mouth, having had a lackluster hop-picking experience that led to Eddowes' pawning Kelly's boots so he could have enough money to pay for a lodging-house bed. Eddowes was meant to have spent her last day visiting her daughter to ask for money, but it came out during the inquest that her daughter had moved with no forwarding address to prevent Eddowes from once again doing just that. Even Eddowes' previous common-law husband, the father of her three children, seemed to have changed his name to keep her from finding him. Later investigation suggests that Thomas Conway had been using a fake name for his own purposes long before he parted from Eddowes, but the picture painted was of a woman very down on her luck and in desperate need of money—so desperate that she would indeed sell sex, despite Kelly's protests that this was not true.

After the night that was quickly dubbed the Double Event, there was a long pause in the violence, but the story continued to grow. Up until this point, the killer was called the Whitechapel Killer or the Whitechapel Knife. Four of the five Canonical victims never heard him called by another name. "Jack the Ripper" was the signature in a letter received by the Central News Agency—not the police—on September 27, 1888. Although it was forwarded to Scotland Yard two days later, it was ignored until after the Double Event seemed to prove some of its predictions true. The contents of the letter, including the Jack the Ripper name, were spread far and wide, and the police reproduced the letter on large placards in the hopes that someone might recognize the handwriting. These actions did not help identify the killer, but they did start a frenzy of new letters purporting to be from the killer and now generally using the headline-making name.

This timing means that, of the Canonical Five victims, only the fifth, Mary Jane Kelly, would have known the killer as Jack the Ripper. At her death inquest, her estranged boyfriend Joseph Barnett said that he had even read to Kelly newspaper articles concerning the murders. In fact, the reason Barnett left Kelly alone in the small room at 13 Miller's Court was because she allowed another woman to stay with them in the tiny space so that she would not be out on the streets as a possible next victim.

Kelly's body was discovered on November 9, 1888, when her landlord sent someone to try to collect some of her outstanding payments. Likely because Kelly had this rented room and the killer was able to shut a door between himself and the outside world, her body was the most mutilated. The Ripper had more than fourteen minutes within that small room, and that same door that allowed him such privacy also meant the police could secure the scene long enough to fetch a camera. There were police sketches of Catherine Eddowes in Mitre Square, but there are police photos of 13 Miller's Court and, since their public release, they have been included in nearly every book about the Ripper murders, ostensibly for educational purposes while really for shock value.

It is unclear exactly how long the Ripper spent in Kelly's room, based on conflicting reports of those who saw Kelly or heard her singing, and this, combined with the extensive mutilation of her body—Barnett is said to have identified her by "ear and eyes,"[17] which has been speculated to be a misprint of "hair and eyes"—and an almost complete lack of background information on Kelly has played into so many theories about the Ripper's motive. Aside from being killed indoors, Kelly stands apart from the other women by being much younger and universally acknowledged as having been pretty, although reports differ greatly about whether this means she was thin or stout or even what color her recognizable hair was.

As the last of the Canonical Five, Kelly also holds an important narrative place in the murders simply because she is qualified as last. If narratives accept the number of victims as five, or only extend that number to murders prior to Nichols,' then there needs to be an explanation for why the killer, who seemed to be accelerating, suddenly stopped. One popular theory was that the Ripper killed himself shortly after November 9, which has led to accusations being leveled against people who died then without any other connection to the crimes.

Other explanations focus on Mary Jane Kelly as either the true target of the Ripper or the final victim in a line of targets leading to her. All that we think we know about Kelly comes through what Barnett reported during the inquest, since she had no known relatives, friends, or prior relationships coming forward to speak about her. The story Barnett told is on par with Stride's use of the *Princess Alice* to gain sympathy, since hardly any of it can be confirmed. Kelly told Barnett a story of her past that included going to France with "a gentleman," deciding she did not like it there, and returning home alone—a difficult tale to grasp, since it would mean leaving the security inherent in such a relationship and seems to coincide with her arrival in the East End. If she went from the arm of "a gentleman" to the poorest part of London, it was a quick and fatal trip. Because of this lack of corroborating evidence, Kelly's history is the most confusing and the most malleable of the Canonical Five and she, above the others, tends to take on a central and at times incriminating role in the Ripper narrative.

Beyond the Canonical Five

Although Ripper narratives are all but required to address the murders of the Canonical Five, they were clearly not the only murders to occur in the East End during 1888. Some narratives argue that the Ripper did not in fact murder all five, while others seek to expand the number of victims. However, Ripper murders have long been troubled by confusion in the press and a lack of evidence supporting some of the reported cases of murder. One such example is that of a woman known only as "Fairy Fay," who was supposedly murdered on December 26, 1887, and who would have been perhaps the earliest Ripper victim. She is said to have been found in a doorway "after a stake had been thrust through her abdomen."[18] Since the Ripper was known to later engage in abdominal mutilations and had killed women in the same area, Fairy Fay was added to the possible victim list although there were no murders recorded in Whitechapel around Christmas that year. Although Fairy Fay has been used in the past to boost the Ripper's victim count, she is generally dismissed as a creation of the press.

Emma Elizabeth Smith, however, was a real woman who died on April 4, 1888, after a brutal attack. This attack occurred on April 3, which was the day after the Easter Monday bank holiday—many of the Canonical attacks happened on or around bank holidays—but managed to walk back to her lodging house afterward. Smith was then taken to the London Hospital, where she slipped into a coma and died the next day, although not before she reported that she had been attacked by two or three men.

Smith either could not, or refused to, describe the men in detail, and no one came forward to report being a witness to the attack. She is commonly described as being a sex worker, and her attackers are generally theorized to be either part of a roving gang who attacked sex workers and stole their money, or perhaps men hired by her pimp for an act of intimidation or reprisal.[19] If Smith sold sex for a living, then she is easily put into the same category as the Canonical Five women who have historically, and continuously, been labeled "prostitutes" and said to have been attacked by the Ripper while out looking for clients. The nature of Smith's injuries, as well as her own report of being attacked by more than one man, seem to indicate that she was not, in fact, the Ripper's first victim.

Martha Tabram was the most likely candidate for the Ripper's first victim outside of the Canonical Five. She spent the night of August 6, 1888—the summer bank holiday—with her friend Mary Ann Connelly, who reported that the pair had split up to each go with a soldier to sell sex. While Connelly and her soldier went to an alley, Tabram was last seen going into George Yard with hers. Although she was seen by a tenant of the building around 3:30 in the morning on the seventh, it was known that the homeless regularly slept on the first-floor landing, so she was ignored. It was not until 5 a.m. that another tenant, leaving for work, realized that she was dead instead of drunk or sleeping.

She had been stabbed thirty-nine times in the throat and torso, including injuries to her lungs, heart, liver, spleen, stomach, and genitals. Although the physician declared that she had been killed between 2 and 3:30 that morning, the building's residents had heard nothing—yet another element of the narrative that would be repeated in future Ripper murders.

Multiple attempts were made to identify the soldiers who had gone with Tabram and Connelly that night. A police officer who had questioned a soldier waiting on the street for a friend who had "gone with a girl"[20] was unable to identify that soldier. Connelly first failed to show up for an inspection of the troops, then revealed she had been shown the wrong unit, selected men who had alibis, and finally could not narrow her selection to a single man. Although the coroner's inquest concluded that Tabram had been murdered, no one was ever accused of, or arrested for, her murder.

These earlier murders were included in the newspapers to sell more copies and have been included since in attempts to piece together the Ripper's "real" beginnings. We now believe that serial killers do not simply start as full-blown murderers, and that they likewise do not simply stop killing, either. When the FBI is faced with a case in which it seems the killer has suddenly stopped, they look for someone who has died, been incarcerated, or moved away. This is especially true in cases where the killer was escalating, murdering more frequently and more violently.

At least one Ripper suspect has been accused largely based on the fact that he died shortly after Mary Jane Kelly's murder, which would provide the explanation for why the murders suddenly stopped. Although others can argue that Kelly was only mutilated to such an extent because she was found indoors, while the other women were murdered outside where anyone could walk by and interrupt, there is still a notable increase in violence from Polly Nichols to Catherine Eddowes. There are also therefore some women who were thought, either at the time or in the decades since, to have been further Ripper victims.

Rose Mylett was found dead on December 20, 1888, although there were arguments about whether or not she had been murdered. The police argued that she had either accidentally suffocated on her collar while drunk or had completed suicide. Others believed that Mylett had been strangled due to the faint markings left on the side of her neck, since there were no knife wounds on her body. Although the death inquest resulted in a verdict of murder, no one was ever accused.

Alice McKenzie was murdered shortly after midnight on July 17, 1889, in Whitechapel with two stab wounds to the neck. There was another, superficial wound to her torso. Doctors who had examined victims of the Ripper were themselves divided[21] over whether McKenzie was another one, or if her murderer had attempted to imitate the Ripper murders to throw suspicion off himself.

A victim known only as "the Pinchin Street torso" was found

beneath a railway arch in Pinchin Street on September 10, 1889. There was extensive bruising on the torso, suggesting that the woman had been beaten prior to her death, and her abdomen was also mutilated. The Pinchin Street torso was reminiscent of "the Whitehall Mystery," a headless woman's torso found on October 2, 1888, in the basement of the new Metropolitan Police headquarters that was being built in Whitehall. An arm and shoulder were found floating in the Thames, and the left leg was also found near where the torso had been buried, but the other body parts were never recovered and the victim never identified. Both of these cases are frequently grouped together as victims of the "Torso Killer," who is unlikely to have been Jack the Ripper, but possibly claimed four victims of his own.

The final generally-suggested Ripper victim was Frances Coles, who was found on February 13, 1891. Her throat had been cut but there were no other injuries, reminiscent of Elizabeth Stride and giving rise to the theory that the Ripper had once again been disturbed at his work. Coles was still alive when a policeman discovered her, but died before a physician could arrive.[22] A man was identified as having been drinking, and then fighting, with Coles in the hours prior to her death. He was arrested and initially thought to have been the Ripper, but released for a lack of evidence.

In a case so full of questions as the Ripper murders, these earlier and later deaths can be ignored and dismissed if they do not fit someone's ideal suspect. Although the Canonical Five must be addressed, not even all of them have to be concluded to be "real" Ripper victims—indeed, Elizabeth Stride is often discounted and removed from the series due to the lack of mutilations that followed her murder. Despite this allowance for personal preference and the opportunity to pick and choose, much of this evidence must be included in any retelling of the story because so much information has been cemented by simple repetition.

Connecting the Dots

A Ripper narrative, then, has to address many of these points in order to "make sense" to readers. Even the books that argue canonical victim Elizabeth Stride was in fact murdered by someone who was not in fact the Ripper need to mention her name, as well as the reasoning behind this decision. Each of the Canonical Five victims should be not only discussed, but also examined for evidence that can point to the author's chosen Ripper. Descriptions of the crime scenes as well as the coroners' reports, any sketches or photographs of the victims' bodies, and lists of the belongings found on or near the women have been examined time and time again for clues about the person who killed them.

The most-examined moments of these women's lives are their final hours because it is generally agreed that we will not find the Ripper any earlier. He was a stranger. Once we have figured out the last time any of them were seen alive, we can narrow down the window during which they encountered their killer. Catherine Eddowes has the most compact of any such timeline, since she had to have met the Ripper after being released from custody, and her murder took place between circuits of PC Wilkins' beat.

Other victims were spotted by witnesses earlier that night in various locations, alone or with a man, whose presence has then led to various possible eyewitness descriptions of the murderer. Elizabeth Stride was reported to be with either one or two men, and George Hutchinson stood outside Mary Jane Kelly's room and reported watching her take a man inside with her. All of these various eyewitness descriptions have been examined, accepted, or dismissed in turn. Authors with a specific Ripper in mind are therefore more likely to believe the descriptions that align with their chosen suspect or to argue that, as their suspect was a trained stage actor, he was able to disguise himself in such a way as to match the description.

Dr. Thomas Bond is frequently credited with creating the first criminal profile in his contemporary assessment of Jack the Ripper, which was mirrored in 1988 at the hundredth anniversary of the murders by FBI Special Agent John Douglas, one of the founders of modern criminal profiling. Douglas even includes the Ripper in his 2000 book *The Cases That Haunt Us*. Much effort, both professional and amateur, has been spent on the Ripper case.

Many, but not all, of the men involved in the original investigation wrote about the Ripper in later years, either in their memoirs or in notes that have been awarded "Marginalia" or "Memorandum" status. The fact remains that any man taken into custody during the Autumn of Terror could be neither held nor charged with the murders. Theories were flying and the pressure they felt was immense, but the murders seemed to stop and the police file was sealed without an arrest. All the same, these memoirs and cryptic notes written by the men involved with the crimes, however tangentially, have likewise been examined, dissected, and decoded to support or reject various suspects.

Books have been published purely as encyclopedias of suspects, rating them on likelihood of having actually been the Ripper. Paul

Williams' 2018 book *Jack the Ripper Suspects: The Definitive Guide and Encyclopedia* covers 333 suspects. He attempts to organize them in an easy-to-assess manner, starting with those who were arrested on suspicion or accused during or after the murders and then moving on to other possibilities. Although his book is nearly 300 pages, fewer than fifty of those relate contemporary suspects, which just shows how much fascination with the crimes has continued to grow. If someone can be proved to have been alive in 1888 and anywhere near Whitechapel, it seems he—or she, or they—must be examined and under suspicion.

What we see here, though, in both these encyclopedic surveys and the hundreds of books about the case, is how many ways the recorded evidence can be interpreted. While much is known about some of the suspects, like Prince Albert Victor, Duke of Clarence and Avondale, whose life was carefully documented, other suspects of lower classes must be tracked through scant records. The holes in Prince Eddy's schedule must be found and carefully exploited in order to name him as a reasonable Ripper suspect, but others are largely blank slates themselves. Such blank spaces are where authors can rely on Mark Seltzer's observation that today's true crime is the practice of "writing by numbers"[23] and editing a strict template, filling in the blanks of their suspects' lives in the expected ways. After all, who would doubt that a child growing up in poverty in Victorian England could have abuse or absent parents in his past?

Presenting a new Ripper suspect is therefore not just about connecting the dots in the puzzle of the murder victims, but filling in the blanks when it comes to the suspect's story. It is almost easier to make a case for a man—or woman—history knows little about, because there is far less information to contradict assessments of background or character. Not only can the details of the murders, the Ripper letters, and the coroners' inquests be emphasized or ignored to fit a theory, but vast swatches of a suspect's life can be created from whole cloth as well. There are simply so many gaps when approaching the Ripper story that it is possible to accuse almost anyone, and nearly impossible to clear them of suspicion.

These gray areas are why the Ripper case makes such a unique Thematic Aptitude Test. Throughout the more than 130 years since the murders, various authors, coming from various societies and cultures, have attempted to make sense of the murders through a lens that makes their story comprehensible to their contemporaries. They ascribe not only an identity to the Ripper, but also motive, exploring not just how he committed these murders, but a full explanation of why. These narratives do not seek to satisfy purely the author alone, but to resonate with his audience. None of these stories were created in a vacuum. With the Ripper murders as a basic framework, authors draw not only on research but also on cultural myths and social norms to flesh out their narratives and make them not only worth telling, but also worth reading.

This, then, is what this book examines: how the various Jack the Ripper narratives reflect our social expectations back to us, showing us not the Ripper's internal motivations, but a reflection of our own culture—one which has now, in the twenty-first century, made quite a science of studying the serial killer.

Filling in the Blanks

Anyone who comes to the Ripper story today therefore does not come empty-handed, with nothing to work with but the name and likely scant facts of a chosen suspect. The murders themselves form at least five points in the timeline that must be addressed and somehow explained: why those women at those times? Why were some of them mutilated and others murdered without further injury? What made the Ripper start, and what then made him stop? Although authors can look for instigating or mitigating factors in their suspects' biographies, they are not left with absolute blanks.

Filling in the gaps in the timeline left by both the murders and any known facts about the chosen suspect is easier because of current popular and professional knowledge about serial killers in general. Writers prior to the 1980s had their own ideas and explanations for their accused Rippers, based on what made sense to them—and therefore society—at the time. More recently, the FBI and the Behavioral Analysis Unit have offered us a framework upon which serial killers both factual and fictional can be, and have been, built. While the police in 1888 seemed to have been confronting a criminal entirely new and strange, we now have generic expectations that make true crime follow Seltzer's formula of murder by numbers. There are expectations for what must have occurred in a violent criminal's childhood, as well as numerous possibilities for motive. As long as there is no concrete evidence that contradicts any of these aspects in the chosen suspect's biography, then authors can flesh out their narratives based on what feels right within the genre, given current cultural knowledge and opinions.

True crime as a genre, bolstered by the professional language and narratives published by the FBI, also outlines the ways victims should be presented, relying on what criminal justice professor Steven Egger has critiqued as the language surrounding the less-dead in order to uphold the generic function of reassuring audiences and presenting them with the restoration of order at the end of the narrative. The criminal is apprehended, however eventually, and his victims are largely presented as being no great loss to society, so clearly the system works and nothing needs to be done to change it. This is one area in which the Ripper narratives must confront the fact that no one was tried for the murders and no arrests panned out. Considering the fact that the Ripper was active during the Victorian era and the police were both relatively new and occupied a very different position than their late twentieth- and early twenty-first-century counterparts, their failure in this case can largely be excused.

This does not mean, however, that detectives both professional and armchair of the more recent decades might not be able to do what Chief Inspector Frederick Abberline and all the men of the London Metropolitan Police could not: identify the Ripper, if not once and for all, then at least for a full-length narrative. We have been trying to pin him down for years, changing our perceptions of the sort of person who could have committed these murders as we learn more about serial murder—and look more deeply at ourselves.

Chapter 1: Sketching the Ripper, 1888 takes us back to the information provided during the Autumn of Terror. We still have copies of contemporary newspapers, and they provide us not only with news about the murders, but also with the general public's response in the form of letters to the editor. Here is where the Ripper first began to take on form and develop according to current thought and prejudice surrounding violent murder. It is important to remember that, although the police and reading public in 1888 did not have access to current knowledge about serial killers, those of us today do not have access to all of the documentation produced during the murders, since much of it has gone missing.

Chapter 2: The Changing of the Guard addresses the vast changes and developments in both experts and their expertise since 1888. First, the men who worked one or more of the murders may have written their memoirs before they died, and some reflected back on the case from a distance of decades. Then the rise of the FBI and the creation of the Behavioral Science Unit—today called the Behavioral Analysis Unit—and psychological profiling shifted our understanding of such murderers while at the same time providing us with a basic backstory for such people. The FBI's dominance and expertise allows not only laymen to tackle the Riper story with this new information but also spurred a founding member of the BSU to tackle a report on Jack the Ripper in 1988.

Chapter 3: Fit to Print covers just some of the published theories

Introduction: The Fact of a Crime

and identities of Jack the Ripper as they have been presented in single-subject book-length writings. As there have been more than 100 books about the Ripper, this survey covers the more interesting trends and deviations that emerge during specific eras. We have not always imagined the Ripper in the same way, but there are still elements of his identity we cling to in every iteration.

Chapter 4: The New Experts covers the idea of the "Ripperologists" and their role in preserving and continuing the Ripper story. Although the term was not invented until the 1970s, it has been retroactively granted to previous Ripper researchers. With growing interest in different aspects of the Ripper case, the term has become diffuse and uncertain: does it apply to all who read and write about the Ripper, or only a certain core group? This chapter explores the expertise and advantages held by those who claim or reject the title.

Chapter 5: Lights, Camera ... Murder looks at the role documentaries play in the Ripper narrative as filmed artifacts concerned with telling the truth about the crime. We have seen a drastic shift in the true crime documentary in recent years, especially in its expectations of viewers, but the shift from written to visual narrative has its own impacts on the Ripper story. The Autumn of Terror is adaptable to many forms, although it is suited to some more than others.

Chapter 6: Once Upon a Time addresses fictional versions of the Ripper narrative in various formats including the novel, the graphic novel, and the movie. Fiction allows authors to fill in the gaps in the narrative and answer questions that do not have real-life references, meaning that fictional retellings of the Ripper story can solve the case and wrap things up neatly. Some versions of the tale have moved through their own various media formats as they catch our attention and demand refinements and new approaches, now unencumbered by the expectations of nonfiction.

Chapter 7: Reach Out and Touch Someone turns to the various three-dimensional methods that have been employed over the decades to present the Ripper murders to audiences. It begins with both slumming and contemporary walking tours of the East End, indications that only the women who truly lived there were at risk from the killer. Walking tours continue today as various guides herd groups through the East End to gaze at the murder sites and describe what they used to look like, calling upon their guests to use their imaginations to travel back in time. Waxworks and wax museums have presented audiences with snapshots of the murders since 1888, inviting them to gaze upon still and lifeless forms, while operas, musicals, and other stage productions present audiences with living, breathing subjects to examine.

Chapter 8: Raised Voices delves more deeply into the ideas of shifting expertise and narratives as the subject of contention instead of as a single story. It covers the evolution of crime narratives in American history and the introduction of the adversarial trial, which is well-known and accepted today but had to be introduced to newspaper readers and those attending the trials to experience them firsthand. This changing understanding of crime and eventual "true crime boom" of the 1980s has vast effects on the Ripper narrative and how today's audiences expect the narrative to be told … and concluded.

Chapter 9: I'm No Expert, But… focuses on the emerging and highly popular format of the true crime podcast, addressing changes in presentation and audience expectations that have already begun in recent documentaries. With the runaway success of *Serial*, we may be seeing a change in how listeners want to relate to, and engage in, true crime narratives. If this trend continues, then perhaps we might leave the Ripper behind, after all.

Conclusion: Connect the Dots takes an overview of these various authors, media, and messages to find the enduring, underlying narrative of the Ripper. This is a story we keep coming back to, and keep renewing, based on new information and deeper understandings of human nature. This is a narrative that somehow cries for a solution even across the years, and we long for that neat, simple conclusion without realizing that, when we tell the Ripper's story yet again, we say far more about ourselves than we do the shadowy figure of the Autumn of Terror.

Chapter 1

Sketching the Ripper, 1888

The Autumn of Terror was not simply a series of crimes, but rather a media event out of proportion to anything that had come before. "We owe Jack the Ripper to the pioneering editors and unscrupulous hacks of the Victorian press"[1] not only because the creation of the name was cemented by the papers but also because, by telling the story, they were the first to shape it. We do not have records of the oral transmission of the Ripper story from person to person, but we do have these printed versions.

Newspapers themselves were evolving as technology advanced to allow cheaper printing and distribution, and "the Whitechapel murders occurred in the midst of the resulting circulation war."[2] It was not just the brutality of the murders but their timing that allowed them to take the front page and continually command not only headlines but also increasing column space. Each paper tried to outdo the others with information about the murders, searching out witnesses to interview and details to publish without necessarily confirming them. The goal of these papers was to sell more copies, and although William Randolph Hearst would not declare the correlation between bleeding and leading until the late 1890s, Victorian newspapers in 1888 were already moving in that direction.

Literacy rates among the general population were increasing along with this ability to produce reading material, although "many of those who were illiterate had the opportunity to hear the most compelling stories of the day (which were probably, due to their content, stories containing violence) read aloud to them in public."[3] Decreasing costs of the dailies did not necessarily put them into the hands of every citizen, but groups pooled their money to buy a copy of the paper and read it communally. The terror of the Whitechapel murderer was not limited to the East End, but those who lived there felt the danger much more keenly than those who did not and wanted to remain on top of the information available to them.

Newspapers "helped to inflate the Whitechapel murders into an often extravagant narrative of shock and horror"[4] with the purpose of selling more copies. A serial murderer is already a serial story, but reporters relied on all their skills—and not a little trickery—to draw the story out. They searched for new angles and new information, using anything they could think of to add to what had already been written. Unfortunately, "journalists do not simply entertain readers with tales of crime, scandal, or sports, but wield real power"[5] with the information they give, and the reporters of 1888 played a solid role in creating the myth of Jack the Ripper.

Read All About It

The late Victorian Era was perhaps not quite so innocent as the average twenty-first-century person might think. A look at the content of newspapers not just from the 1880s, shortly before the Ripper murders, but the decades leading up to it reveals much about the sorts of stories Victorians were willing to pay money to consume. Literacy rose throughout the nineteenth century in England, and even those who could not themselves read newspapers could listen to others read them out loud. Indeed, Joseph Barnett recounted during his inquest testimony that he read stories of the Whitechapel murders to Mary Jane Kelly prior to her own murder.[6] Engagement with news stories did not have to be isolating, and stories such as those about murder were fodder for gossip long before the era of office water coolers. The Ripper was not the start of Victorian crime news reporting, but the next step in its development.

"By 1888 London had thirteen morning and nine evening national dailies"[7] on offer for prices that were at an all-time low. The news was more accessible not just because of advances in printing technology and changing tax laws, but because of increased literacy and the telegraph's means of transmitting news at hitherto unknown speeds. Indeed, as the Ripper murders unfolded, "[n]ewspapers around the globe were now becoming more than familiar with the unravelling events, reporting on the crimes as if they were happening on their own doorstep"[8] thanks to these advances. News that would have once only traveled by word of mouth and been known to the immediate area was repeated, and created a culture of fear, in places where the Ripper himself would never step. The news terrified people who were never threatened by the Ripper's knife and led to calls for action from people who had never set foot in Whitechapel.

Chapter 1. Sketching the Ripper, 1888

Newspapers were so common in Victorian England that "readers knew more or less what to expect from form or layout, if not content,"[9] and much of that content involved crime. More involved coverage of crime, especially crimes committed in areas like Whitechapel, not only increased awareness of the conditions of such areas but also inflated the average readers' impression of how much crime was actually being committed. The press was able to frame this reporting as being for the good of the general public, and papers "called for more funding for civic improvements"[10] in their columns as well as printing letters to the editor demanding the same. If the Ripper had not arisen to direct this focus to the East End, then the papers would have found their cause elsewhere. Crime reporting sold, reflected by the content of the papers and their circulation numbers, and "[t]he nineteenth-century media created a culture more conversant with violent crime than any society of the previous century, or perhaps any society of any century."[11] Despite this familiarity with crime and crime stories, the press was still not prepared for the Whitechapel murders.

Although newspapers had been reporting on crime prior to the Autumn of Terror, "Ripper reporting inspired shifts in column presentation, changes in the content and role of illustration, and impacted the rhetoric of newspaper advertising."[12] The popularity of the story and resulting increase in circulation fed back into the reporting of the story, changing what newspapers looked like overall as well as what, and how much, they chose to report. This was not an entirely new means of reporting, but the increasing circulation wars meant "the right spark could ignite the press into an orgy of sensationalist reporting as papers battled for circulation.... [and] Jack the Ripper provided that spark."[13] The murders and the resulting public response, including those letters purported to have been written by the killer, all fed not only into the myth of Jack the Ripper, but also into the rise of yellow journalism and various papers' attempts to control the media.

While some of the changes to the papers themselves involved the printing of illustrations such as maps, the impact of which is discussed in more detail in Chapter 7, the feedback between the papers and their audience was such that the demand for more impacted the way papers told the story ... as well as the way those papers included advertisements. As the Autumn of Terror continued, the space for advertisements in the paper increased, "suggest[ing] that advertisers were as keen to profit from the public interest in Jack the Ripper as the papers themselves, and recognised that close material association with Ripper reporting increased product exposure."[14] The murders were news and, in their battle for circulation numbers, the papers blurred the line between reporting the news and creating it. Not every reporter made so many strides as the one who "dressed as a woman and roamed the streets of Whitechapel hoping to be attacked by the killer, risking death for the scoop of a lifetime"[15] and perhaps writing the next headlines in his own blood, but even the most respectable papers of the day found themselves involved in the sensation.

Reporters during the murders found themselves facing multiple challenges as far as telling the story while it unfolded. For one thing, the police did not want to talk to the press for many of the same reasons law enforcement refrains from speaking to reporters today. They did not want to reveal their full plans or the true extent of their knowledge. This backfired in that, according to what the press could report, the police had neither plans nor knowledge. "The attitude of the police to the press, moreover, exacerbated the already strained relationship between the two"[16] and led to reports that made light, if not fun, of the police attempt to capture the killer. The Ripper is frequently called "the world's first serial killer" and while this is not in fact true, the case *is* the first to receive such concerted public attention. There was no FBI to be called in for consultation, and the creation of behavioral profiling was still almost a century in the future.

Just as the police did not know what they were facing or the sort of criminal they were meant to catch, so the press had no precedent for reporting on such a case. Single incidents of crime, much more common, have a shorter lifespan as far as reporting goes. Once the crime itself is over, the suspect is either captured or at large. If captured, the papers can report on the trial and sentencing and give readers a proper ending that supports the idea that the justice system is indeed justice. If still at large, the suspect can be minimized based on his personal history and relation to the victims. Here, motive and backstory play into the idea that the general public is safe, since the readers themselves have done nothing to personally wrong the suspect.

When it came to Jack the Ripper, the crime was multiple instead of single. The seriality of the murders was not an issue for the papers which were themselves serial and already engaged in extending finite stories via methods of interviewing further witnesses or providing summaries and rehashes of events after the events themselves were over. Each further murder during the Autumn of Terror provided not only a new scene and new witnesses, but also the opportunity to revisit each preceding crime and remind readers of details that had already been published. All papers participated in such practices, but "[a]ny prize for wringing copy out of the situation would probably go to the Pal Mall gazette"[17]—a prize earned only after a hard fight, considering how many papers struggled to maintain relevance and reader interest as time passed.

A major challenge to the press, and one that likewise faced the police, was the question of motive. Although used to relating a narrative of events when it came to everyday crime in the East End, reporters were at a loss to explain why someone would commit serial murder. Due to the identity of the victims, robbery was likely not a factor. If the women were married, they were estranged from their husbands, and none of their current boyfriends came under serious scrutiny as suspects. The usual, apparently explicable, causes for murder were absent, and the reporters rushed to outdo each other in filling the void.

Contemporary reporters such as *Daily Telegraph* correspondent J. Hall Richardson "complained that newspapers during the 'Ripper' crimes were constantly up against the inventions and fictitious stories of competitors in journalism."[18] When there were gaps in the narrative, they had to be filled before being presented to the reading public, and the inventiveness escalated as the crimes continued. Later writers have complained that "no newspaper to-day would print such awful details as the more reputable sections of the Press did"[19] during the Autumn of Terror and that the papers' use of "the most sensational language imaginable, did much to promote alarm."[20] Although the press had previously published crime news, the Ripper murders led papers to make a shift in their choice of language so that "[r]eaders were confronted with words never before printed in their newspapers"[21]—and, alongside with complaints about the choice of the words used to describe the crimes, there were issues with the details the papers chose to print.

Although most of the sensationalism focused on descriptions of the crime scenes and the violence done to the murdered women, some of it revolved around introducing greater London—and the world beyond—to the conditions within the East End. Perhaps the attitude is best expressed by *The Times*: "Who is my neighbour? Unhappily for all of us, the Whitechapel murderers and their victims are the neighbours of every Londoner."[22] That "unhappily" emphasizes general public opinion about the East End, an area largely ignored by those who could afford to do so. Reporting on the crimes meant reporting about conditions in Whitechapel and commenting on the (presumed) occupations of the murdered women. Discussing the murders meant discussing the perceived immorality of sex work.

In large part the women were maligned as having chosen both to leave the safety of their marriages and protection of their husbands, and also to engage in sex work as one apparent choice among many. Their reasons for leaving their marital homes were discounted and downplayed in part because still-living husbands were able to express their perceptions and opinions unchallenged by their murdered wives.

Newspaper articles "reflected the Victorian obsession with character and virtuous conduct,"[23] using the women's pasts to justify their violent deaths. After all, if they had stayed with their men, they would not have been in the East End on the nights of their murders, many of them on the street because they had no money to pay for a bed.

This blaming of the victim for her own demise is an approach still seen today and has a hold on us for multiple reasons. First, if we support the narrative that leaving marriage and engaging in sex work is a completely free choice, uninfluenced by abusive or cheating spouses and a lack of employment opportunities, then it seems that being put in such a dangerous situation is entirely in our own hands, since we frame it as being entirely in theirs. We can therefore protect ourselves and not worry about our loved ones who make apparently better, presumably safer decisions and therefore avoid becoming victims ourselves.

The women whose murders made headlines were reported as being from the category Steven Egger calls the less-dead, which was already identified in newspapers during the Autumn of Terror as "people [who] can disappear from their haunts, and their departure is not noted."[24] Egger identifies multiple categories of identity within the broader less-dead definition, including sex workers and the homeless: identities that the murdered women shared. Only Mary Jane Kelly, the fifth Canonical victim, had her own room and a regular address, and she was the only one murdered indoors. Further, she was the only one of the five with "prostitute"—the term of the era, now outdated—listed as her occupation on her death certificate. The Ripper murders shed light on the conditions in the East End and led to social change, although even these changes highlighted the prejudices against the poor and unhoused.

Further adding to the Otherness of the location and people discussed in the papers was how "reports of the murders included descriptions of the area's destitution and foreign ways."[25] The East End was home to many immigrants, and then many Jewish immigrants specifically. The murders, and accusations of Jewish suspects, increased the antisemitism already present within the broader communities, threatening Jewish or any "foreign-looking" men alongside the area's women. Early accusations were leveled at a Jewish man known only as "Leather Apron," leading to the arrest—and release—of John Pizer, who was known by that nickname. The fact that Pizer was cleared of the murders did not end suspicions against the Jewish people. Jewish suspects abound in the case, including the proposed slaughterman in Robin Odell's 1965 *Jack the Ripper in Fact and Fiction* and the recent focus on Polish Jew Aaron Kosminski, an immigrant hairdresser who was institutionalized in 1891. While Othering the victims leads readers to feel safer for themselves or their loved ones, Othering the killer provides a way of creating distance between one's own background—in this case, fine upstanding British gentlemen—and the violence of the crimes.

In such cases, "[t]he minority group is doubly maligned, first to be the focal point of community rage while at the same time being the most at risk."[26] Mobs chased men they accused of being the Ripper on the smallest perception of evidence, endangering their lives and forcing them to turn to the police for protection. Suspicion abounded as strangers were scrutinized, but the East End was full of itinerant residents and day laborers, so it was not always possible to remain within circles of friends and acquaintances. Further, women still needed money for their beds or else they would find themselves on the streets at night, open to threats from the killer. If sex work was the only work they had, then they routinely took strangers into more secluded areas and risked an attack to pay their doss.

Sensationalizing identities and details of the murders allowed papers to both tantalize and reassure their readers. Those who did not live in the East End could relax in the safety of their homes and "assume such violent dealings are the natural consequence of illicit behaviour,"[27] further arguing to themselves that avoiding such behavior—leaving a marriage, alcoholism, and sex work—would protect them personally. If they followed the social rules and expectations, then they would be shielded by dint of their position in society. The sensationalism in the daily papers, however, meant that they felt neither safe nor secure, no matter how distant the murdered women or the killer seemed to be.

Although it cannot be argued that the Ripper purposefully sought social change, "the issue of poverty and the problems it generated in the east London slums were brought into sharp focus"[28] during the Whitechapel murders. Those who had done their best to avoid acknowledging the slums and the people living there were confronted with descriptions not only of the living conditions, but also the knowledge that screams of "Murder!" were frequent and therefore frequently ignored. The good, upstanding citizens of London who had more than enough found themselves pressured to contribute to social programs supporting the poor, an issue discussed in more detail in the next section concerning letters to the editor. The Ripper may have murdered the less-dead, but he encouraged the haves to recognize and then address the conditions of the have-nots.

The newspapers milked the story as much as they could, using new crimes as an opportunity to once again dredge up the details of prior crimes. Reporters often spoke to witnesses before the police did, either because those witnesses mistrusted authority or wished to make something up just to see their names in print. So much was done not just to serialize the story but to drag it out and rehash it given the slightest cause, to the point where identifying a suspect "would be profitable only so long as he could not be found."[29] Indeed, our continued fascination with the case more than a century later is rooted in this lack of a solid identity.

Newspapers not only reported information, but also gave birth to theories about the Ripper that attempted to both entertain and explain. "Some newspapers started publishing stories about a rather lofty motivation for the Ripper's ghastly murders,"[30] but this was a struggle in an era where a killer like the Ripper was seen as something new. This is hardly surprising, since the question of motive, so inextricably tied with that of identity, is one that still troubles us today. While murder was nothing new in the East End, what sort of person would kill strangers so brutally and leave them on display?

The figure of "Leather Apron" was indeed an initial, if vague, suspect as women reported being threatened by such a man and his knife. It was hardly a rare nickname in an area where many working men wore such garments in their line of work as butchers or shoemakers, and the figure of Leather Apron played into the era's antisemitism. However, Leather Apron first turned into an individual named John Pizer and then was more or less dismissed when it was determined that Pizer, despite his history of threatening women, had an alibi for two of the murders. It seems that the nickname of "Leather Apron" was solely connected to Pizer despite the popularity of the item—one was even found in the yard where Annie Chapman died—and no other man with the nickname was identified or arrested.

It was *The Times* that "gave birth to the 'lodger' theory and to the notion which has persisted to this day, namely that the Whitechapel murderer was not a member of the working class,"[31] early in September. While Leather Apron was a working man of the East End, likely Jewish, who was comfortable with knives and also likely with blood thanks to his occupation, the lodger was an outsider from the upper class. More will be discussed about the lodger as a fictional character in Chapter 6, but here we already see an intriguing split in the perception of the suspect as outsider. Leather Apron was likely a Jewish foreigner who was not born in the East End but had come to live there, while the lodger was also a transplant from a better, or at least richer, part of the city. Leather Apron could blend in with the crowd and conceivably knew the ins and outs of Whitechapel's twisting streets, but the lodger would stand out, and it is more difficult to imagine that he knew his way around and could travel without catching someone's attention.

One other question that needs to be answered in any Ripper retelling is how the chosen suspect would have been able to approach the murdered women, especially later in the series when they would presumably have been on their guard. Many have argued that a man from the upper class would put a woman on alert more than one who seemed to belong there, but the number of young men slumming in the East End might help balance out the strangeness of the lodger's dress or accent. Indeed, since the Jekyll and Hyde theory also took hold early on, the idea that the Ripper managed to disappear into the London fog, or perhaps just into any crowd, has been put forward since the beginning. In fact, "'the Ripper' so quickly took on a mythic quality"[32] that he could be almost anyone, or anything, with any conceivable motive.

Victorian Message Boards

Letters to the editor are where the news becomes interactive and anyone with access to a pen and postage can attempt to see their words in print. In fact, they are "the 1888 equivalent to a modern day internet message board"[33] in that anyone could write a letter claiming any sort of expertise or background, but there was no way of proving if they were who they said. For example, "*The Times* had a policy that while a person did not have to publish his name and address, the information must be included in the original letter to show good faith,"[34] but there was no requirement that the address be confirmed or the sender tracked down prior to publication, which could be under a pseudonym. Other letter writers could respond to previous letters either by name or pseudonym, or by referencing the title the letter had been given in the paper. It was a place to react publicly not only to what had been written by reporters, but also by others from the general population and "the printed letters—whether emanating from elite or plebian circles—revealed much more about the writers than about the crimes."[35]

Thematically, letters about the Ripper murders could be broken down into a few themes. First, and perhaps most confusing, was the idea of motive. Since the public was faced with a serial killer for the first time they were aware of it, they struggled to explain why someone would kill numerous strangers. Robbery could not have been a motive since the women were all poor, and it seemed inexplicable that a stranger would so brutally mutilate their bodies and leave them in public places on display. Victorians, especially in the East End, were used to ideas of violence, whether it was between couples or for monetary gain, but it seemed there was nothing personal about the Ripper murders, and thus they did not fall into the easily explicable.

Although Robin Odell laments that, "while the murders were still relatively recent, no one with an investigative turn of mind applied their talents to solving them,"[36] many letter writers still tried even with their lack of expertise. Although some lamented that "no intelligible motive can be ascribed to the perpetration of any of these crimes,"[37] others reached for explanations that included madness, religious ritual, or the completion of black magic. The reading public was faced with the same desire that still holds us today: to shape the violent crimes into a narrative with a cause and an explanation, including an ending that restores the previous order so dramatically interrupted by the murders.

Part of this frustration with their personal search for a motive was an increasing animosity toward the police whose job, it seemed, was to identify and apprehend the murderer so that the public could have these answers without having to come up with them themselves. Multiple writers criticized the selection process for the police, arguing that "to-day the public are made to pay for height and not for brains"[38] because applicants had to be a certain height or else they would be rejected, regardless of other qualifications. The police were critiqued for how they walked their beats, since their presence was too obvious to potential criminals due to both the clockwork nature of their stride and the sound of their boot heels on the cobbles. Many suggested that the force would do well to invest in rubber coverings for their shoes so that officers could sneak up on criminals and presumably catch them in the act. The question of whether bloodhounds would be useful—and what, exactly, was meant by the term "bloodhounds"—was bandied about in these letters before Sir Charles Warren experimented with dogs, but they were never tested at a murder site. Even newspapers that were generally supportive, such as *The Times*, "opened [their] columns to letters critical of the police"[39] and gave in to overwhelming public feeling and opinion. Whatever the police did—or at least whatever they did and allowed the press to print—was criticized because, while arrests were made, no real suspects surfaced, no man went to trial, and the murders continued.

Some interesting math surfaced in these letters criticizing the police. One hopeful writer argued that "it was estimated in New York that every street electric lamp saved one policeman and was less expensive to maintain,"[40] combining a critique of the police force with one about lighting conditions in the East End. Later, another suggested that "[t]en well-trained bloodhounds would be of more use than a hundred constables,"[41] making each bloodhound worth at least ten street lamps. No matter what was suggested, be it nonhuman animal or inanimate object, writers seemed convinced that their ideas would surpass the current police force as far as effectiveness against crime. As Donald McCormick observes, "[i]t was quite a novel experience for the police to be getting so much assistance from the public"[42] and, despite the letters that proclaimed their authors' backgrounds as being related to police work, many of the suggestions were unreasonable or downright fantastical. Readers' frustration, fear, and perceived helplessness in the face of a killer who may very well come after them next tried to assume some measure of control through these suggestions, which stretched beyond suggestions for revolutionizing the police force and extended to propositions for improving the social situation of the East End.

The living conditions of the poor as reported in the newspapers was new information to so many readers who "were in large part normal, everyday Londoners"[43] and had never previously had a reason to venture into the East End. These readers were shocked not only by the brutality of the murders, which seemed beyond their control, but also by the living conditions of so many, which seemed to be an easier issue to tackle. It only appeared to be easier, however, as many letters started to pick apart the various issues facing those from a class lower than they currently occupied.

In a much-alluded-to letter given the title of WOMAN KILLING NO MURDER, Florence Fenwick Miller called attention to a number of court cases where men who murdered their wives or girlfriends were released free of apparent consequences, depending on the identity of the woman who had been killed.[44] This, Miller argued, led to the current situation where women of a certain class and presumed occupation are generally considered expendable or, perhaps like vermin, *ought* to be destroyed. Miller's critique of this social stance sparked myriad responses from other authors who either supported her argument or willfully misinterpreted what she had to say, bringing up other cases as counterarguments or otherwise taking the man's side even after he had committed murder. The gendering of killer and victim was just one flash point in the middle of all these fears.

There was also the narrative that all of the murdered women were sex workers, and therefore an apparently simple reorganization of housing for the poor would not be the solution it appeared to be. "So long as the class exists they will have their haunts and resorts," one writer pointed out. "You do not destroy the vermin by simply destroying their nests."[45] At the time, and in many versions of the Ripper narrative since, it was assumed that the women chose to be sex workers of their own free will. Indeed, such women in the Victorian era were assumed to be oversexed and to desire continual sexual intercourse with strangers for their own pleasure, with the money they received as incidental to their real goal. Even if the plans for tearing down doss houses and creating new opportunities for housing were as easy and apparently inexpensive as some writers argued, this letter's author believes the problem goes deeper than basic human needs.

Even then, those who want to offer monetary, food, or housing assistance clearly want to tie personal notions of respectability to this aid. One letter-writer acknowledges that "the first difficulty, I apprehend, will be to draw the line of distinction clearly between the vicious and the casual poor"[46]—that is, determining who "deserves" to be fed and housed based on apparent morality. There were already standing rules about what items were allowed in doss houses, as well as what could or could not be brought into casual wards and what inmates had to do to pay for their accommodations, carefully controlling the lives of the poor and unhoused. What seems to have been lost in these discussions is how there were not enough beds or enough "respectable" jobs for the entire population of the East End.

Indeed, just as the public's suggestions for improving the police may have been well-intentioned but failed to grasp the complexities and realities of the situation, so did their suggestions for "improving" the conditions of the poor. In fact, Arthur J. Robinson, Rector of Whitechapel, took it upon himself to write his own letter and sign his name to it, arguing that "every single agency suggested for the amelioration of Whitechapel is already in existence."[47] All of the apparently good ideas had already been thought of and, instead of taking the time to create an entirely new aid program from the ground up, the money that so many people apparently thought would be easy to raise could be directed toward those already doing the work. There is frustration in these counterarguments from those who have already been engaging with the East End poor and for whom the living conditions are not a new and appalling discovery, in part because this means all of their work has been ignored.

Whether their work is appreciated and encouraged by the people they are helping is not addressed in these letters. Despite the increased literacy rate and the access people of all classes had to newspapers, it seems that few to none of the people actively being threatened by the Ripper's crimes had the time or money to send in their own letters. Their words and reactions could be reported by others, both in the regular newspaper columns and in the letters to the editor as well as in police reports, but it seems that, if anyone more closely associated with Whitechapel *did* write a letter, it did not make the editorial cut to be "selected from among vast numbers which reach us by every post."[48] Even when writers had personally been to the East End instead

Chapter 1. Sketching the Ripper, 1888

of speculating from a distance, the voices of those at the heart of these suggestions were not heard.

Early on in the Autumn of Terror, however, it was shown that the columns of letters to the editor were indeed a place where someone who felt he had been overlooked could make his voice heard. William Nichols, estranged husband of the first Canonical victim Polly Nichols, wrote to correct information that had appeared about his marriage and relationship with his wife in a previous edition—or at least to elaborate in a way that made him look better socially. Nichols argued that his wife was the one who had left him, rather than the other way around, and that "it was proved at Lambeth police-court that she had misconducted herself"[49]—in other words, that she had been sexually active with at least one other man, committing adultery if not selling sex—after their separation. William Nichols had been interviewed by the police and was able to speak and tell his side of the story at the death inquest, and he was also able to write directly to the newspaper and therefore the reading public to correct what he saw as an inaccuracy in how his character had been represented. He did not write to offer advice or more information that might lead to the killer's apprehension, but to ensure that the public was not led astray by what, to him, was misinformation. He understood that a letter to the editor would indeed provide him with such a platform.

Writers did not have to have such a close personal connection to one of the victims to both write in and have their letters published and entered into contemporary record. Philanthropist Thomas Barnardo, founder of various homes and schools for the children of the East End, wrote such a letter after Elizabeth Stride's murder to say that he had met her shortly before her death when she was a member of a group of women discussing how hopeless and helpless they felt, and how they feared they would be the next victim.[50] Since Barnardo did not know Stride personally during her lifetime, and made this connection only after he had viewed her body in the mortuary, it is difficult to say how accurate his identification might have been. Followed by Joe Barnett's testimony that he used to read the newspapers out loud to Mary Jane Kelly, who also feared the murderer, it certainly seems like a believable story, especially coming from a man whose character seemed beyond reproach.

Barnardo's letter to the editor includes his name and therefore uses his ethos to make the contents of that letter believable, the same way William Nichols wrote as husband of one of the victims to provide information about both Polly and himself. Other authors included statements about their own backgrounds or experience as they related to police work either in England or abroad to support their suggestions about police approach, or their involvement with dogs and tracking when discussing the idea of the police using bloodhounds. Such statements can give weight to the following suggestions, although without a well-known name at the end of the letter, this expertise can be impossible to prove. Readers who have no background themselves have no touchpoint for determining whether or not the author should be trusted.

These authors, guided by what they read in previous letters to the editor and newspaper articles as well as their own personal experiences, may have been guided by maxims that continue to rule over true crime today: if there are gaps in the narrative that cannot be known, such as the final thoughts of a murder victim, then the author writes what *feels* true and will therefore be accepted by others living in the same time and culture. While it was difficult for reporters and letter-writers alike to discover the killer's motive based on their known cultural narratives, it was believable that a philanthropist working among in the poor in the East End could indeed have met one of the victims prior to her murder, or that the husband of one of the victims might wish to correct the story about himself that had been made public. Whether truthful in their identity or honestly backed by such experience, these letters still provide us with portions of the cultural myth that fed into the narrative of the Ripper murders.

One final important aspect of these letters is that they published not only critiques of the police, but of the papers themselves—at times with a comment from the editor defending the paper's choices. One reader wrote to say "I think, in common with all the female inhabitants of the Metropolis, I have a right to complain of a sensational morning paper,"[51] voicing her displeasure with the changes in reporting that came along with the murders. The papers found themselves walking the same thin line as true crime does today: is it informative or sensational? Does it educate or entertain? At what point do these stories cross the line from enlightening the general public to glorifying in violence done to others?

Part of the disservice done by this media attention to the case was reported to the papers by, for example, AN ELDERLY GENTLEMAN who informed readers that "I myself have been taken for the murderer"[52] during a journey where he was identified as a stranger to the area and then followed by a group of locals who still did not attack him or even stop him from entering a nearby house. They did wait outside, presumably ready to run for help if they heard a commotion, but the people living there knew the elderly gentleman and confirmed his identity to the waiting crowd. The man was thus able to go on his way unmolested, unlike others who were forced to run into the nearest police stations to avoid mob violence, and the tone of his letter is one of great offense that anyone might suspect him of such horrific crimes. It seems that the Ripper is not merely a threat to poor women in the East End, but to men everywhere who have no one to vouch for them.

The newspapers thus not only set about informing the reading public of London and around the world of the facts concerning the murders, but also provided a place for the readers to air their own opinions, grievances, and arguments with the paper, the police, and each other. Greater literacy contributed to more than just circulation wars and increased desire for daily papers. Readers could also be writers and contribute to the growing documentation of, and speculation around, the Autumn of Terror. Writing letters to the editor was an outlet for members of the public to find an audience beyond their immediate circle, but it was not the only way the average citizen could insert him- or herself into this unfolding story.

Interactive Murder Narratives

Of course the most important letters during the Autumn of Terror were not the reading public's letters to the editor, but the letters sent purporting to be from the killer himself. The most famous of these was sent to the Central News Agency and is known as the "Dear Boss" letter for its salutation. The most important aspect of this letter, however, was the fact that it was signed *Jack the Ripper*. "With a few lines in red and a brilliantly-chosen pseudonym, someone gave the Whitechapel Murders to the public and propelled them into legend"[53] to the point where we still discuss him today. This first letter that named the Ripper added fuel to the media fire not only because it gave the killer a name other than the Whitechapel Killer, but also because this first missive, once publicized, paved the way for so many more.

The "Dear Boss" letter was dated September 25 but postmarked and received by the Central News Agency on September 27. Later speculation has given rise to the question of whether the letter was written shortly before it was posted and not, in fact, on the 25th, further leading to speculation that the writer may have gotten his hands on an early edition newspaper and culled it for information rather than being the actual murderer. Paul Begg and John Bennett likewise point out that "[t]he first known example [of a letter purportedly from the killer] was written on 24 September and sent to Charles Warren,"[54] the head of the

London Metropolitan Police, but it is the "Dear Boss" letter that has assumed a place in mythic history. A letter sent by the supposed killer to the police makes one sort of statement, but a letter sent by the supposed killer to a news distribution center sends another. After all, "this letter-writing culprit was tailor-made for the media,"[55] and the letter aided various papers in their battle for greater circulation.

If the letter naming the killer as Jack the Ripper had merely been received by the Central News Agency and passed on to Scotland Yard two days later, the killer might still have been called the Whitechapel Knife and the legend surrounding him might not have grown to such heights. However, "[t]he police took the fateful decision to publicise the letters,"[56] not only making the pseudonym public knowledge but also inspiring others to follow suit and providing today's audience with multiple new sources of information. The police made enlarged reproductions of the letter to be displayed in case anyone recognized the handwriting, and the contents of the letter were published in the papers. In this way "editors could claim to be performing an important public service"[57] rather than inflaming panic, arguing that their readers needed all the information about the murders that could be provided. If this letter and future letters held threats, then the papers could argue that forewarned readers would be forearmed, and not simply panicked.

This decision to publicize the initial letter, leading to a flood of letters in different handwriting and on different paper, all claiming to be from the killer, has been highly criticized in the years since. Although contemporary decision-makers may have reasoned that someone might recognize the writer's handwriting or rhetorical style, as Ted Kaczynski was identified after the Unabomber Manifesto was published over a century later, this did not happen in the Ripper case. Rather, the media and police found themselves inundated with letters purporting to be from the killer, but which "usually exploited the popular theories about the murders that were current in the newspapers"[58] rather than offering anything new. Although some would-be senders were caught in the act and punished for it, others were never caught.

Aside from the "Dear Boss" letter, the "From Hell" letter sent to Whitechapel Vigilance Committee Chairman George Lusk is the other missive most often given the benefit of the doubt as having perhaps honestly come from the killer. The letter to Lusk, which accompanied a parcel, was postmarked October 15, 1888, after the Double Event of September 30. Because the package contained part of a human kidney, and because Catherine Eddowes' kidney had been removed by her killer, there are reasons to believe that this letter came from the real Ripper. However, there are also arguments as to how an innocent man might have procured a human kidney without murdering to obtain it, and forensic medicine of the day could not conclude without a doubt that it was indeed part of Eddowes' missing kidney. Hundreds of other letters contained neither human organs nor specific information that would be enough to convince the majority of readers of their validity, and even though the last of the Canonical Five murders occurred on November 9, 1888, letters purporting to be from the killer continued to be sent until October 14, 1896.[59]

The publication of the "Dear Boss" letter not only gave us the killer's pseudonym, but also opened the door for others to participate in the story of the murders by adding their own voices while posing as the killer. The newspapers' role in creating the narrative refracted: they published the letters, which were written by people who read the newspaper and added details from the papers to their letters, which the newspapers published. It has even been suggested that the original letter was written by Tom Bulling, himself a Central News journalist,[60] which would explain why the killer seemed so perfectly formed for the media. The continued letters, sent by so many others and based so concretely on what the papers themselves reported, created an echo chamber about the case.

What that echo chamber did, aside from sell more newspapers, was to cement a culturally-created image of the Ripper's identity, personality, and motive. There are elements in many of the letters that show a certain amount of playfulness or lightheartedness, indicating an enjoyment with teasing the public and not merely taunting the police. Had all of the letters been sent to the police rather than the media, this would indicate a different goal for the senders; however, the letters may still have been made public and contributed to the sudden inflow of hundreds more.

While letters to the editor allowed the average citizen to feel that his or her voice had been heard, these Ripper letters meant the authors put on the persona of the killer. Like letters to the editor, it was a competition to write something that would be deemed worthy of publication, especially once it became clear that competition was so fierce. Although "[t]he authorities roundly dismissed them as the work of a hoaxer,"[61] the letters still received public attention and became central to the Ripper myth. Once a letter gave the Ripper his name, the gates were opened for all sorts of contributions from writers attempting to both have their secret fifteen minutes of fame and also explain why these murders were happening. By drawing on the newspaper reports, these letter-writers attempted to make believable threats about future murders based on the given narrative of why the Ripper was killing, the sorts of people he chose as his victims, and how he murdered.

Even if none of the letters was written by the real killer, they still have an important place in the Ripper myth above and beyond the creation of the Ripper name. Whether a reporter or an average citizen, each letter-writer drew on personal knowledge, the information provided in the newspapers, and the current cultural environment to write those letters. Repeated elements—taunts to the police, declarations of being a foreigner, references to the most recent news stories and declarations of their inaccuracies—tell us not only what narratives sold, but also which were believable to the general population.

None of the letter writers were experts on serial killers or criminal profiling because the term "serial killer" was not in use and the FBI's invention, modification, and heavy publicization of criminal profiling were still a century away. These were not letters written by people who had read the core narrative handed down by experts and filled in the blanks between the facts with expert-accepted narratives; rather, these were everyday people attempting to make sense of a new phenomenon and to assimilate these brutal crimes into what they knew about their own time and place.

It is interesting how many of these supposed Ripper letters reflect the messages in letters to the editor. The authors did not use this interactive medium to "correct misconceptions" about the killer, but rather in general leaned into what was already being said or speculated about the killer. Granted, some of the taunting to the police pushed back against current theories—even the "Dear Boss" letter includes "They say I'm a doctor now ha ha"[62]—but we do not see theories originating from the letters alone. Although the myth around the Ripper crystallizes in part because of these letters, they add to the growing lore rather than veering off to a new branch or attempting to school the public about what honestly would motivate such a killer—a question that has yet to be fully answered and will be addressed further in Chapter 3. All in all, the Ripper letters contributed to the mediated narrative of Jack the Ripper and helped to shape not only his name, but also to flesh out more of his shadowy figure.

The End of the Ripper

Jack the Ripper emerged at the perfect time to both shape late nineteenth-century new journalism and to be shaped by it. Prior to the Autumn of Terror and the murders being linked to a single perpetrator, "the press were already in a state of frenzy"[63] as they negotiated access to new and cheaper printing technologies and faster means of communicating news across long distances. Circulation increased, as did competition, and a story as intriguing as the Whitechapel murders of course fought for dominance among the various papers and their reporting styles. Reporters were not held to rigid standards as to the truth of what they wrote, so competing stories with different information were common. Many of our current myths about Jack the Ripper originated in these pages and, although some have been proved factually untrue by police documentation, the stories still linger.

In part, this is because we still agree with many of the conclusions drawn back in the day. Even though these reporters did not have the benefit of the FBI, criminal profiling, *The Silence of the Lambs*, and police procedurals, they still concluded that the killer was most likely a man who knew the area well and was able to blend in at least enough to go to secluded places with his intended victims and to leave the scenes of the crimes without being stopped. Granted, the social and economic factors of the day led the general consensus to follow current feelings of xenophobia and antisemitism in identifying what sort of man this could have been, but even that is a feeling that continues to hold sway today: such violent killers must be Other, not one of us.

Jack the Ripper, as the first serial killer to receive such media attention, "personified the tabloid sensibility (all scandal, all the time)"[64] that made up newspaper reporting in the late 1800s and is generally relegated to tabloids, be they print or digital, today. Because the events being reported were themselves serial, and because the killer's identity and motive were never confirmed, this left the story open to speculation. Newspapers engaged in circulation wars with each other based on their headlines, content, and column space devoted to the murders, not minding that they published "conflicting accounts in their thirst for 'the big story.'"[65] The media may have helped create Jack the Ripper, but the Ripper also helped create the media.

The format of the newspapers was not entirely one-way. Columns, published without bylines at the time, indeed worked as a one-to-many form of communication as the paper functioned at least in part to inform its readers of events, but the letters to the editor allowed readers to then respond to what was written, both by the paper and by other letter writers. Those who had strong reactions, be they positive or negative, to what they read in the papers did not have to remain silent or express these thoughts merely to their friends. By writing letters, they had the chance to then read their own words in print.

As the Autumn of Terror progressed, common themes emerged and papers were so inundated with letters that they had to summarize the contents of multiple letters so as to allow enough space for the rest of what was deemed publishable. Concerned citizens wrote with suggestions to the police about how they might catch the killer; to the general public with ideas about how to improve living conditions and morality in the East End; and to explain their own individual experiences in their own words, such as in the case of William Nichols after his wife's murder or the elderly gentleman incensed that strangers thought he might have been the murderer. For Nichols, the letter provided an opportunity for him to respond to the paper that had already published something about him and to add his corrections. For the others, it allowed them the chance to be heard beyond their circle of friends.

It is difficult at times to tell which letters came from inherently good-hearted authors who were not aware of the details of the situation and which were penned by nineteenth-century trolls. Those already performing social work in the East End wearily countered that many of the suggestions given by other letter-writers were, in fact, already in place, suggesting that the original authors were Johnny-come-latelies to the social realities of the poorest area of London who only cared because of the lurid headlines. Others, such as Florence Fenwick Miller with her letter titled WOMEN KILLING NO MURDER, invited misogynistic responses that filled the letters columns with vitriolic responses especially from men who wished to inform her that life was hard for them, too. She clearly touched a nerve with her chosen topic, and if readers purchased the papers to discover how this argument progressed rather than for the headlines, the newspapers were still being sold. The Ripper touched on so many sore spots in Victorian society that there was always something to complain about.

A further means of public participation through letters came in the form of letters supposedly penned by the killer. Considering that "[t]he real importance of the famous Jack the Ripper letters lies in their creation of the name,"[66] and that the letter bearing that signature has been attributed to a newsman wanting to sell more papers, the Ripper has truly been an interactive media event since the beginning. Since the publication of the letter bearing that sobriquet, the police collected well over 300 letters as individuals playacted as the murderer. It is highly unlikely that any of the letters purporting to be from the killer were actually written by him, although the package sent to George Lusk containing a piece of human kidney meant to belong to Catherine Eddowes seems likelier than others to have come from the killer.

Enough people were caught sending letters from the Ripper, however, to indicate that members of the public felt that this was a way to involve themselves in the narrative. Because the Ripper murders occurred at this period in newspaper development, it was the first time

Chapter 1. Sketching the Ripper, 1888

a killer wrote and sent letters to a news agency—and the first time the contents of those letters were published, ostensibly so readers might recognize either the diction or the handwriting on the enlarged reproductions. Once it was clear that such letters would receive attention, many people decided to engage in this new means of storytelling concerning violent crime. The police as well as the press were overwhelmed, and the instances in which senders were prosecuted for contributing to public panic did not dissuade others from writing.

Although these initial newspaper reports were meant to be factual, they did not stick to the same expectations of today's journalists, and "the potential was established for future commentators to employ the imagination of a novelist as much as the objective of a dedicated researcher in order to convince a skeptical public of a particular analysis and conclusion."[67] Fact and fiction were already blurred in 1888 as reporters used novelistic conventions to convey their stories and keep the suspense ongoing in order to sell more papers, while public participation through witness statements, letters to the editor, and letters purporting to come from the killer continued to twist the facts and cloud what little evidence there was.

The lack of cooperation between the police and the news played into the newspapers' tendency to exaggerate information, seek out those possible witnesses for their breathless statements, and to criticize the police for their lack of action. Because the Metropolitan Police did not issue many public statements about what they were doing to halt the murders, and because they did not keep any suspect under arrest, the papers and the public both quickly found fault with them and their methods. Officials remained quiet for decades and only publicly wrote about the Ripper again at the end of their careers, reflecting back on the events with both the benefit of hindsight and the challenge of distant memory.

Chapter 2

The Changing of the Guard

After the murder of Mary Jane Kelly, Jack the Ripper quickly left the newspapers. Things were hushed up and the case declared closed, even though no one had been sent to trial for the murders. The killer, and the media sensation, were quickly swept under the rug as headlines moved on to other topics. Even later murders—such as Rose Mylett, Alice McKenzie, and Frances Coles—that might be tangentially related to the Ripper were dismissed, albeit also never solved. The police had failed to catch the Ripper, the newspapers had made their money on the case, and it was time to move on. The Ripper murders were a once-in-a-lifetime occurrence and best dismissed.

The men who worked on the case also moved on. Frederick Abberline became involved in the infamous Cleveland Street scandal in 1889, which became his last major case. Queen Victoria's grandson was accused of having been a frequent visitor to the homosexual brothel in question, and Abberline was convinced his superiors participated in the coverups. He retired from police work in 1892 and never wrote his memoirs.

Detective Chief Inspector Walter Dew did indeed write his memoirs, but instead of the Ripper case, his title capitalizes on a better-known success. *I Caught Crippen*, published in 1938, begins with Dew's tale of arresting Dr. Hawley Harvey Crippen for the murder of his second wife, Cora Turner. Dew's pursuit of Crippen, including his reliance on the wireless, is documented in Erik Larson's *Thunderstruck* (2006). Copy for *Thunderstruck* identifies Crippen as Britain's second most famous murderer, after Jack the Ripper, although the back cover does not indicate whether that fame is judged within Britain itself or throughout the rest of the world. Dew, however, opens his memoirs with "The Whole Truth about the Crippen Case" and immediately follows it up with a like number of pages about "My Hunt for Jack the Ripper."

It can be corroborated that Dew was transferred to Whitechapel in 1887 and that he was indeed a detective constable in the Criminal

Chapter 2. The Changing of the Guard 43

Investigation Department during the Autumn of Terror, but otherwise his autobiography is questioned. He wrote it nearly fifty years after the Ripper murders, after all, and does not seem to have kept a diary he could refer back to. Thus Dew's claims to have known Mary Jane Kelly well enough to recognize her by sight have to be taken with a grain of salt since, although he claims to have been involved in her death investigation, police records of the men involved do not include his name. It is Dew who gave us the tidbit that the dead woman's eyes were photographed in the belief that they would contain the last thing she saw in life and thus identify her killer,[1] but again, official records contradict him. It seems the doctors had already agreed that it would not, in fact, work.

Despite the pages he devotes to the case, Dew does not offer Jack the Ripper's real name. He believes that the killer *must* be dead, because otherwise he would not have stopped killing, but that is as far as Dew goes.

Sir Melville Macnaghten also wrote an autobiography, *Days of My Years* (1914), but his biggest contribution to the Ripper's identity was written in 1894 and is now referred to as "the Macnaghten Memoranda." Granted, Macnaghten himself was not part of the investigation into the Canonical Five victims, but he worked on the possible later victims of 1889–1891. The Macnaghten Memoranda is a tricky document for multiple reasons.

First, although Macnaghten names the men he believes to be the three most likely Ripper suspects, he gets his information wrong. His three suspects are "A Mr. M.J. Druitt," "Kosminski, a Polish Jew," and "Michael Ostrog, a Russian Doctor." While a young man named Druitt was found drowned in the Thames after Mary Jane Kelly's murder, he was a decade younger than Macnaghten describes him, and a lawyer instead of a doctor. "Kosminski" presented more of a rabbit hole than a solution, but recent thought seems to point to an Aaron Kosminski who was committed to an insane asylum in 1891. Michael Ostrog has since been found to have been imprisoned in France during the fall of 1888 under one of his pseudonyms.

Second, although Macnaghten wrote these pages in 1894, they were in a private memo that he is said to have written twice, although not as exact copies, and one version has never been seen. His daughter apparently made a copy of this other version, thought to be a draft, and allowed some of it to be televised in 1959. The full text of the sole remaining version in Macnaghten's own handwriting was only made public in 1975.

Despite these difficulties, Macnaghten does give us more than some of the other men who worked the case, and more in his memoranda than he does in his memoirs. The names, however vague or factually problematic, at least give us a place to start. He calls Druitt a doctor, leaning into the idea that the Ripper must have had some medical training, and names Kosminski and Ostrog in support of the idea that the Ripper had to have been a "foreigner," and also Jewish, to make him as much of a monster and unlike the upright British men as possible. (Druitt is excused because, while he is a British man, he is a *mad* British man.)

Macnaghten's suggestion of Kosminski seems to be supported by "the Swanson Marginalia," the other set of notes given such a specific name in the Ripper Case. Chief Inspector Donald Swanson was placed in charge of the overall case after Annie Chapman's murder and, although he did not write his own memoirs, his grandson discovered that he had written notes within Robert Anderson's published memoirs, further discussed below. In 1981, James Swanson revealed that his grandfather had agreed with Anderson's claim that the only known witness to the Ripper was Jewish and, recognizing a fellow Jew as the killer, refused to identify him. Swanson himself wrote the name Kosminski in the margin.[2]

Sir Robert Anderson, the Second Assistant Commissioner of the London Metropolitan Police from 1888 to 1901, was the author of those annotated memoirs. He published *The Lighter Side of My Official Life* in 1910, eight years before his death. Although his Chapter IX does address "The Whitechapel Murderer," Anderson was in fact out of the country on medical leave for many of the murders. He also argues that it was not his responsibility to find the murderer, since the police of the district should have done so. Anderson does not leave behind any Memoranda or Marginalia, but his autobiography does include the following declaration: "One did not need to be a Sherlock Holmes to discover that the criminal was a sexual maniac of a virulent type; that he was living in the immediate vicinity of the scenes of the murders; and that, if he was not living absolutely alone, his people knew of his guilt and refused to give him up to justice."[3]

As shockingly modern as Anderson's statement seems, he was not the first to pen what we now refer to as a criminal profile. The earliest known example was written by police surgeon Thomas Bond in 1888—at the behest of Anderson, no less. Anderson simply repeats some of Bond's arguments and observations here, avoiding getting into the more sensational aspects of the case and indeed sounding like he very much wishes he did not have to cover the case at all. Anderson dispenses with the Ripper in less than seven pages, but not before claiming he knows

Chapter 2. The Changing of the Guard 45

the killer's true identity. Anderson even coyly argues that all of Scotland Yard knows the Ripper's identity, but anyone who spoke up would be telling tales out of school, so he cannot say who it was. He just insists that the Ripper murders were not, in fact, unsolved, even if they appear that way on paper. Perhaps it sounded more convincing in 1910.

Whether or not they knew the true identity of Jack the Ripper, and whether or not they left any notes behind, the men who had worked the case died in the early part of the twentieth century. It seems that, for some of them, the Ripper case played a major role in their lives—Dew, for example, devotes about a third of his autobiography to it, although it comes second and misses out on the title to a case that he did in fact solve. Macnaghten barely mentions the Ripper, giving the case only spare references instead of the few concentrated pages Anderson devotes to it. Abberline and Swanson did not write their memoirs, leaving us nothing to work from to either guess at the Ripper's identity or the case's continued prominence in their lives.

With the police files sealed and not opened for decades—and, when opened, discovered to be largely missing—the bulk of expertise concerning the Ripper case seemed to have passed with the men. The murders themselves drifted out of living memory. Possible witnesses, as well as friends and family members of the victims, would have been valuable sources of information about the case, but only written documents were left as evidence and, as historians lament, few "average citizens" kept notes or diaries about their lives. Newspaper articles became vital for anyone looking into the case after the police files were sealed, and remain important components of research because of how much official documentation has been lost. If it was not written down in 1888, it had no hope of surviving, and even that was not a guarantee. Even the men's memoirs, penned years later, relied on their memories and not on written journals from the time of the murders.

Memories are tricky enough things when they are not wrapped up in international cases of intrigue when the men remembering were at the center of heated criticism for their apparent inability to solve the ongoing case. It makes sense for them to want to say nothing about the case, or to gloss over it as quickly as possible, but it also makes sense for them to attempt to change that narrative by insisting the case *was* solved, the killer *was* known, and the public was made safe by direct police action rather than coincidentally. This is still a difficult argument to make, however. Because the murders themselves were such widely circulated headlines, the identification and neutralization of the murderer should also have been such widespread news. Attempting to claim secret justice years after the fact instead directs attention toward the embarrassing situation that means we still call him "Jack the Ripper" and cannot agree on his—or her, or their—real name.

But the first eight decades of the twentieth century were largely a lull when it came to the Ripper. Over that initial century after Jack first struck, he was a curiosity that popped up from time to time, in fiction—such as in *The Lodger*, first in the novel by Marie Belloc Lowndes in 1913 and the silent Hitchcock film in 1927—and fact: the first book-length study of the Ripper was Leonard Matters' *The Mystery of Jack the Ripper* in 1929, and in 1939 William Stewart proposed that the Ripper had in fact been a woman in *Jack the Ripper: A New Theory*. But it was not until the 1970s and then the hundredth anniversary of the murders in 1988 that things really began to pick up for the Ripper story.

Shift Change

Sir Melville Macnaghten may have been the first person to declare expertise and in effect play Monday morning quarterback on the Ripper case, having come in so soon after the Canonical Five murders. He would have gained an intimate knowledge not only of Whitechapel from a policeman's perspective, but of Victorian policing itself. He would not have needed as much explanation about what it meant to live in Whitechapel in the 1880s, or the social expectations for women and cultural consequences for those who left their marriages and struck out on their own. Macnaghten was, at least, a man existing in the same time and structures as those who had worked the case, even if he was not of the gender or class of the murder victims. But Macnaghten is not the only man who has stepped in and claimed to know better than the men best positioned to have solved the Ripper murders at the time.

For one thing, we have seen significant scientific and technological developments since 1888. Although they were already moving past "photograph a dead woman's eyes to capture the last thing she saw," fingerprinting was not used by the police until 1892. While the police apparently had a field day testing out the tracking skills of bloodhounds, which was mocked by the newspapers, the dogs—not trained scent dogs—never ended up being used, since they were returned to their owner before Mary Jane Kelly's murder. Granted, we do not see CSIs today using bloodhounds after a murder, but even this attempt at modern methods was mocked. It cannot be considered a failure, however, since it was never tested.

The Uhlenhuth test to determine if blood was of animal or human origin was not invented until 1901. Men, assumed to be butchers, and women, who might have been Stewart's midwife, could walk the streets of Whitechapel with visible bloodstains on their clothing and still go unquestioned. This has been put forward as one more reason why the murderer himself was not stopped immediately, even though some of the crimes were committed late enough that he escaped in the early light. Karl Landsteiner first discovered that humans had different blood types in 1900, but it was not until 1907 that we knew there were a total of four. Once a stain was determined to be human blood, blood typing was the first means of narrowing down *whose* blood it might be. DNA was not used to identify criminals until a century after the Ripper's crimes.

Today we have no hope of employing blood hounds or dusting for fingerprints to identify the Ripper, considering the number of people who have walked the streets and touched important surfaces in the intervening years. Construction has further changed the face of Whitechapel, removing some of the landmarks completely. Today's Ripper tours invite visitors to look at a parking deck while imagining the fate of Mary Jane Kelly. Some popular recent claims, such as Patricia Cornwell's identification of artist Walter Sickert as the Ripper, or Russell Edwards' claim that the Ripper was Aaron Kosminski, do indeed rely on DNA analysis. Each of them has tracked down items purported to have been licked or ejaculated on by the Ripper—envelopes of the Ripper letters and a shawl apparently stolen from Mitre Square that had once belonged to Kate Eddowes, respectively—and had scientists test envelope flaps, stamps, and fabric for any traces of DNA.

The impressive news was that genetic material was indeed recoverable in each case, and it could be compared to known descendants of Sickert, Eddowes, and Kosminski. The small print that comes with every triumphant headline declaring a match is that, as advanced as science has become, the only possible comparison was of mitochondrial DNA and not nuclear DNA. Nuclear DNA is considered the gold standard for matching a sample to a distinct individual. When a tech in a police procedural finds a DNA match, it means they have caught the killer. But everyone in a line of matrilineal descent shares the same mitochondrial DNA. Instead of finding a perfect match, each of these Ripper tests concluded that the sample *could* have come from the same family line as the suspects' descendants, although it also could have been one of 40,000—or perhaps 400,000—other people. Until the time comes when science has sufficiently advanced to perform nuclear DNA tests on such old, degraded, and unprotected samples—none of the letters can be proved to have been written, much less sealed, by the Ripper, and the famous shawl had been in a room with Eddowes' descendants prior to testing and has no clear line of provenance—we cannot identify the Ripper through bodily secretions.

So what does that leave us? Old newspapers that have to be treated with some measure of caution, since they were written to sell and not for accuracy. The materials that remained in the official files once they were unsealed. Whatever documents intrepid researchers—or curious descendants—happen to unearth.

If only we had some experts in violent crime who could make sense of such things for us.

It Started with BS

Science has changed since 1888, and so has policing. The job of Victorian police—our original experts—was preventing crime, not solving it. They stood in the same spot their entire shift, as per orders, or walked their beats so precisely that criminals could time their actions between appearances. This was apparently the case with Kate Eddowes' murder, since it occurred in the fourteen minutes it took PC Edward Watkins to complete one circuit of his route. There were advances from scientists, including those forwarded by "The Sherlock Holmes of France" Edmond Locard; "American Sherlock" Edward Oscar Heinrich, the father of forensic criminology; and Calvin Goddard's work with firearms, but none of these help with the Ripper case. For that, we need to venture into social science.

The Netflix show *Mindhunter* (2017) introduced audience members to the idea of a maverick young FBI agent with a new idea on how to approach violent crime. The character of Holden Ford first engages help from a more experienced agent and then the pair join forces with trained psychologist Dr. Carr as they conduct interviews with incarcerated violent criminals to perform the ultimate crime prevention: identifying budding criminals before they escalate. By examining trends in the lives of such serial killers as Edmund Kemper and David Berkowitz, Ford and his colleagues seek to map the commonalities in the offenders' backstories and use what they learn to identify and capture unknown subjects in open cases.

The show is a mix of fiction and reality. Kemper, Berkowitz, and the other offenders are taken from real life and given their real names, while others are fictionalized versions of real-life former FBI Special Agent John Douglas—who wrote the book *Mindhunter: Inside the FBI's Elite Serial Crime Unit* (1995) with co-author Mark Olshaker—his co-interviewer Special Agent Robert Ressler, and Dr. Ann Burgess. Although Douglas and Ressler did not found the FBI's Behavioral Science Unit (BSU, later changed to Behavioral Analysis Unit, BAU), their

Chapter 2. The Changing of the Guard 49

work with Burgess contributed to the official creation of psychological profiling.

Like Bond and Anderson before them, the BSU looked at the evidence offered by crime scenes in order to tease out information about the person who committed the violent acts. Their interviews helped them create a more solid framework for the sorts of statements Bond and Anderson had already suggested: a perpetrator's race could be assumed based on how easily he was overlooked in the neighborhood where the crime was committed, his age determined because of the average age of first offense indicated by their interviews, and his job and marital status based on the times of the murders. Although psychological profiling was still ridiculed as little more than guessing, the BSU was first bolstered by Burgess' academic background and training and then assisted by both the U.S. Senate hearings on serial murder in 1983 and the emerging boom in the genre of true crime. Thus, the FBI presented itself as the expert on this newly identified, wide-reaching threat of serial murder. The cinematic success of *The Silence of the Lambs* (1991), with character Jack Crawford based heavily on John Douglas and Jodie Foster playing a young agent interested in criminal profiling, was just a final layer of cement. Although the "world's first serial killer" Jack the Ripper may have terrorized England, by the 1980s serial killers were a profoundly American product and all great knowledge about this violent threat resided within the FBI.

It was not just the FBI, the Senate hearings, and *The Silence of the Lambs* that taught the average American about this new specialized knowledge, either. True crime as a genre flourished in the 1980s, adding single-subject book-length narratives to a history that goes all the way back to the Puritan execution sermons of the pre-revolutionary colonies. Crime had long been the subject of these shorter documents, from pamphlets to trial reports to newspaper articles to magazines, but books were a relatively new area for the genre. Truman Capote first published *In Cold Blood* as a serial in *The New Yorker* in 1965 before his "non-fiction novel"[4] was published by Random House in 1966. Capote may have led the way for others to follow in his footsteps, including Vincent Bugliosi's best-selling *Helter Skelter* (1974) about the Manson Family murders from the perspective of the prosecutor at Manson's trial, and *In Cold Blood* and *Helter Skelter* remain the top two best-selling true crime books, but the 1980s saw an incredible boom in competition.

It was also smack dab in the middle of what Peter Vronsky has called "the 'Golden Age' of Serial Killers."[5] Ted Bundy had been arrested in 1978 and sentenced to death for the third time in 1980, although that sentence was not carried out until 1989, after Ann Rule had written her first true crime book about him (*The Stranger Beside Me*, 1980) and a made-for-TV-movie had Mark Harmon playing Bundy (*The Deliberate Stranger*, 1986; based on the book of the same name, 1980). Harmon was declared *People*'s sexiest man alive the same year he played Bundy, driving attention to that portrayal and legitimizing the choice to take on the character of a serial killer the way *The Silence of the Lambs*' multiple Oscars authorized interest in the movie and its own subjects of serial killers and the BSU.

All of this together—the interviews and published material that form the basis of criminal profiling; the legitimization of the serial killer threat in the Senate hearings; the boom of true crime books; and the acceptance of less factual crime retellings with central characters of serial killers or criminal profilers—means that the FBI's expertise was very quickly disseminated through various forms of popular culture. Their initial information, as well as their hold on the position of expert, continues today.

The Basic Backstory

The FBI and therefore popular media have educated all of us in the background of a serial killer. As a child, he likely displayed some of the warning triad: lighting fires, torturing animals, or wetting the bed far past a "normal" age. (This last is usually stated without the further explanation that such bed-wetting is generally an indication of mental or emotional distress in the child's life, and not simply an embarrassing occurrence that might, by itself, fuel anger.) The serial killer's father is usually absent, and his mother is frequently abusive, often sexually. He is a loner with few friends and an outcast who has no idea how to relate to girls or women. He chooses victims from his own race who excite him sexually and kills them in specific ways—modus operandi and signatures—to fulfill his sexual desires. When he is not killing, he is a very unassuming Clark Kent sort of figure with nothing special about him, even though there are always signs and something strange about his eyes for those who know what to look for. He starts killing in his mid-twenties and will not stop until something makes him stop, be it incarceration for an unrelated crime or his own death. If a sudden rash of murders suddenly halts, suspects should be sought in prison, the obituaries, or a new city. And finally, killers are either "organized," carefully planning out the entirety of their crimes and making it more difficult to catch them, or "disorganized" men who suddenly fall victim to their own violent urges and are more likely to leave evidence behind.

Chapter 2. The Changing of the Guard

Although "organized" and "disorganized" are two FBI-specific terms for categories that have since been dismissed, the FBI also offers other expert terminology and categories in the form of "high-risk" and "low-risk." When applied to a victim's lifestyle, "high-risk" means that the person in question has made choices that mean her disappearance will go unnoticed for a long period of time, making it difficult to pin down exactly when and where she went missing. Women who hitchhike, are homeless, or who engage in sex work tend to fall into this category. Victims who lead "low-risk" lifestyles have steady jobs and secure housing with coworkers, bosses, friends, roommates, and/or spouses who will immediately notice if they deviate from their normal schedule and report them missing.

When taken out of the FBI's context, these terms seem to support the idea that a victim can be blamed for her own demise. It is her apparent choices that have allowed the serial killer not only to cross paths with her, but also to murder her. This matters because of the oft-repeated long-standing belief that the Canonical Five victims of Jack the Ripper were not only sex workers but also were out searching for their next client when they were murdered. The FBI, however, does not record this information and let it lie, but uses it to ask the question "What sort of criminal would choose such a person as a victim?" For them, using their expert language for its intended purpose, the final question is always one of the perpetrator's identity. Unfortunately, for the rest of us, the high-risk/low-risk lifestyle discussion turns into one of morals and value judgments.

The second area where risk is categorized concerns the crime itself. Snatching a lone woman walking through a darkened alley is, for the criminal, a low-risk situation because it is highly unlikely that he will be seen. He might have no control over whether his victim was meant to meet someone in five minutes who will quickly sound the alarm, but he has a better chance of kidnapping her without the events being seen or recorded. A high-risk crime is one where the criminal put himself in a position where he could easily be spotted, stopped, or captured shortly after attempting the crime. Again, the FBI evaluates the risk level of a crime to then ask "What sort of criminal would choose to act this way?" By comparing situations with unknown subjects against past crimes committed by violent offenders who have been caught and interviewed, they can make statements as to what sort of person is more likely to have committed the unsolved crime and point toward certain personality aspects that will help law enforcement narrow down their search for a suspect.

Note that all of this talk has been gendered with the serial killer as "he" and the victims as "she." One criticism of the FBI's work on criminal profiling, especially the early work, is that their interview subjects were overwhelmingly male. It is to the point where we look at Aileen Wuornos, subject of the movie *Monster* (2003) and the role for which Charlize Theron won multiple awards, including the Oscar for Best Actress, and dub her "the world's first female serial killer." The question of whether women *can* be serial killers tends to dissolve into one of the definition of the term and the multiple categories the FBI recognizes, as opposed to popular culture's fixation on the lust killer: someone who kills for sexual satisfaction. Women, it seems, do not kill in the same ways, or for the same reason, as men, although books about female serial killers have become more popular in the twenty-first century as they argue between erasure and equality.

It should also be noted that the FBI's careful wording of serial killers choosing victims from their own race and of the gender that sexually attracts them means that killers like Dennis Nilsen, Jeffrey Dahmer, and John Wayne Gacy are sites of discussion not only because they are serial murderers, but because of their sexualities. They are Othered not only through their crimes but through non-heteronormative orientations, and discussions of their crimes reflect concerns about perceived threats to heteronormative culture, heterosexual men and boys, and the idea of "homosexual overkill" that arose in response to both these fears and the HIV/AIDS epidemic of the late twentieth century. Men acting violently toward women might not be an entirely *comfortable* topic, but it is more socially accepted and culturally acceptable for men to display this kind of sexually charged violence toward women rather than to other men.

In 1888, the police, as well as the newspapers and the public in general, had trouble answering the question "What sort of person could have done this?" when confronted with the Ripper murders. Murder was such a common occurrence in the East End that many witnesses reported ignoring cries of that very word, but the Ripper murders showed a brutality that many others did not. The Ripper was not content with making sure his victims were no longer alive—he (or she, or they, depending on the argument) mutilated the corpse he had created, spending more time at the scene and putting himself at higher risk for being caught.

This incredible increase of information from the FBI about what sort of person would commit violent crimes was an advance that could, and has been, applied to the Ripper case many times over. Through the 1970s, a total of twelve books had been published about the Ripper; that number is now well over one hundred. It is not that suspects are easier to find, since the most famous—including members of the royal family—were readily named in earlier texts, but that suspects who appear only rarely in historical records now have a complete backstory that can be used to flesh them out. We understand the sort of past that can make a serial killer, and accept it when authors fill in the blanks in historical records with the story that the FBI has taught us is realistic.

For the specific case of the Ripper, though, Special Agent John Douglas took things a step further.

UNSUB Jack the Ripper

In a document dated July 6, 1988, and written for the hundredth anniversary of the Ripper murders, Douglas compiled a criminal profile for "UNSUB; AKA JACK THE RIPPER."[6] The document, now available on the FBI website, consists of seven typewritten pages apparently laid out exactly as the BSU would present a psychological profile in an ongoing, contemporary criminal investigation. It includes sections on victimology, medical examination, crime and crime scene analysis, and a short paragraph on the so-called Ripper letters before engaging in the meat of the profile: offender traits and characteristics, an overview of pre- and post-offense behavior, and a short section with suggestions on how the Ripper should be interrogated.

The final paragraph of the document indicates that Douglas prepared it for the use of Cosgrove-Meurer Productions, Inc. They were producing the television special that interviewed both Douglas and Special Agent Roy Hazelwood, presenting them with four suspects and asking them to choose which one aligned most closely with the profile. Both agreed that the best fit was Aaron Kosminski,[7] although this was hardly enough to solve the mystery once and for all. Hazelwood did, however, write the foreword to Robert House's 2010 book *Jack the Ripper and the Case for Scotland Yard's Prime Suspect* which makes the case for Kozminski (the book's preferred spelling).

Again we have the intersection of the historic crime, the rising new approach to identifying and categorizing violent offenders, and entertainment. Douglas' profile was created specifically for the show because this was not the situation in which such documents were generally constructed. The final section, suggesting that the Ripper should be interviewed early in the morning and would be comfortable writing about his crimes, shows the usual purpose of such a profile: to track down and identify the offender. Since the Ripper crimes were a century in the past, there was no hope of finding a living suspect. There was, however, a chance to display the BSU's powers of perception to a wider audience and to give a more nuanced and supported version of the profile originally created by Sir Thomas Bond.

Douglas starts by acknowledging that the information provided about the Ripper murders does not match what he would usually be given about a case, considering the advances in forensics and psychology that have come about in the past century, and the incomplete police files. He acknowledges that he "filled in the missing pieces of information by making certain probable assumptions,"[8] likely based on his experience interviewing violent criminals of the 1970s and 1980s. Although technology—and society—have changed, the profile proceeds with the assumption that current trends would accurately reflect violent offenders of the 1880s.

The victimology section makes much of the fact that the murdered women were "female prostitutes[s] who drank heavily."[9] Douglas explains what a high-risk victim is, a definition he likely would not need for an official FBI document, and clarifies that, even if DNA evidence had been preserved, it would have been difficult to separate what came from the Ripper from other clients or close contacts the women may have had. He also stresses that the Ripper would have dressed up for his nightly prowls, presenting himself as a man of means, so that the women would have been the ones to approach him. While the mythologized Ripper is usually depicted as a silhouette in a top hat carrying a walking stick, Douglas adds a deeper meaning to the idea that the Ripper would have been well-dressed. It would not have been so over-the-top to get him especially noticed and therefore remembered in poor Whitechapel, the way the traditional Ripper costume would have been, but enough that he did not have to make the first move and initiate contact. (Douglas dismisses the idea that the Ripper could have been a woman simply because he, personally, has never professionally encountered a lust killer who was a woman.)

The profile leans heavily on the commonalities of violent offenders' pasts: overbearing mother, absent father, and either fire-setting or torturing small animals as anger outlets in his childhood. The Ripper developed a violent fantasy life and preferred to keep to himself rather than be in company, and the profession he pursued would have reflected that. If he had ever been married, it would have been a short marriage to a much-older woman, and he was not married at the time of the murders. He likely started murdering in his mid- to late twenties, but Douglas cautions that suspects should not be eliminated purely based on age. All of this information comes not from the Ripper files, but from the common biography Douglas put together from the FBI interviews.

Why does that matter? This document, structured as an official

Chapter 2. The Changing of the Guard 55

FBI profile, was not written for police to use within an ongoing investigation, or even to be kept to a limited audience. It was composed for television, with explanations composed specifically for a large public audience with no law enforcement background. First used for the documentary, it is now available on the FBI's own website. Anyone curious about the case, or about what the FBI's foundational profiler has to say about it, can download it and read Douglas' declarations. And, at this point, we have been taught—or trained—to accept all of this as basically true, with few exceptions and outliers.

It is the story the FBI developed for in-house use and then disseminated through various public and popular venues like this television special, the Senate hearings, and the booming true crime genre. Anthony Hopkins won the Academy Award for Best Actor as Hannibal Lecter offering his own psychological profile of unsub "Buffalo Bill," not only bringing a sense of prestige to *The Silence of the Lambs* but, along with Jodie Foster and Scott Glenn, shining light on the FBI's BSU and the apparently fantastic methods of accurately identifying, and then disarming, the unknown serial killer threats. This general sort of serial killer background, a combination of fill-in-the-blanks and connect-the-dots, was disseminated by the Bureau, acting as expert, and then repeated frequently enough that it is simply accepted.

It is really this aspect of the profile, and not the specific attributes Douglas lists, that opened up an entire world of Ripper suspects for the taking. It is difficult and possibly morally questionable to accuse someone of having been a serial killer posthumously, considering the lack of evidence that can be used to positively link someone to the case, but this generalized biography can be used to fill in the gaps when records are sparse. Very little information is known or can be confirmed about many of these suspects, especially the poor whose movements were not continually documented, but, thanks to the BSU and this general profile, we can fill in the blanks of any suspect's past. If a man—or even a woman, at this point—can be shown to have been alive in 1888, old enough to have reasonably committed the murders, and anywhere near London, then gaps in their past can be filled in using a story that audiences have already been conditioned to accept. Suppositions can be built off the barest hint of factual information as long as lines can be drawn between official records and this FBI-sanctioned backstory.

Douglas does help add some specifics to the Ripper case, however, that may or may not help amateur sleuths shine the light on their own preferred suspect. If the suspect's story aligns with Douglas,' then the profile can be considered reliable; if not, then profiling is more art than science, and has likely increased in accuracy in the decades since

Douglas composed it. He suggests that the murdered women were not the only ones who had problems with alcohol, saying that the Ripper drank prior to each murder. Douglas argues that the Ripper would not have been involved with the police investigation—and that the so-called "Ripper letters" are more likely to be a dead end than evidence—and also declares that the Ripper would not have completed suicide following Mary Jane Kelly's murder, eliminating longstanding Ripper suspect Montague John Druitt. He also adds that interviewers would have found a pressure point in reminding the Ripper that he had been "soiled" with the victim's blood, ending with the observation that "Jack the Ripper believed the homicides were justified and he was only removing perishable items—who were like garbage."[10]

Even these more specific observations might make us say "So what?" because they seem so commonplace ... now. We somehow all know that serial killers are unstable, but manage to hold it together in public for long enough to complete multiple murders; that there has always been something "off" about them that is obvious in hindsight; and that they have a hate/attraction relationship with their victims and with murder. These are simply accepted as facts when it comes to the way twenty-first-century Americans address and consume serial killer narratives. We know it, and the FBI backs us up, because the FBI told us in the first place.

It is a cycle that feeds and refreshes itself as it gets reaffirmed in each further retelling. True crime books have become "murder by numbers,"[11] a strict outline formed by this BSU-approved backstory that only needs authors to fill in the proper names and dates in the spaces provided—and, since the late 1980s, so many authors have stepped up to the challenge.

Chapter 3

Fit to Print

Although it might be hard to believe these days, considering the vast—or perhaps overwhelming—number of Ripper texts available, full-length books about the Ripper had a slow start. Once the Ripper left the newspapers, there was a time when no one seemed to want to print anything about him at all. Perhaps the same pressure that shortened Mary Jane Kelly's death inquest and limited those headlines acted on all publications. Although the police and others connected to the case wrote about it in their memoirs, as outlined in Chapter 2, they largely did so with the insistence that the killer had indeed been identified and was no longer a threat. The mystery may have been unsolved in the headlines, but those "in the know" knew better, although they could only hint at the solution.

Once pushed out of the headlines, the Ripper story was also largely suppressed in other print formats. Although the men who had worked the case reflected on the Ripper in their autobiographies, time quickly moved past, and then "the Second World War put a brake on speculation about the Ripper and drew a line under an era when first-hand knowledge and recollections could be passed on."[1] The sealed police files also limited access to information about the Ripper, making it all the more difficult for early authors to find and confirm data. Many elements were introduced into the Ripper narrative in these early decades that were later found to be untrue, such as the idea that Mary Jane Kelly was pregnant at the time of her death and, despite work done to update and clarify the facts, myths remain in circulation.

Changing cultural and societal norms also influenced the Ripper stories presented in different generations, such as how the "Cold War brought about further conjectures of Jack the Ripper as the demonized personage of rogue social and political systems."[2] Considered an outsider from the beginning, always Other and not "one of us," the nature of the Ripper's marginalized identity has experienced certain telling shifts while other aspects have remained more or less stable. This is not to say that there have been no wild theories that have disrupted the general narrative—indeed, "the seventies did untold harm to the search for Jack the Ripper and its effects are still being felt today"[3]—but we can still make connections, if not through the history of the entire Ripper story, then to the time period in which these deviations were composed.

The Early Rippers

One of the first full-length texts about the Ripper was the Danish *Hvem Var Jack the Ripper?* by Carl Muusmann, published in 1908, but "the first serious case study of the crimes in English"[4] was Leonard Matters' 1929 *The Mystery of Jack the Ripper*. Matters includes photos of many of the murder locations as they appeared at the time and forwarded the "Dr. Stanley" theory: a man going by that pseudonym apparently gave a deathbed confession to the murders, explaining that his motive was finding the woman who had infected—and then killed—his beloved son with syphilis. This woman was in fact Mary Jane Kelly, but Dr. Stanley had a hard time finding her and thus had to kill everyone who pointed him along the way.

Matters does not give us "Dr. Stanley's" real name, so there is no way for researchers to follow up on the veracity of this story. It has, however, been argued first that syphilis would not have killed Dr. Stanley's son in as short a timeline as the narrative claims, and second, that there is no record of Mary Jane Kelly having been diagnosed with syphilis. What *The Mystery of Jack the Ripper* does is bring the case back into public light and tackle the tricky question of motive.

From the beginning, motive was "always the bugbear when it concerns Jack the Ripper."[5] It was a struggle in newspaper reporting and for the police, since they had not come across such a series of crimes before. This is also the reason the Ripper frequently gets billed as "the world's first serial killer." Although serial killers predate both the phrase and the Ripper, the Autumn of Terror was the first time that such connected and gruesome murders were recorded, reported, and splashed about in the news of not only the region but also the world. As the murders were happening, and as reporters needed to fill in the gaps between them by rehashing the crimes, they kept trying to explain why one person would kill these women in this specific way. A narrative that could connect and explain the deaths would include a motive, but no firm theories were forthcoming in 1888.

In 1929, Matters' book attempted to answer numerous questions about the case. Why would someone choose to murder sex workers? Dr.

Stanley was after one particular sex worker, but he did not want Mary Jane Kelly to know he was coming, so he murdered anyone he questioned in his search. Did Jack the Ripper have medical training? He did, in fact. Why did the murders end with Marie Jeanette Kelly? Because she was the one Dr. Stanley felt was responsible for his son's death and the ultimate target of his revenge. She was the youngest and apparently the most beautiful of the women killed during the Autumn of Terror because she had entranced the younger Dr. Stanley and seduced him, and Matters describes Kelly as "just one of those light-hearted creatures who seemed to have been destined for the night-life into which she fitted so naturally."[6]

Catherine Eddowes' murder was one of mistaken identity, since she frequently used her boyfriend's last name and was known to introduce herself as Kate Kelly. As the second victim of the Double Event and the fourth of the Canonical Five, Eddowes was murdered both quickly and the most brutally of the series thus far. Matters explains this by indicating Dr. Stanley thought he had found his intended prey, but he then realized "[s]he was old and ugly"[7] and thus could not have captured his son's attention. Marie Jeanette was both young and beautiful despite being an East End sex worker, and this should have helped Dr. Stanley on his quest to track her down, but Matters also reported that Marie Jeanette rarely walked the streets alone. Perhaps she was aware that her status as both seductress and murderess of "respectable" young men made her position all the more precarious.

By making the tale of the Whitechapel murders into one of revenge, Matters assigned a reason for these murders and provided a narrative connection that was lacking in the contemporary newspaper reports. By using Dr. Stanley, Matters did not have to provide a known connection between the five victims—the mad doctor, one of the theories of the Autumn of Terror, simply assumed the women he accosted would know of the younger, prettier, and apparently charismatic Kelly. The brutality of the murders came from the doctor's grief and anger over his lost son, with the increasing horror correlating to his thoughts that he had the woman at fault. The murders stopped with Kelly because they had, in fact, started with Kelly—a theme that will continue through the decades in new forms. Although Matters' theory of "Dr. Stanley" has been left behind, many elements of his tale continue.

Two more books were published in the following decade, Edwin T. Woodhall's *Jack the Ripper; or, When London Walked in Terror* in 1937 and William Stewart's *Jack the Ripper: A New Theory* in 1939. Although Stewart's title is the only one to advertise it, both of these books include the theory that the Ripper was, in fact, a woman. This was not an entirely new theory as the flashy title of Stewart's book indicates. Indeed, such titles were not left behind in the early twentieth century, as John Morris' 2012 book *Jack the Ripper: The Hand of a Woman* includes a further *The Compelling New Account* on the cover. In the 1930s as in the 2010s, readers are expected to be shocked at the idea that a serial killer—especially one of the world's most famous serial killers—might have been a woman.

At one point Woodhall suggests that the Ripper was in fact a woman named Olga Tchkersoff who, like Dr. Stanley, sought revenge for a beloved family member. Rather than having a son who died because of a sexually transmitted disease passed on by a sex worker, Olga murdered sex workers because they had enticed her own sister to "fall" and become one of their number. After her younger sister's return home and tragic death, Olga decided that "all women of that type were her enemy, innocent or otherwise,"[8] and that she would extract her revenge by dressing as a man when leaving the home she shared with an elderly couple in order to commit the murders. The husband of the pair, it should be mentioned, allowed Olga to run away, swore his wife to secrecy, and made sure to eliminate any evidence should the police come around, having identified the Ripper at last. It seems that Olga's motive for committing the horrific and bloody murders was understandable.

Stewart's suggested Ripper likewise did not care about the identity of her victims beyond their occupation as sex workers. He does not forward a name but rather indicates that the Ripper might have been a midwife who, after serving out a sentence for performing an illegal operation—an abortion—on a sex worker who then reported her to the police, decided to avenge herself against the entire profession. Although Woodhall does not go into such detail, Stewart argues that the murdered women would have accepted, and even invited, a midwife to go with them into a private location, the same way the papers and reading public accused the women of assisting in their own murders by leading the Ripper to isolated places as a client. Stewart's identification of the Ripper as a midwife also gives his suspect the medical training afforded to Dr. Stanley and under such discussion during 1888.

All three of these earliest English books largely intertwine their identification of the Ripper with the motive of personal revenge. Dr. Stanley and Olga Tchkersoff seek justice for a beloved and wronged deceased loved one, while Stewart's midwife was betrayed for helping the poorest and most helpless class of women. If the reporters and police in 1888 could not connect the murder victims, it is because there *was* no connection beyond their occupation—Dr. Stanley simply used the women to track down his true goal, while Olga Tchkersoff and the midwife were unconcerned with anything beyond the women's occupation. Although there is no neat and tidy reason as to why Olga Tchkersoff fled and the midwife stopped killing after Mary Jane Kelly, she was Dr. Stanley's intended victim all along.

The Great Ripper Conspiracy

In 1970, British surgeon Thomas E.A. Stowell began a trend that still holds audiences in thrall today: the royal conspiracy and coverup explanations for the Ripper murders. Stowell combined a few common threads when he wrote that the Ripper had contracted syphilis and the disease was driving him insane, which led to the murders.[9] He did not name his chosen suspect in the article, but readers concluded from his myriad hints that he meant to implicate Queen Victoria's grandson, Prince Albert Victor, Duke of Clarence and Avondale, fondly known as Prince Eddy. Stowell wrote a letter to the editor firmly denying this claim,[10] and it was published the day after he died. Although Stowell was no longer around to further his argument and put forth another possible Ripper, the damage—or perhaps the intrigue—was done. The 1970s were a fruitful time for conspiracy theories, and the idea that the Ripper murders might be connected in some way to the crown was far too juicy to let lie.

Michael Harrison approached the royal family idea in book form with *Clarence* in 1972. Despite the title, Harrison suggests that the murderer was not in fact Prince Eddy, but his friend and apparent former lover James Kenneth Stephen. The murders began when the couple parted ways and Stephen apparently had difficulty coping with the end of the affair. The murders were supposedly his means of working through his feelings, especially since he had received a head injury in 1886 that may have unbalanced him. The fact that he was admitted to an asylum in 1891 and died there in 1892 adds to his appeal as a suspect, hearkening back to the madness motive already suggested in 1888. If a man is mad, then there is no other explanation necessary for his actions. Although Harrison's book predates the media's obsession with "homosexual overkill," which surfaced after the arrest of Jeffrey Dahmer in 1991,[11] Stephen's apparent hatred of women, supported by choice lines from his writings, provided the explanation for why he would have become the Ripper. Madness and homosexuality combined to form an acceptable explanation for why he would have killed strangers so brutally.

In 1978, Frank Spiering's book *Prince Jack* was published, and it did what Harrison's title suggested: outright accused Prince Eddy of being the Ripper. Part of Spiering's evidence was a previously undiscovered journal of Sir William Gull, Queen Victoria's personal physician, although Spiering seems to be the only person to ever have seen the artifact. Journals and diaries are a central component of many Ripper theories as authors claim to be the first to have uncovered a previously-hidden link but, unfortunately for Spiering, his theory was unsupportable. Even if he had such evidence to present to the public, it could be countered with, for example, Prince Eddy's royal schedule and his duties to the crown. The heir to the throne could not be so immediately connected to the Ripper murders, but a theory arose in the 1970s that placed him at the center of events that led to the Ripper's creation all the same.

Perhaps the most famous Ripper conspiracy theory is Stephen Knight's 1976 *Jack the Ripper: The Final Solution*, adapted into both the graphic novel (1989) and the movie (2001) *From Hell*. *The Final Solution* takes full advantage of the decade's propensity for conspiracy theories: Prince Albert Victor had not only a secret marriage but also a secret child, and Queen Victoria's personal physician, Sir William Gull, took it upon himself to institutionalize the prince's wife and perform experiments on her to cause brain damage and erase her memory. Unfortunately the child ended up in the care of Mary Jane Kelly, who told her friends Polly Nichols, Annie Chapman, and Liz Stride all about the child's father. Since she wanted to blackmail the crown with this information, the Freemasons decided that all of the women involved in the plot needed to die. Gull and his coachman became Jack the Ripper in order to protect the royal family and ensure that no one would either blackmail the Queen or make it known that the prince had married a commoner, and a Catholic, to boot.

The story is not one of Knight's own making and did not originate in his book. In 1973 a man named Joseph Gorman appeared on the BBC's television series *Jack the Ripper* and first presented this story to a rather confused audience. The series became a book, *The Ripper File*, published in 1975. Knight only published *The Final Solution* after further conversations with Gorman, who claimed he knew the story because it was his own grandmother who had married the prince. As the apparent descendant of Prince Eddy's heretofore unknown child, Gorman presented himself as a man with an interesting—and potentially groundbreaking—heritage. Knight himself could not confirm all of Gorman's story and indeed, many details were provably wrong. Fellow Ripper researcher and friend Colin Wilson wrote after Knight's death at the age of thirty-three that he suspected Knight "wrote the book with his tongue in his cheek, then found himself caught up in a success that prevented him from retracting or quietly disowning it."[12] Knight, like Stowell, did not have the time to fully gain perspective on the impact of his writing and offer a more complete explanation for what was said.

Although the role of the Freemasons in the Ripper murders has intrigued many, Ripperologists have dismissed Knight's complicated, convoluted theory in large part based on Gull's health in the autumn of 1888. Absence of proof is not proof of absence, since naturally Freemasons at all levels would have worked to cover up the plot, had it existed. However, Gull was physically unwell after several strokes and could hardly have traveled around the East End in his carriage, committing five murders, even if he did indeed subdue his victims in advance by offering them drugged grapes. Despite the fact that Gorman's—and therefore Knight's—chosen suspect could not have been the killer, other authors have drawn out elements of Knight's tale and continued to forward at least some variation of the royal Ripper conspiracy.

Although no longer the most famous proponent of this theory, in 1990 Jean Overton Fuller was the first to indicate that Knight had nevertheless found himself close to the truth with her book *Sickert and the Ripper Crimes: 1888 Ripper Murders and the Artist Walter Richard Sickert*. Knight recognized Sickert as a player in the events leading up to the murders, since he was the one meant to have introduced Prince Eddy to his Catholic bride and then brought in Mary Jane Kelly as the baby's nursemaid, but Fuller argued that Gorman and Knight had the real killer wrong. Drawing on a story passed down by a friend of her mother's, Fuller argued that the artist Walter Sickert, whose work showed a familiarity with the murders, was in fact the murderer himself.

In 2002, Patricia Cornwell, perhaps most famous for her series about fictional medical examiner Kay Scarpetta, published *Portrait of a Killer: Jack the Ripper—Case Closed* with much fanfare. The book references neither Knight nor Fuller, although Cornwell argues that Sickert was indeed the Ripper. She spent a great deal of her own money to buy Sickert's belongings, including some paintings, and paid for DNA tests to be run comparing samples from Sickert against the envelopes and stamps of selected Ripper letters. Cornwell does not address the fact that few if any of the Ripper letters are likely to have come from the killer himself, or the possibility that letters could have been sealed and stamps licked by postal employees. Indeed, she doubles down on her evidence in her 2017 follow up, *Ripper: The Secret Life of Walter Sickert*.

While continuing to keep a longstanding Ripper conspiracy theory relevant, Cornwell engages in two newer themes of twenty-first-century Ripperology: using DNA testing to "prove" that a given suspect was a killer, and opting to ignore previous work by established Ripper theorists and choosing to go her own way as a lone wolf in search of the truth. These two aspects commonly go hand in hand and will be discussed shortly. First, however, we must address another royal conspiracy theory from the 1990s: one which did not catch on nearly as well as Knight's version, and might be more complicated, but which highlights a number of contemporary fears.

The Ripper's Sexuality

John Wilding's 1993 *Jack the Ripper: Revealed* was not the first to question whether the Ripper might have actually been two people, or that the two people involved might have been gay. Indeed, Harrison's suggestion that J.K. Stephen was the Ripper centered the motive on a hatred of women and the instigating event as the end of his relationship with Prince Eddy. However, the 1990s had new fears surrounding not only homosexual men, but homosexual men as serial killers, following John Wayne Gacy's arrest in late 1978 and the more recent arrest of Jeffrey Dahmer in 1991. While Gacy and Dahmer worked alone, other pairs such as Leonard Lake and Charles Ng, apprehended in 1985, and Kenneth Bianchi and Angelo Buono, apprehend in 1989, killed together without being suspected of having a romantic or sexual relationship with each other. Wilding combines the ideas of homosexual overkill and platonic partners in murder with his new theory.

Like many others, Wilding puts the blame for the Ripper on Mary Jane Kelly's shoulders. She is at the center of his story because she has been carrying on an affair not with Prince Eddy, but with his father Bertie, the future King Edward VII. Two of Prince Eddy's friends came together in fear that this impending baby might somehow interfere with Eddy's inheritance: the aforementioned J.K. Stephen and a young lawyer/schoolteacher Montague John Druitt, a perennial Ripper suspected because he completed suicide by drowning himself in the Thames shortly after the Autumn of Terror was over.

Wilding offers some interesting explanations as to why Stephen and Druitt killed so many before reaching Mary Jane Kelly. For example, he takes Polly's well-known final words about her new bonnet and interprets it as Kelly noticing she was being followed and quickly giving Polly her bonnet, thereby distracting the murderers so she could escape. When she confides in her friend Annie Chapman, Kelly signs her death warrant. It transpires that Queen Victoria learns of the pregnancy and intervenes on Kelly's behalf, declaring that any part of her beloved Albert must be saved, and here Wilding places even more blame on Kelly: she works with the murdering duo to choose the next few victims, ending by helping them fake her own death so she might be whisked away to give birth to the queen's grandson in peace.

This seems to be the only Ripper narrative in which the killers' plans change in the middle. Dr. Stanley, Olga Tchkersoff, the avenging midwife, the Freemasons, and other Rippers have one goal from the beginning and, either coincidentally or purposefully, complete that goal with murdering Mary Jane Kelly. The killer duo of Stephen and Druitt are caught before they can complete their intended murder, identified, and then forced to work with their intended victim to complete further murders. Instead of killing the woman pregnant with their friend's half-sibling, they end up helping her fake her own death so she can be taken away and the child raised in safety.

Wilding also takes this extra step to implicate Kelly in the murders. Although many narratives place her as the cause for the Ripper's spree, be it because she infected a beloved son with a deadly disease or because she roped her friends into a plot against the crown, only here does she play an active role in the murders themselves. Wilding has her personally choosing Kate Eddowes and plying her with alcohol so that she might not be aware of the murder, a plan that backfires because Eddowes was arrested for public drunkenness before she could be killed. Kelly is also responsible for choosing the woman to be found murdered and mutilated in her own room, specifically picking someone to die in her stead and be buried with her name on the headstone. Perhaps she did not wield the knife, but she chose those who would die.

The motive Wilding gives his pair of Rippers is questionable—why would a baby younger than Eddy, born of a woman who was not the crown princess, have any effect whatsoever on his inheritance?—but it is perhaps difficult to explain why two homosexual men would choose to murder women, especially when the FBI by then made it clear that sexual serial killers choose victims of their own race and of the gender that sexually attracts them. The Ripper murders have long been considered sex murders for a number of reasons, including the women's apparent profession and the locations of the mutilations, and while authors have struggled to explain why the Ripper might have felt this attraction-repulsion toward these specific women, it becomes even more difficult when the Ripper himself is meant to feel no sexual attraction toward any women.

David Abrahamsen, a forensic psychiatrist who interviewed, among others, David Berkowitz, takes his own approach to the Ripper narrative in his 1993 book *Murder and Madness: The Secret Life of Jack the Ripper* when he decides that his own killer pair is Prince Eddy and J.K. Stephen. For Abrahamsen, the pair is a romantically and sexually involved couple at the time of the murders. As a motive, Abrahamsen opts for misogyny and childhood abuse. Indeed, he ends his book by telling readers "Prince Eddy and J.K. Stephen were victims but so were those who raised them. In a significant way, we are all victims of victims,"[13] indicating that the Ripper murders were in fact the result of intergenerational trauma and overall cycles of abuse. It seems that the men killed because they could not help themselves from perpetuating violence and therefore cannot be held responsible for their actions, since they were themselves reactions against their own pasts.

Abrahamsen writes from a position of authority due to his education and past experience with real-life twentieth-century murder and serial murder cases, so readers are primed for a certain level of expertise and insight into the Ripper murders. Indeed, he relies on discussions of psychology and takes the time to inform his readers of apparently expected and known behavior of both homosexual men and "transvestites," conclusions that were seen as outdated and offensive even at the time. Because of his personal involvement in famous cases and the degrees that follow his name on the cover, Abrahamsen is expected to be able to make trustworthy leaps when it comes to the psychology of the people in question, although he seems to always opt for the deviant explanations rather than the mundane. Granted, as this is his background it might be a simple case of viewing everything as a nail so that he can use his hammer, but all of this put together makes his narrative more off-putting than intriguing.

The dismissal of Wilding's and Abrahamsen's theories comes not only because of the lack of evidence to support their chosen Ripper suspects, but also because their choice of Rippers—gay men—is not supported by the evidence the FBI has gathered and publicized concerning serial killers. Since 1888, the most common theory is that the Ripper was a man working alone, and even the FBI's extensive bank of evidence supports this idea. Identifying the Ripper as a pair of gay men in the late twentieth century is similar to ideas of the Ripper's foreignness or Jewishness in the late nineteenth century as a society attempts to identify the killer as Other and place him within a marginalized, and therefore feared, population.

In each case those Othered were isolated and forced to rely on each other for support. The Jewish population of the East End in 1888 was denied state support and thus created their own systems to care for their own people, and the gay population was suppressed and left to its own devices during the AIDS epidemic. Further, individual members of the given marginalized peoples—Israel Lipski, Dahmer, and Gacy—had been publicly convicted of violent crimes and were at the forefront of the general population's mind due to media coverage of the murders. By centering the identity of the Ripper within these populations, dominant culture was able to once again declare that the Ripper was one of Them, not one of Us, and therefore not a product of our own society.

Although suggestions that the Ripper was Jewish have endured past the 1880s, suggestions that the Ripper was a gay man or a pair of gay men have largely been dismissed. The FBI's information about serial killers, as well as the general population of the East End, suggested that the Ripper could indeed have been a Jewish man—although his Jewishness would not have been a main cause for the murders—but do not support that a gay man or men would kill women in such a way, despite misogyny's hold. Indeed, it is far more likely that gay men would become victims of violent crimes rather than perpetrators. Although the United Kingdom has guidance against using gay panic or "The Portsmouth Defense"[14] in cases of violent crime, the United States has no such national ban and allows individual states to decide whether perceived sexual orientation is a viable defense. In states where it is allowed, it is now generally used as a supplemental or secondary defense to bolster another initial defense in order to be more acceptable and to have a better chance of swaying the jury.

The idea of a homosexual Ripper or Rippers is therefore dismissed these days, even without needing to add in more arguments about the specific individuals chosen to occupy that role. The twenty-first century has, however, given rise to a new narrative of the Ripper murders.

Technology Versus the Ripper

Patricia Cornwell used advances in DNA technology to match the artist Walter Sickert to samples she obtained from the envelopes and stamps of a selection of Ripper letters. In this case, "match" means that Sickert was not excluded as one of the tens of thousands—if not hundreds of thousands—of people who might have licked either the stamp or the envelope. Despite these long odds and the fact that no one has been able to prove that the Ripper himself penned, much less sealed, those letters, she continues to stand by her identification. Although Cornwell uses historical documents and some of Sickert's paintings to support her theories and suppositions, the DNA identification took center stage when her book was announced.

DNA evidence was also at the center of Russell Edwards' 2014 book

Naming Jack the Ripper. Like Cornwell, Edwards was not the first person to bring up the name of his chosen suspect—although, also like Cornwell, Edwards emphasized the fact that he refused to engage with established Ripper experts or even take their advice. He wanted to participate in the mystery on his own, unencumbered by the research or advice offered by those who had already been working on the case. Indeed, in his introduction Edwards tells how established authority Stewart Evans attended the auction of the shawl that forms the center of Edwards' argument and told him that "nobody should buy it."[15] Intent on "proving" the identification of the Ripper once and for all, Edwards ignored him, purchased the shawl, and paid for Dr. Jari Louhelainen to perform tests on it.

The shawl has the same issues as the Ripper letters: despite Edwards' claims, there is no evidence that it once belonged to Catherine Eddowes and was found at the scene of her murder in Mitre Square. Louhelainen's tests supposedly proved that the blood on the shawl belonged to Eddowes and the semen stains matched Aaron Kosminski, a Polish barber and hairdresser initially connected to the Ripper murders in The Macnaghten Memoranda in 1894. (See Chapter 2 for more information on Macnaghten.) Kosminski was not a new name in the Ripper game and had even recently been named in *Jack the Ripper and the Case for Scotland Yard's Prime Suspect* in 2011. What Edwards brought to the table—and what made up much of the marketing for *Naming Jack the Ripper*—was this supposedly conclusive DNA evidence.

Edwards' argument suffers from many of the same critiques of Cornwell's. Despite advances in technology, the tests they ordered could only identify mitochondrial DNA and not nuclear DNA. Although nuclear DNA testing is famous in police procedurals for identifying the one single person who could have left such a sample behind, mitochondrial DNA establishes family lines instead of individual identities. Yes, Eddowes and Kosminski *could* have been the ones to contribute to the stains on the shawl, but so could tens or hundreds of thousands of others. The tests did not eliminate them, but they did not narrow things down to them and only them.

The shawl also suffers from an unclear provenance. Twenty-first-century fans raised on shows like *CSI* understand that evidence must be carefully collected and traced in its movements from the crime scene to the lab to ensure that it was neither lost nor swapped out for a similar item, and that it has not been contaminated. One of the reasons Evans told Edwards not to buy the shawl was that there was no evidence it actually came from the scene at Mitre Square, and Edwards received critique for allowing Eddowes' descendants to be in the room with the shawl without protecting it from contamination. Since the test was for mitochondrial DNA, the samples matched might have been from her living descendants and not from 1888.

Further, although Edwards' book was available in 2014, Louhelainen did not publish his own work until years later. His case report "Forensic Investigation of a Shawl Linked to the 'Jack the Ripper' Murders" was published in the *Journal of Forensic Sciences* in 2020 and only then were his processes and procedures fully open to scrutiny. This publication allowed headlines to once again trumpet that Jack the Ripper had been identified due to DNA testing, but they were once again wrong. Louhelainen's work was critiqued by his peers and the results once again dismissed.

The idea that we might be able to finally conclusively identify the Ripper after more than a century is a tempting one. Just as we like to think—and the FBI likes us to think—that the Ripper could not have gotten away with his crimes today, we like to believe that technology as well as psychology has outpaced the rudimentary "world's first serial killer." Police procedurals have primed us to believe in the conclusive power of the DNA test and to accept that it is indeed possible to know, beyond a doubt, that an individual has committed a crime. Why not use such powerful modern technology to reach back in time and solve the most famous unsolved case?

From a marketing point of view it of course makes sense to announce such testing as irrefutable and declare that it has, indeed, solved the question of the Ripper's identity once and for all. Cornwell and Edwards support their arguments with their own research—as lone wolves, they have no one else's to call upon, and would not trust anything they did find—into the biographies of their chosen Rippers, but each is foiled by the lack of records that others have already found. Yes, it is possible to fill in the gaps by relying on the FBI's accepted serial killer backstory, but even then the authors find themselves having to shoehorn known information into this narrative.

Cornwell has even pushed back against critique of her book by saying that Ripperologists, discussed further in Chapter 4, "don't want somebody else to find out the suspect."[16] She frames it as resistance solely because she is an outsider and argues that Ripperologists do not, in fact, want the mystery to be solved rather than addressing concerns with her scientific procedure. Cornwell and Edwards both position themselves as the underdogs in opposition to the established experts, fighting against the longstanding dominant narrative and individually uncovering the real truth in a world that prefers the mystery. Americans especially love the underdog trope and the idea that a single hardworking person can topple established norms in order to shine light on something that has long been ignored or purposefully hidden. Indeed, this is one of the reasons conspiracy theories hold so much sway. By arguing that established experts will want to bury their work because it does not come from their preferred inner circle and because it reveals information they would rather keep hidden, Cornwell and Edwards situate their work in the context of this emotional appeal to gain support and sympathy.

Unfortunately for them both, despite Cornwell's second book expounding on her theory and Louhelainen's academic article, the issues with their methods and conclusions remain. Granted, no book proposing a conclusive identity of the Ripper likes to direct attention toward its assumptions, probabilities, and any information that may have been suppressed in order to sustain the story, but the emphasized use of science to support their theories places a higher expectation on the scientific method and a specific approach to the data. Whereas in scientific experiments no result is still a result, Cornwell and Edwards suppress many elements of the tests they paid for in order to emphasize the fact that they, above all others, have found the solution.

Secret Journals

DNA is not the only element authors can find and use to stake their claims while also suggesting that those who have gone before them were misled or outright incorrect. In some cases the "newly rediscovered" information was due to the fact that the Metropolitan Police Files concerning the case were sealed and not publicly available until 1976.[17] These files were, however, incomplete, since it seems that pieces had been removed in the intervening decades, possibly as souvenirs. Some of the missing documents have emerged since then, and other pieces of evidence, such as the Swanson Marginalia and The Littlechild Letter,[18] have likewise come to light.

Many of these papers have been made public in the wake of their discovery. Although they lend support to given suspects or offer insight into the thought processes of those who were involved in the case, they do not positively identify a single person as having been the Ripper. Still other documents apparently do exactly that, although they do not stand up to intense scrutiny nearly as well as these individual notes.

In 1992, Michael Barrett presented the world with a diary he said was written by James Maybrick. The book does not name its author, but it does confess to the Canonical Five murders, as well as two others that have yet to be identified. Like Cornwell and Edwards, Barrett struggled with explaining how, exactly, the diary was concealed and then revealed, explaining first that a friend gave it to him and then changing his story to say that the diary had been in his wife's family for years. Shirley Harrison's *The Diary of Jack the Ripper* came out in 1993, and despite controversy over the diary, she followed it up a decade later with *Jack the Ripper: The American Connection*, the cover of which advertises that it includes Maybrick's diary. The stated American connection is not just that of his wife, a woman from Alabama who was convicted of Maybrick's murder, but the apparent fact that Maybrick had also been in Austin, Texas, at the same time as a string of brutal murders in that city. Connecting one "known" serial killer to another series of unsolved murders is a recent trend that helps solve unsolved murders, supports the FBI's assertion that a serial killer will continue killing unless stopped by an outside force, and adds new layers of horror to the presented story.

Not everyone was as supportive of the diaries as Harrison, but tests of the diary's ink and paper were inconclusive. The diary was written in a genuine Victorian scrapbook, but pages at the front—that might have originally held photographs—were torn out, and the handwriting likewise divided experts. To add to the confusion, Barrett swore not one but two affidavits in 1995 that he dictated the entire diary to his wife. Despite this, and in part because Barrett later withdrew the affidavits, Harrison and others still stand by the authenticity of the diary. Adding to the convoluted story was the appearance of a pocket watch in 1993 that contains multiple etchings inside its brass case, including "J. Maybrick," "I am Jack," and the initials of the murdered women—that is, the Canonical Five, and not the two more mentioned in the diary but still unidentified. The watch was studied under an electron microscope and Dr. Robert Wild concluded that the engravings were "at least several tens of years" old.[19] Although not discovered together, and despite the questions of the diary's authenticity, it seems that the pocket watch supports Maybrick's guilt.

We are once again confronted with a complicated explanation of the Ripper's identity that, quite honestly, fails to explain anything. Both Maybricks had affairs during their marriage, although his were more numerous and thought to have predated hers, except the diary indicates that the murders began because he knew of her affair. The diary does not include Maybrick's name, and the pocket watch has no reference to the other two murders. The two pieces of evidence were connected by their content and not by their owners, and yet Barrett first changed his story about how he came into possession of the diary and then confessed that it was a forgery.

It was the diary and the diary alone that forwarded Maybrick's name as a Ripper suspect. He was not a contemporary suspect or one mentioned in the biographies and reflections of the men who worked the case. Until Barrett, Maybrick was simply a cotton merchant who overdosed on arsenic in early 1889. His wife's story may have been more intriguing, since Florence—an American—was sentenced to death for his murder and later released, although she never saw their children again. Had she known, or anyone suspected, that Maybrick was the Ripper, it could have been brought out during her defense.

Oddly enough, it is not only the *presence* of a diary that can lead to a heretofore unlikely suspect being named. Tony Williams, great-great-nephew of Welsh physician and baronet Sir John Williams, put forth his famous ancestor as a suspect because he discovered a *gap* in Sir John's diaries. Although the physician's papers were collected and housed at the National Library of Wales, Tony discovered that there were no entries for 1888. In fact, that year seemed to have been deliberately cut out.

Because of this absence, some letters Tony found indicating Sir John was in Whitechapel, and a knife found among Sir John's collected slides, Tony argued that his ancestor had been Jack the Ripper. The diary had been edited to remove the sort of evidence and confessions that were present within the Ripper diary apparently written by James Maybrick. *Uncle Jack* once again recalls the Autumn of Terror's fear that the murders were being carried out by a doctor, and possibly a mad one, but Tony gives his great-great-uncle a motive of sorts: Sir John was, among other accomplishments, an obstetric surgeon. The wounds on the murdered women, and especially the fact that Annie Chapman's uterus was removed, seemed to indicate not only a physician, but specifically a physician of women.

Tony Williams gives his great-great-uncle a sort of mad scientist approach to the murders. Sir John and his wife had no children, and thus he is meant to have practiced in the East End in order to learn more about fertility. Sir John apparently also carried on an affair with Mary Jane Kelly, whom he hoped to impregnate. When he ended up murdering his mistress, as well, he suffered a breakdown and the murders ended.

In 2012, as previously mentioned, John Morris published *Jack the Ripper: The Hand of a Woman* and referenced exactly the same gap in Sir John's personal accounts, as well as speculating about a breakdown, but Morris pointed the finger at someone else: Mary Elizabeth Anne Hughes Williams, Sir John's wife. Instead of being a physician herself, Lizzie, as Morris calls her, learned enough from her husband's practice to indicate that the Ripper was indeed a doctor. Her motive combines multiple elements of Tony Williams' story as well as those that place Mary Jane Kelly as the cause of the murders: Lizzie knew her husband was upset at their lack of children, and she also knew that he sought out a sex worker in the East End to have his child. Her search for Mary Jane Kelly is reminiscent of Dr. Stanley's, including the misidentification of Kate Eddowes as Mary Jane Kelly, and the murders end with Kelly because she was the object of the Ripper's fury this entire time. The mental breakdown Tony Williams speculates now comes because of Sir John's realizations of his wife's murder spree, and the missing diary pages do not implicate Sir John, but express concerns about Lizzie.

It is perhaps easier for us to accept that the Ripper might have known a physician and learned practices unofficially rather than accepting that a trained physician might ignore the Hippocratic oath and commit murder, but these two narratives indicate that we have not yet given up on the Ripper-as-doctor theory. It was so prevalent during the murders that men were mistrusted simply for carrying doctors' bags, and there was not agreement at the time over whether the Ripper had any medical training. The records are not clear enough for today's experts to conclusively answer that question, and the example of serial killer Harold Shipman, known as "Doctor Death" and convicted of fifteen murders although suspected of over 200, at least proves a serial-killing physician is possible. For women, the concept of the "angel of death" or the "angel of mercy" establishes that nurses have been known to kill sickly or elderly patients under their care, presumably to end their suffering, although this concept does not apply to any woman accused of being Jack the Ripper.

Evolving the Ripper

One of the reasons we keep returning to the Ripper story is this lack of conclusive answers. It is not only a question of who the Ripper was, but why he—or she, or they—killed, both in the selection of victims and the manner of death. What in the world would make someone not only cut the throats of, but then mutilate the bodies of, poor East End sex workers who seem to have no connection to each other? If the women were victims of opportunity, then why kill so violently? What is the killer meant to have gotten out of these murders and, if he did get something out of them, why did he stop?

Possible answers to these questions change over time as our understanding of serial murder and psychology have clarified. Fears, especially when connected to violent death, have also changed over time, and there is always the possibility of good shock value by presenting a theory that seems to come out of left field. We both keep trying to explain the Ripper and keep trying to scare ourselves with the story like children around a campfire. Clearly *we* are safe, being so far removed from the Ripper's time and place, but, even wrapped up so carefully in these narratives, he is not entirely benign. The Ripper is a threat, but not to us. To us, he is a puzzle.

A puzzle that has yet to be solved, despite more than 100 full-length books devoted to the subject. These "are usually characterized by a painstaking build-up of facts and theories followed by a vertiginous leap into a fantasy in the closing chapters"[20] to provide an advertised solution to the mystery that, in many cases, is unsupported. As Robin Odell observed, "while a great deal of heat has been generated by this activity, there has been very little illumination."[21] Indeed, for all the theories and the hundreds of named suspects, it seems we are no closer to solving the case than they were in 1888. What we can learn from all these writings, however, are the points of interest related to the narrative, both the short-lived and the still-enduring.

The question of identity is inextricably linked to that of motive, and Ripper authors have offered us many common narratives to consider. The idea of revenge continually circles back so that the Ripper might be avenging the death of a loved one—as in the cases of Dr. Stanley and Olga Tchkersoff—or, perhaps, avenging him- or herself: the wronged midwife seeks to kill the class of women who first used and then reported her, or Lizzie Williams wishes to avenge her own marriage. Even James Maybrick is meant to have murdered because he realized his wife was cheating on him. In only a handful of these cases is one of the women, generally Mary Jane Kelly, the actual object of the Ripper's revenge. At other times it is the class of women—poor East End sex workers—that serves the Ripper's purpose.

Although conspiracies, especially those involving the royal family, made a big splash in the 1970s, they have not entirely died out in the intervening decades. Rather ironically it was Stephen Knight who observed that "[w]hen the tale is as compelling and ghastly as the Whitechapel Murders it cannot fail to be embellished and distorted beyond measure,"[22] since his own *Final Solution* is generally considered to be both embellished and distorted. Elements of Knight's narrative, however, have caught popular attention and continue to be repeated. Royal family members sneaking around and denying the wishes of Queen Victoria, Mary Jane Kelly scheming and therefore being at fault for the series of murders, and the question of identity of the woman found at 13 Miller's Court all continue to be present in Ripper narratives. As the last of the Canonical Five victims, the youngest, and apparently the most beautiful, Mary Jane Kelly has always had a central role in speculations about the Ripper's motives, and authors like Knight and Wilding give her agency in causing the murders. They are not the only ones, since placing the blame on a murdered woman—especially a sex worker—has been a long-accepted narrative move. By "choosing" a life of sex work, a woman signs her own death warrant, and death is the natural end of a woman who sold sex. Indeed, in many cases the Ripper was considered to be cleaning up the streets and helping society by ridding the East End of the morally questionable.

Not all proposals for motive and identity are as enduring as these, however. Claiming that the Ripper was indeed a member of the royal family or arguing that he—or they—were a homosexual man have fallen out of style. It might still be acceptable to argue that Prince Eddy defied his grandmother and married a commoner, but not that he held the Ripper's knife. Speculation about his sexual orientation might likewise continue, but arguments that the Ripper or Rippers were gay men brutally murdering women no longer fit our understanding of serial killers, sexual orientation, and victim selection. Indeed, the idea of homosexual overkill has more recently been inverted to acknowledge that homophobia means not only the inflated reporting of such cases, but also the fact that members of the queer community are many times more likely to be the victim of violence rather than the perpetrator. Changing cultural perceptions of Otherness and evolving understandings of marginalized communities change the way we approach many subjects, including murder.

Alongside evolving ideas of psychology and cultural norms, scientific advances have also impacted the Ripper story. The idea that technology has progressed enough to prove the Ripper's identity once and for all through DNA testing is a tantalizing one, and it has been trumpeted through the headlines multiple times that our search for the answer is indeed over. However, a closer reading of the results indicates that, while for example Cornwell's and Edwards' preferred suspects have not been eliminated by the completed DNA testing, results were not as singularly conclusive as needed to declare someone the once and for all Ripper.

Part of the influence on these various Ripper tales is the sudden increase of books and authors concerned with the Ripper. From the first full-length English language book in 1929 up until the 1980s, a total of twelve such books were published. With the centennial mark of the murders in 1988, that number began to rise steeply. In the 1990s alone, the number of published Ripper books more than doubled, and the number of books and authors continues to grow in the twenty-first century as established authors publish more and newcomers begin their Ripper journey. The following chapter takes a closer look at those authors who fall under the title "Ripperologist" and their influences on the continued storytelling.

Chapter 4

The New Experts

What, exactly, is a Ripperologist? The broad definition seems to be "anyone who examines the Jack the Ripper case," but is there a difference between a Ripperologist who publishes books and one who publishes online posts? There is no degree in Ripperology and indeed recent events have highlighted the fact that Ripperologists are generally anti-academic. This is hardly a surprise, since academia as a whole does not embrace true crime, much less their specific area of study.

The origin of the term lies with Colin Wilson, although even here there is some confusion. In his introduction to Alexander Kelly's *Jack the Ripper: A Bibliography and Review of the Literature* in 1973, Wilson writes, "Ripperologists (if I may suggest the word),"[1] to indicate those who have addressed the question of the Ripper's identity. Later, in a book co-written by Colin Wilson and Robin Odell in 1987, they write about "'Ripperology' (a word coined by Colin Wilson in 1972),"[2] although other sources declare, "In 1976, he coined the umbrella term 'ripperology' in a review of Stephen Knight's hugely influential (and highly contentious) *Jack the Ripper: The Final Solution*."[3] Since Donald Rumbelow's 1975 *The Complete Jack the Ripper* is dedicated to "Ripperologists," we can assume that the term, or versions of it, were in common usage in the mid–1970s, and Colin Wilson is the origin of the word.

Although the first journal associated with Jack the Ripper was *Ripperana*,[4] which began publication in 1992, *Ripperologist* was quick to follow in 1995 and is billed as "the leading publication in the field."[5] While *Ripperana* includes pieces that are more generally true crime-related, *Ripperologist* focuses on Jack the Ripper, the East End, and Victorian studies, including articles, editorials, and book reviews of both fiction and nonfiction. It would seem, then, that anyone whose work is accepted for publication is a Ripperologist, and that the term is one adopted from the inside. What does it mean to be part of this presumably exclusive group?

The Ins and the Outs

Even those who write about Jack the Ripper and are presumably themselves Ripperologists do not always have good things to say about the group. Philip Sugden, for example, wishes to set himself apart from them and observes that, "as far as most Ripperologists are concerned, the truth runs a very poor second to selling a pet theory on the identity of the killer."[6] Indeed, that is the stereotype of the Ripperologist: someone with a rabid interest in proving that his own chosen suspect is indeed the killer, writing to emphasize the evidence that supports this theory and ignoring or minimizing evidence that does not. William Beadle argues that "Ripperology ... is a more sophisticated version of witch burning, a game of mock trials without any rules of evidence ending in character assassination as a substitute for the victim's execution."[7] Perhaps ironically Beadle's book argues for his own chosen suspect, while Sugden prefers to make a survey of the most popular suspects without arguing for one in particular.

"But that's the wonderful thing about Ripperology—it's as nigh-on impossible to refute a theory as it is to prove it,"[8] leading to continued arguments about which of the hundreds of already-named suspects, as well as a few newcomers as time passes, is most likely to have done it. This, too, is the outside perception of Ripperologists: that they only want to prove the identity of the Ripper—or, as Patricia Cornwell argues, they do not want to know and instead prefer the eternal, ongoing mystery.[9] While such comments might adequately describe individual researchers, there are so many authors who have either called themselves or been called Ripperologists that it can be difficult to make sweeping judgments, especially when concerning a field that does not have well-defined boundaries.

Ripperologists are, by and large, "amateur criminologists"[10] whose sole focus lies on the Autumn of Terror. While some come to the case through their backgrounds in policing, many more seem drawn by the mystery and the chance to examine evidence, if not discover more of it. As time passes, the likelihood of uncovering documents seems to diminish, although there remains hope that some of the missing evidence from the police file might resurface. To a great extent, however, evidence about the Ripper has stabilized to a set number of data points, although of course there are still arguments over whether, for example, any of the supposed "Ripper letters" were written by the killer and which, if any, eyewitness statements could be considered reliable. In the twenty-first century, thanks to the sharing of information over the internet as well as documents held in archives, Ripperologists tend to be working from the same evidence and, at times, battling the same apocryphal tales that still cling to life.

There is no single background shared by all who come to the field, although Robin Odell observes that "[c]onfidence is one characteristic that binds Ripperologists, especially the theorists."[11] Those who have a pet theory about the Ripper's identity cling to it, refusing to be shaken even in the face of evidence that seems to disprove it. Since solid evidence is hard to come by—or agree upon—in this case, cherry-picking details that support a theory, over-emphasizing some and completely dismissing others, is common in Ripper narratives. Part of what Ripperologists hope to achieve in recent years is this continued dispelling of myth and an emphasis on the facts and evidence that cannot, or should not, be ignored. This has led to tensions when it comes to discussing the narrative of the Ripper, from both within Ripperology and without.

Even those who have published about the Ripper and whose work has been well-received offer some cautions for those wishing to follow in their footsteps. "The whole subject is now a minefield to the unwary," warns English historian Philp Sugden. "Even true crime experts venture there at their peril."[12] As the first academic historian to write about the case, Sugden was hailed for bringing scholarship to an area where many do not have a background that has trained them for research. Indeed, even recognized experts Martin Howells and Keith Skinner have added that "most of us who have ventured in the past to opt for a particular suspect have been torn apart limb from limb."[13] It seems dangerous to venture toward, much less into, Ripperology, even for those who have already made their mark.

Some of the critiques are similar from within Ripperology as from without, such as the observation that "[m]uch of the Ripper story has been a rehash of earlier theories tempered with some new angle or approach."[14] The lack of solid evidence about the murders, as well as the numerous theories and variations that popped up from the beginning, mean that the Ripper narrative has always been open for interpretation. There is no one single story to tell, so numerous people from different backgrounds have brought their perspective to the events and created their own narratives, making their own arguments through their variations.

The popularity of the story "allowed ill-researched and uncorroborated theories to flourish as popular journalism"[15] and the struggle, especially in recent decades, has been to make the transition from splashy tabloid headlines to a presentation of the information as educational and factual, if not fully academic. Apocryphal tales must still be overcome, since they are now so deeply embedded in the Ripper mythos, and the popularity of the Freemason conspiracy continues into the twenty-first century despite its lack of reliance on evidence. The fact remains that the majority of the world does not wish to engage in Ripper media beyond a single instance and does not care to be bogged down in the discussions of such minutiae as whether or not Elizabeth Stride actually ate grapes and whether the one version they read left out some apparently important information in order to shoehorn the author's personal pet suspect into the narrative. The casually curious might embark on a walking tour or pick up a single book, but they are hardly likely to delve into a podcast that now has hundreds of episodes, or wade through pages of forum posts, or get their hands on multiple books to compare the contents.

This is one reason why, for example, Cornwell's 2002 *Portrait of a Killer* made such waves not only in the wider world, thanks to her platform as a fiction author, but also within the circle of Ripperologists. When such individuals—and their theories—are given headlines, the concern is that the general public will be misinformed, but think themselves well-educated by this "new" information. While some theories fall by the wayside, others create larger impacts in the general media and have impacts long after other works have been published.

Woodhall, Stewart, and Matters, for example, are largely dismissed and not considered suggested reading except in cases where newcomers are interested in the history of Ripperology. Their theories have not withstood the test of time or the opening of the sealed police file. This is perhaps at odds with Robin Odell's declaration that, "once a suspect's name has been placed in the frame of guilt, it stays there to be resurrected at a later stage, cloaked in different arguments,"[16] but it follows with this book's argument that changing approaches to the Ripper story follow cultural and societal evolutions. The adaptability of the theories to be picked up and reused in a new form is part of what keeps the Ripper current, since he can be molded to contemporary fears and ideas of deviance and Otherness. Some theories have to be dismissed as a product of their times, unsustainable in a more politically correct society, but others continually rise to the surface and make a public splash, if not one among the Ripperologists themselves, before dying down again.

One such recent splash, the ripples of which are still being felt, is the 2019 publication of Hallie Rubenhold's *The Five: The Untold Lives of the Women Killed by Jack the Ripper*. A social historian known for her research on sex work, Rubenhold's book dismisses the figure of the Ripper and ignores the murders while exploring the lives of the Canonical Five victims. Her story of each of the women stops when they lie down to sleep for the night, a controversial decision because the acceptable narrative is that each of the women was soliciting at the time of her death and therefore both wide awake and responsible for inviting the killer into her presence.

Although Robin Odell declared in 2008 that "hitherto described disparagingly simply as whores and seen as pawns in some serial killer's mad scheming, [the victims] are now viewed as individuals with personalities and family backgrounds contained in a social environment,"[17] Rubenhold's book took this depiction of the women as women further than the Ripperologists had taken it. Granted, Neal Stubbings Sheldon's 2007 book *The Victims of Jack the Ripper* did push the boundaries at the time, but his 112 pages, many of which include photographs of the women's descendants, does not cover all that Rubenhold's more than 300 pages does. Here we see researchers building on the work of previous authors in order to add depth and breadth to a subject, introducing it not only to a wider audience but also including insight from a neighboring field of research to flesh out an understanding of the time and place in which these women lived. Repeated books about the Ripper have done so for the killer himself, offering at times sympathetic biographies of the chosen suspect, and these books—such as Cornwell's—have engendered negative reactions from the circle of Ripperologists.

Part of what makes books like Sheldon's, Rubenhold's, and John Bennett and Paul Begg's 2014 *Jack the Ripper: The Forgotten Victims* stand apart is their focus on something other than the Ripper's identity—in this case, those who died as a result of the Ripper's existence. Bennett and Begg's book briefly touches upon the Canonical Five before moving to a broader discussion of women who suffered from the resulting fear and violent male outbursts that sprang from the Ripper story rather than those who died directly by the Ripper's knife. These approaches engender grumblings in online reviews from readers who have not grasped that the point of the book was not, in fact, the Ripper's identity or a rehashing of the Ripper's crimes, but rather to focus on another element of the narrative entirely.

Even presenting readers with an expected narrative of identity surrounding the Ripper comes with its own pitfalls. Philip Sugden argues that "we cannot seriously accuse anyone … of crimes like those of the Ripper without clear and positive evidence to back us up,"[18] although the history of Ripper narratives shows that many have done exactly that. The issue with the Ripper crimes, and that which allows us to keep returning to the narrative, is that facts and evidence are hard to come by, and even that which was reported in 1888 and has been repeated since then cannot be depended on. How trustworthy are eyewitness statements? What if they were given to the papers instead of to the police? All too often there is simply no documentation to support or refute claims and turn them into facts or apocrypha, and anyone who ventures into the world of publishing about the Ripper leaves himself open to critique from all sides.

Curating a Heritage

Established Ripperologists come from many backgrounds. Some, like Edwin Woodhall, have a history within law enforcement—Woodhall declares he is a "detective turned author"[19]—thereby establishing an ethos and expertise beyond that of the written word. Indeed, in order to have a book accepted for publication, an author needs to make the case that his point of view brings something new, important, or unexpected to the narrative. Anyone with a background in law enforcement would therefore have the advantage over readers who do not, just as historians likewise bring specific knowledge and skills to their narratives. Before these comparisons can be made of a group , however, that group must be identified.

Although his work predates the creation of the term, Begg and Bennett have declared that "Edward Knight Larkins, through his persistence, could be considered the first 'Ripperologist,'"[20] a statement that only holds value insofar as Begg and Bennett themselves were established Ripperologists at the time of making the claim. Larkins, who worked as a clerk in the Customs Statistical Department and did not have any legal background, was obsessed with the case as it unfolded in 1888. He was a proponent of the merchant seaman theory which has once again recently come back into vogue. Larkins was clearly not the last person to suggest a solution to the case, although there was a lull in such intense study before others, such as Woodhall, one again took up the mantle.

The earliest phase reintroduced the then-known details of the case to the reading public and grappled, as all narratives concerned with the Ripper's identity must, with the question of motive. Motive and identity are intrinsically linked so that a theory of one can support a theory of the other. A suggestion that the Ripper was a woman, for example, lends itself to theories of revenge for her arrest as a midwife assisting in abortions or because one of the women carried on a relationship with her husband, but not specifically of revenge against a sex worker who passed on a sexually transmitted disease to the killer. Some of these suggestions were general, naming a profession rather than a specific individual, and thus the Ripper was presented as a midwife or a Jewish butcher. However, the great influx of named suspects was still to come.

These initial declarations of the Ripper's identity asked audiences to rely heavily on what the author told them, although their information was "primary anecdotal by source, then anecdotal with supporting 'evidence' of an esoteric and often dubious nature."[21] Before the reopening of the official police files, and especially before the days of the internet, access to such information was limited and involved traveling or obtaining single hard copies of newspapers which were not always compared to other reports for discrepancies. This is perhaps in part where Ripperology picked up a reputation for being un- or even anti-academic and a playground where anyone, regardless of background or training, could engage with the narrative and make a claim.

As more books were published, more authors came into the conversation, and more information was revealed. For example, Donald Rumbelow parenthetically informs his readers that "(This is the first complete description of the mutilations that has appeared in a book)"[22] in his 1975 *The Complete Jack the Ripper*. It is apparently the mark of a true Ripperologist to remember which piece of information, be it image, description, or document, was discovered by which person and be able to recite this information from memory with Quiz-bowl-like accuracy. If one cannot uncover new information oneself—a task becoming increasingly more difficult as the years pass and we can seem to do little more than wait for something to come up in an estate sale—then at least one can track the history of such discoveries.

Begg and Bennett mark the emergence of "a new, improved era of 'Ripperology'"[23] in 1965 with the publication of Tom Cullen's *Autumn of Terror: Jack the Ripper, His Crimes and Times* and Robin Odell's *Jack the Ripper: In Fact and Fiction*. Cullen himself critiqued previous authors for simply following the lead of those who came first, not bothering to check information before repeating it. Specifically, he laments that some others "have obviously been misled by Annie's pretensions to respectability,"[24] referencing the way the second of the Canonical Five victims told others her husband had worked for nobility. Cullen, and many who followed, argued that the women themselves were untrustworthy sources for information about their pasts, although usually Liz Stride and Mary Jane Kelly come under the most scrutiny for this presumed fault. Cullen and Odell, however, marked a short era instead of a complete turn in Ripperology, which descended into royal theories and elaborate conspiracies in the 1970s, as explained further in Chapter 3.

1988 marked renewed interest in the case with the centenary of the murders, introducing many authors who are still active within

Ripperology to this day. Even more books emerged in the 1990s, some continuing the trend of naming new suspects with little evidence while *The Complete History of Jack the Ripper*, written by Philip Sugden and first published in 1994, acted again as Cullen's and Odell's books had by directing the focus back toward supportable evidence. Sugden also marked a shift in authors of Ripper books. Previously amateurs, journalists, and former police officers had entered the fray, but Sugden was the first academic to bring his training to the narrative. His book carefully examined the leading theories surrounding the Ripper's identity and cataloged evidence to dispel longstanding myths, but Sugden did not introduce any new or shocking theories. When social historian Hallie Rubenhold's *The Five: The Untold Lives of the Women Killed by Jack the Ripper* was published in 2019, her book created a much bigger uproar because of two declarations that go against every previous Ripper narrative. Rubenhold points out that there is only evidence for two of the Canonical Five having ever worked as sex workers, and contends that the women were killed in their sleep rather than after soliciting their final customer: the Ripper himself.

While Rubenhold holds an M.A. in British History and an MPhil in British History from the University of Leeds and brought this experience to bear on her book and new theories, she is hardly the only author of late to push back against established Ripperologists and longstanding theories. There have been other renegades coming from other fields to make their marks in the long history of Ripper books and theories, claiming their own unique perspectives and attempting to shake things up in other ways.

Renegades and Newcomers

Due in part to the large number of books and means of communicating about the Ripper—through forums and podcasts, to name but two—there has also recently been a tendency for newcomers to declare themselves as being different from all the other Ripperologists. They need their work to stand out in some way in order to entice a publisher to take a chance on it, or to get eyes on their words online. At times they even want to play into the overwhelming amount of information that keeps flooding the market, as though to give a wink and a nudge to weary readers who honestly do not believe anything more needs to be said.

Some outright declare their special status, informing readers that "this book is not like any other Jack the Ripper book"[25] and thus indicating that audiences should not treat it as such. They may, in fact, need to forget everything they have ever learned about the Ripper—not because the theory is untenable otherwise, but because the author brings such a fresh voice and point of view to the question. Considering how much "known" information comes from apparent witnesses without any evidence to back up their statements, this is not an entirely unwise approach to the Ripper story. However, by forgetting everything we have ever read, we would also not be able to notice when authors miss important information.

All the same, some such renegades seem to caution readers about believing them completely even as they paint themselves as bravely forging ahead through uncharted waters. Russell Edwards, who claims to have identified the Ripper through DNA he found on a shawl he claims belonged to Catherine Eddowes, confides early on in his book that, "[w]ith no background as a researcher, I have had to learn as I go along."[26] There is nothing wrong with learning something new; however, more experience with either research or the research subject allows a person to work more effectively and to be better on guard against common tricks and traps. Indeed, the scientific testing on which Edwards bases his whole theory, not to mention the provenance of his star piece of evidence, have both come under heavy questioning and do not stand up beyond a reasonable doubt.

Bruce Robinson, author of *They All Love Jack: Busting the Ripper* (2015), gleefully writes, "By now it had become almost a maxim of my research to go after whatever the authorities tried to dismiss."[27] There seems to be this idea that any newcomers or outsiders who are not themselves Ripperologists will be able to finally solve the case after only a short investigation, the way so many novels rely on amateurs to beat the police at solving crimes. Although this sort of dismissive, irreverent attitude may appeal to some, and it can indeed be wise to investigate further when it seems the work has not been done before, such authors pride themselves in turning their backs on work that has previously been done, no matter what the caliber. Rather than engaging in a conversation with the field and constructing a literature review—something authors like Edwards would have no experience with if they have not been trained in research—they decide to start from scratch and strike off on their own, thereby not even knowing if what they believe has been said before.

One common place for these newcomers to diverge with established thought is in reference to the Ripper letters. Both Cornwell[28] and Robinson[29] choose to argue that they *were* all written by the same person, and that this person was indeed the killer. Each has chosen a creative as their preferred suspect—Cornwell the artist Walter Sickert and Robinson composer and singer Michael Maybrick—in order to explain the different papers, writing utensils, and handwriting found on the various letters, and each dismisses the known cases where people were identified and faced legal consequences for sending fake letters. Cornwell especially relies heavily on the letters as evidence for her suspect, testing some of the stamps and envelopes for DNA, so for her theory and research to work, they *must* have been written by the Ripper. Surely over a century of other minds working the case and concluding that they were fakes must all be wrong, and the authors who singularly declare otherwise must be right.

They are far from the first to dismiss methods and theories of previous authors. Shirley Harrison, writing to argue the authenticity of the Ripper diary and James Maybrick as its author, declares that "so far everyone had tried to solve the Whitechapel murders by examining unreliable evidence,"[30] indicating that the evidence in front of her is, in contrast, reliable ... and not simply new. Again, in order for her theory to work she must believe that the document—here a diary instead of the letters—is authentic and authentically penned by the Ripper. Without this provenance, the new theory falls apart completely and has no support.

There is also the tendency of authors to declare their shock and astonishment at learning something that has, in fact, been associated with the Ripper narrative since the beginning: although there are the Canonical Five generally named as the Ripper's victims, that is not a confirmed number of victims of the same killer. Since the Ripper was never caught, there has never been a solid number of victims, and even reading the papers published back in the day would have indicated this. Instead, we have authors declaring how many victims their personal "investigation revealed"[31] or the rather more dramatic "He left far more victims in his wake than the 'canonical five.'"[32] While this might indeed be a surprising revelation to newcomers, it seems strange and somehow a red flag for those writing books about the subject to be so surprised at this uncertainty. Surely their research should have uncovered this multiple times over, so it would not seem to be some sort of secret tidbit they can confide to their readers, but just one more aspect of the case's gray area.

Some of these renegades like to revel in the difficulty of their research, not just because of the missing documents from the police file but because they feel they are dealing with "experts who just didn't want to know"[33] the truth. The conspiracy seems to be that Ripperologists are not simply acknowledging the complexities of the case and the gaps in evidence when they dismiss theories, but are actively working to ensure that the Ripper is never identified. Perhaps they toil hand in hand with the Freemasons to protect the Ripper's identity and have collectively decided that the best way to do this is to overwhelm the world with suspects so that the real one will never be identified in the haystack of false ones.

One interesting critique of foregoing books surfaces in the introduction to James Tully's 2005 *The Real Jack the Ripper: The Secret of Prisoner 1167* when he writes that "rarely did I sense that an author was really *involved* with what he had written, or that he had researched his subjects to any depth."[34] He refers to the repetition of commonly-repeated elements that could not be proved with evidence—tales which would have come up time and time again in research prior to their being disproved—but his use of "*involved*" is interesting. Although Ripper books by and large cannot be accused of being overbearingly academic, they do not noticeably stand out against other works in the true crime genre. If an author has not, for example, presented the murdered women passionately and empathetically, it is because the genre has not called for it, although Tully himself makes a concerted effort to change this in his own work. On the other hand, so many authors have gotten themselves truly *involved* with their suspects, presenting their choice of brutal murderer with empathy and compassion, minimizing the violence and instead focusing on childhood trauma or the apparently understandable reasoning that goes into becoming "the world's first serial killer."

Although it is important for any area of study to have newcomers to refresh and revive the discipline, it is also important for anyone venturing into a new field to become familiar with what has come before. If someone is going to flat-out reject a commonly-held belief, then there needs to be more explanation beyond a gut feeling or the desire to simply go against the current thought leaders and play devil's advocate. Academics and trained researchers know that they must review the literature before engaging in the conversation and that their work is an extension of what has gone before instead of something entirely new that no one has ever thought of. Critique is an important aspect of a field as it expands to new scholars, new points of view, new technologies, and new evidence, since a stagnant echo chamber will quickly render a group obsolete, but in many cases there is a compromise between the stale and the renegade.

Shades of Gray

While it is tempting to label anyone who writes about, or engages with, the Ripper narrative as a "Ripperologist," the definition does not turn out to be that simple. Some who write about the Ripper declare themselves to be something else, while those who are established Ripperologists reject the use of the title for those they do not deem worthy. Although the term comes from within and is used by established authors for both their magazine and to refer to themselves, it is also frequently used by those wishing to indicate that they stand apart from common beliefs and are therefore somehow more reliable since they have no background in either academic research or Ripperology.

Indeed, those who do understand the process of historical research might think that established Ripperology is inconsistent and arbitrary. Theories and understandings not only of the murders but also of the time period must evolve as new evidence is uncovered and as broader understandings are brought to the case. The murders cannot be removed from their socio-historical context if we hope to understand them, in part because of how little information we have about them. While the "documentation is so vast and disparate that errors are easily and unintentionally made by even the most diligent researchers,"[35] those same researchers must approach the available information with a critical eye. We are hampered not only by missing information, but also by preserved statements that may or may not be true as well as possibly being incomplete or difficult to comprehend. Investigating the Ripper murders is already a minefield before we come to considerations of who is, or is not, a Ripperologist.

By and large, the Autumn of Terror is "a subject that has been almost exclusively a male preserve,"[36] especially when it comes to publication of books. This stands in stark contrast to various polls for audiences of true crimes in all its formats, which skew heavily toward women. The way authors construct their narratives to explain given events depends not only on their background as far as information they have already learned about the murders and the historical period, but also their own lived experiences in the world, including gendered experiences. Writing in 1990, Jean Overton Fuller observes that certain information surrounding Mary Jane Kelly's death stands out to her "[p]erhaps because I am a woman,"[37] separating her observational acumen from that of those Ripper authors who are men. Groups that lack diversity in gender, age, and other personal qualities are more likely to agree on a certain interpretation that aligns with personal experience and values, and therefore stop looking for other possible explanations.

This, perhaps, is one of the reasons why recent authors separate themselves from "Ripperologists" and criticize them for such approaches as "whitewash[ing]"[38] or "giv[ing] unqualified credence to the Victorian police."[39] When coming from a nuanced standpoint of critique, such points of view are valuable and help strengthen the field of study overall as others respond to such comments and further explore the questions raised. Granted, this sort of continual feedback depends on the rigor and investment of both parties along with a willingness to step back and reconsider data as new information comes to light, which is not necessarily standard for those outside of academia. When people feel a certain possessiveness over their subject and its interpretation, it is difficult to separate inquiries into the subject from personal attacks on the self.

Even those long engaged with the study of the Ripper have noted that "[o]ur interest in the death of five Victorian prostitutes has become a curiously antiseptic and painless experience,"[40] and this experience has clearly influenced the way authors write about the Ripper, as well as other true crime. Ripper narratives are therefore affected not only by the amount of time that has passed since the murders occurred, the amount of trustworthy information remaining, and the background and knowledge base of those writing about them, but also by other such narratives and generic expectations. Once again, history influences the way stories are told so that even the apparently new genre of "true crime" has its roots in previous crime narratives. All of this has led to Howells and Skinner's observation in 1987 about our approach to five gruesome and horrific murders and their transition from horror to emotionless logic puzzle.

Even here, though, those who study the Ripper disagree, since Robin Odell counters in 2008 that the murdered women "are now viewed as individuals with personalities and family backgrounds contained in a social environment."[41] Unfortunately my own 2018 survey of written descriptions of the Canonical Five as living women instead of corpses potentially rife with evidence about their killer falls more in line with Howells and Skinner, and the uproar surrounding Hallie Rubenhold's 2019 book exploring the lives of the women above and beyond their presumed identity as sex workers suggests that Ripperology resists not only new approaches, but also the suggestion that the women should be allowed to be individuals. True crime narratives have long been content to agree that violent death is the natural end of the sex worker, and that women therefore choose such an end when they likewise choose the profession, so complications to this longstanding narrative disrupt our comfort by collapsing the distance between us and the murdered women.

Narratives constructed by Ripperologists, or by those proclaiming themselves to be different from Ripperologists, are not created in a vacuum. These stories are not just about presenting impartial evidence, but the point of view and approach of the author involved in shaping said story. These authors are influenced by culture, society, and their own backgrounds, which can include the presence—or absence—of other Ripperologists. Once someone has made a name for himself as a Ripperologist, he may be called upon not only to write, but also to advise or be involved in other forms of media such as documentaries or movies concerned with the case.

Chapter 5

Lights, Camera ... Murder

Although the Ripper crimes have been a written narrative since the murders occurred in 1888, the story is, of course, adaptable. With the rise of film technology, he has stalked his way onscreen as well as on the page. Documentaries purport to be factual and "pretend to have a pedagogical purpose,"[1] but the line between truth and fiction, between education and entertainment, is even more difficult to draw when the narrative in question is that surrounding the Autumn of Terror. "Fact and fiction are so difficult to disentangle in the Ripper epic"[2] that shifting it to a new mode of film, especially a mode more commonly associated with fiction, blurs that line even further.

Simply shaping real-life events into a narrative involves human input and therefore the addition of both perspective and bias. Narratives introduce the idea of cause and effect, and every time we recount even the apparently simplest of actions, we turn distinct occurrences into a story. There is no other way for us to relate events and put them in words. Even something as mundane as "They're predicting rain, so I should bring an umbrella" is a narrative we impose not only on the world and on others, but also on our own lives. One common aspect of the Ripper narrative, for example, is that all of the victims were sex workers and therefore bear some responsibility for their own deaths since they, at the very least, accepted the Ripper as their final client and went off with him to a secluded location, aiding him in their own murders.

Aside from cause and effect, we use narratives to impose the concepts of "beginning" and "ending" on our lives, turning events into sequences that have clear endpoints. Despite the way we have labeled the Canonical Five, the Ripper narrative does not have such fixed points as a clear start and a clear end. If he murdered more than five, then the dates of his active period change. If he did only murder the Five, we are still left with a question mark as to his end. Was he killed? Incarcerated? Relocated? There is no clarity and no true end, but "[t]rust in the organizational value of narrative, however, usually comes hand in hand with a coherent ending."³ Documentaries, especially before the early twenty-first century, seek to explain a narrative and include that coherent ending. This is why so many true crime narratives are not published until after trials have been completed and sentences meted out. Ann Rule did not publish *The Stranger Beside Me* (1980) until after Ted Bundy was sentenced to death for the first time, legally confirming his guilt and reassuring readers with this final consequence to his actions. Since the Ripper was never caught, there is no such reassurance, although the passage of time means he is no longer a threat to audiences approaching the case.

Documentaries offer viewing audiences different experiences of the crime than written accounts. If its subjects are still living, "documentary probes the emotions and interactions of social actors in their intimate and vulnerable moments [and] renders it a form of emotional pornography."⁴ The camera intrudes on private emotions the way true crime intrudes into private spaces, purporting to show audiences the truth. When situations are in the past and cannot themselves be filmed, reenactments are used in their stead. These "[r]e-enactments are not evidence, although it is possible for them to build a convincing narrative about the events they depict"⁵ in a way that written narratives might not be able to achieve. Although written accounts may include hedge words such as "may have" or "must have" when it comes to a criminal's actions, and the narration accompanying a reenactment might do the same, viewers can still witness someone playing the role of the criminal performing those exact actions in front of their eyes without such hedging. What the narration hints as a possibility becomes a certainty onscreen.

Documentaries have evolved from this one-to-many dissemination of information to "asking the audience to reconsider notions of criminality and equal justice"⁶—and then to act on their conclusions. The added element of possible intervention is not entirely new, given previous shows such as *America's Most Wanted* (1988–2012) and the format of asking viewers to help catch fugitive criminals, but this call to action has been recently raised to new levels within the true crime documentary circle.

Documentaries and Social Action

Like other forms of the genre, "[t]rue-crime documentaries are in the ascendant"⁷ and have hit new heights—or perhaps new depths—in the twenty-first century. Documentaries push the boundaries between education and entertainment, claiming to be firmly on the side of the former while making use of many techniques involved in the latter. The main element a documentary offers that written narratives do not is the reenactment.

"Re-enactments never definitively confirm if they are evidence or narrative fiction"[8] since they most often show someone in the role of the criminal performing the crime. They are used to put theories or suggested narratives into three-dimensional space—or four, if we also count time. When we have questions about whether someone could have managed to fit all of the necessary actions within a certain timeline, we reach for the reenactment both for the courtroom and for the documentary. The reenactment becomes, in essence, a MythBusters-style test at which the proposed sequence of events could fail and necessitate a new theory instead.

The most common moments reenacted in true crime documentaries are the commissions of the crimes themselves. Audiences might see a cloaked figure approach a woman in the street and draw out a knife as though we have been transported back to 1888 and can watch the actual events unfold, or they might take place clearly in the present as an expert explains, perhaps in a room made up to look like a morgue, the various blows and injuries that occurred. Dummies might be used to clarify questions of blood spatter and whether the perpetrator would have needed to conceal telltale stains, and computer-generated images can help illustrate injuries to organs and other damage that cannot be inflicted on a real person in front of the camera and might be too technical or fiddly for a dummy. Here MythBusters combines with CSI to let us more fully explore the damage done to murdered bodies in detail we could not achieve with our eyes alone.

The camera allows us to slow down time and examine events on a level unattainable with the human eye, as well as adding in elements of the microscope and CSI's trademark shots that appear to zoom into bodies to illustrate a character's narration of the injuries. Rather than a static medical diagram, documentaries can present viewers with dynamic models or graphics to show the damage inflicted on a human body while couching the description in distant medical terminology and not fully inviting audiences to respond to such representations as a human life.

Reenactments of the criminal completing the crime, such as the Ripper accosting women in the street, also illustrate "the tendency of non-fiction film and television to re-present reality by transforming it into narrative."[9] Part of assigning a narrative to events means including elements such as cause and effect and the idea of motive. Any retelling of the Ripper murders includes the assigning of such narrative elements, but visual reenactments of the crimes solidify the filmed events as probable actual occurrences.

There is an "intimate connection between documentary film and trials"[10] because both are involved with the same process: taking individual events and pieces of evidence and applying a narrative of either innocence or guilt. In recent decades wider audiences have been exposed to courtroom proceedings, in part thanks to "Court TV[, which] emerged in 1991 to provide C-SPAN-like coverage of legal trials."[11] As discussed further in Chapter 8, the media has played a large role in educating the public about the procedures and expectations involved in adversarial trials in the filming and airing of both real-life trials and also fictional police procedurals. Individuals no longer need to be personally involved in a court case or present in the courtroom to watch things unfold.

Documentaries about more recent crimes rely on these taped courtroom proceedings to supplement their video or audio footage by sharing not only the words spoken by their subjects, but spoken in their own voices. Clips allow audiences to assess body language and tone above and beyond a written transcription of their words, a fact that plays into a recent trend in true crime documentaries that invite their audiences to come to their own conclusions. "Audiences now expect to be able to examine the evidence close up and weigh its significance in the same way the producers of these shows do,"[12] thus assessing the dominant narrative of the case—is the convicted person truly guilty?—and coming up with their own ideas about what "really" happened.

We see this especially with shows like *Making a Murderer* (2015–2018) that have been created and curated to call the official legal proceedings into doubt. This is, in fact, the trend in recent true crime documentaries: to address a recent case where the outcome seems unfair and deputize audiences to participate in the investigation and then pressure those in charge to change the outcome or allow for further proceedings. This is a movement toward documentaries as "vehicles of knowledge and power that, in a word, can and are socially obligated to make things happen."[13] Once presented with an injustice, viewers cannot simply rest on their laurels—they must act in order to resist the system and reverse the current outcomes.

Such action carries with it a sense of urgency when a case is unsolved or when the documentary suggests that the wrong person has been arrested for the crime. Just like in *America's Most Wanted*, "many of the actual cases featured in these documentaries remain unresolved and open,"[14] allowing viewers to work together to uncover new evidence or present a new reading of established evidence in order to track down the real criminal. There is not only a sense of miscarried or incomplete justice, but one of danger when a criminal is still free and able to commit more crimes. Such shows managed to deputize audience members—and kept track of how many cases were closed thanks to their involvement—although in such a way that they "glamorized vigilantism while ensuring that it never truly threatened the state."[15] *America's Most Wanted* supported, and was supported by, the FBI, while more recent documentaries criticize the established systems and call for change.

The Ripper murders are, like many of these recent documentary cases, unsolved. There is no trial footage and no trial transcript for documentaries to draw on because no one was arrested for the murders. Many documents related to the crimes have gone missing. Finally, and an especial detriment in the age of active audience involvement, there is no hope of actually capturing the Ripper and bringing him to justice. All of the suspects are long-dead.

In and Out of Focus

Despite this lack of living suspect to be brought to trial, there are numerous documentaries about Jack the Ripper aimed at positively identifying the Ripper, directed toward calling a new figure into question, or created with the intent of being a general introduction to the case. Considering how much information is available about the murders—and how much needs to be sorted through to determine whether it is fact or apocrypha—it is difficult to summarize the Ripper into an hour-long episode. Those who have a working background knowledge of the case might become frustrated with the lack of depth and new insight, while those who have not encountered the Ripper narrative before will have no idea of how much was left out.

Just as twenty-first-century documentaries invite audience members to conduct their own research and "to retell the story to one's own satisfaction,"[16] so documentaries concerning the Ripper tend to focus on the creators' retelling. For example, when Patricia Cornwell makes an appearance, it will be to argue for her own chosen suspect, the artist Walter Sickert. Although other experts might also be interviewed and involved with that particular documentary, Cornwell's segments will focus on Sickert and the information she believes supports her opinion. It is left up to others to question her declarations and mention evidence that she might ignore in favor of her chosen narrative.

The same is true of Jeff Mudgett, great-great-grandson of American serial killer H.H. Holmes—birth name Herman Webster Mudgett—who believes his ancestor was not only a killer in North America but also traveled to commit the Ripper murders. Mudgett is a central figure in the History Channel's eight-episode series *American Ripper* (2017) and has appeared on other documentaries to continue to make his case. It is clear that, when he appears, he will argue for H.H. Holmes being Jack the Ripper, just as Cornwell will argue for Sickert. Once someone has been established as the promoter of a specific Ripper suspect, they will be called upon and expected to continually make the argument for that suspect.

Because so many names have been attached to the Ripper crimes as a suspect, most documentaries concerning the Ripper play into these competing narratives and make use of multiple voices providing their own points of view and, presumably, expertise. This is an extra layer of drama laid over any dramatic reenactments of the crime and can indeed invite viewers to draw their own conclusions about which theory is correct. Rather than inviting—or almost instructing—viewers to conduct their own research, documentaries can present audiences with conflicting narratives similar to adversarial trials in which juries must decide on the most likely narrative to explain the known events. While audiences of Ripper documentaries are denied the opportunity to track down trial transcripts or even the addresses of witnesses and family members involved in the story, they can still play a role in deciding for themselves whether the evidence presented in the documentary makes sense.

Laura Marsh argues that twenty-first-century viewers of true crime documentaries "are just learning to confront their own collective helplessness"[17] when it comes to cases of injustice, and that this is a difficult process. Those who watch documentaries about the Ripper have always been helpless to solve the case due to both lack of hard evidence and the amount of time that has passed since the murders. Although documentaries may present viewers with a solution they believe to be true, the very fact that we keep producing media about Jack the Ripper shows how uncertain we really are. We are indeed collectively helpless to bring the Ripper to justice and thus the murders are a site not only of fascination, but also of frustration.

Frequently Ripper documentaries film on the street in Whitechapel, at night, playing into "an inherent belief that returning to a site where an event, in particular a traumatic event, occurred will bring both subjects and audiences closer to understanding what 'really happened.'"[18] Visiting the murder sites is not a new pastime (see Chapter 7) but, because the Ripper is so connected to such a small physical area, it seems that we need to visit under the proper conditions to evoke the desired mood. Thus, we see Emilia Fox and Professor David Wilson walk the streets at night in *Jack the Ripper—The Case Reopened* (2019), bundled up against the chill of the night, the chill of the murders, or both. Fog, cobbles, and black-and-white film have all been used to indicate that viewers need to transport themselves back to the Victorian Era even if the camera shows modern-day London.

Documentaries also make use of photographs from the proper time period, although there are limits to what Ripper narratives can show. There is only one known photograph of any of the Canonical Five women from when they were alive, showing Annie Chapman on her wedding day. Other photos have circulated purporting to be one of the other four women, but frequently those images are proved to be someone else entirely. The desire to give viewers a human face and inspire empathy can override the factual identity of the woman in the photo, although it is also common for documentaries to show the known photos of the murdered women: the morgue photos taken after their deaths.

Photographs of the crime scene have long been included in true crime retellings. In books, they usually come grouped together near the middle, printed on a higher-quality paper than the text. Readers can flip past them or study them at their own speed, deciding how much they want to see and which details they want to focus on. When used in a filmed documentary, these images are displayed for a given amount of time. The camera might pan across them, zoom in, or focus on a specific part of the image depending on the narration accompanying them. Viewers who wish to avoid such images cannot do so as easily in documentaries as in texts. Although they might be able to close their eyes and open them again once the images are gone, perhaps assisted by another viewer as far as timing, they cannot skip over such things completely without missing some of the audio text.

Seeing a reenactment of a crime using real people, a mannequin, or a computer-generated visual is not the same as viewing images of actual murdered people. Viewers know that, when they see a reenactment, they are not witnessing an actual murder. The man who wielded the knife has not really killed anyone. The woman who gets stabbed and falls to the ground where she lies, unblinking, is in fact still alive and unharmed. When the camera lingers on her unresponsive body, which may or may not have a realistic amount of fake blood, we are looking at a living actress and not an actual murder victim. She has consented to this treatment, by both her fellow actor and the camera, and knows that viewers will be able to scrutinize her body as well as her character's fate. Audiences can also hope she has been fairly compensated for this work. The main point is that the actress has agreed to be put through the scenario and have strangers watch as it happens, while the Canonical Five never gave consent.

Such ogling of non-male bodies, be they live or dead, is part of the male gaze and frequently seen in movies and other fictional visual creations, once more showing an area where "the contrast between factual news and fictional entertainment is not so clear-cut."[19] Audiences have been trained to expect such sequences and to look from this point of view, giving them the right to examine especially murdered women's bodies. The true crime genre has worked in tandem with the male gaze of fictional theater to turn murdered people into evidence rather than human beings, giving readers and viewers the feeling of not only the right but also the obligation to look closely and uncover clues to the killer's identity. The new approach to true crime documentaries enlisting viewers as new detectives just adds to this approach, asking us to examine not only the crime scene photographs but also the reenactment for anything law enforcement might have overlooked.

The proliferation of true crime series on television has contributed to what Stella Bruzzi names "factual entertainment" and the blurring between real and imaginary. She argues that the various forms of media, both nonfiction and fiction, mean that we as audiences "no longer feel the need to adjust our perspective or attitude as viewers depending on whether we are sitting in front of a television, cinema, computer or phone screen enjoying a documentary or a drama."[20] We can enjoy video entertainment anywhere we have internet—and even places we do not if we download media onto our phones first—and at any time. We can view things alone or with others and, once we have taken something in, we can go online and find the proper subreddit to engage with others who have likewise been stirred by what they saw.

With all of these changes introducing a new relationship between audience and documentary, and added expectations that audiences will engage with the subject beyond the documentary, has Jack the Ripper also adapted to serve this evolving genre?

Celluloid Justice

While "the true crime genre's malleability is crucial to its longevity,"[21] and the same can be said for the narrative of Jack the Ripper, the Ripper narrative is not served well by these new changes to the film documentary. Initially documentaries were a one-to-many mode of informing audiences of facts, much like the nightly news, where experts explain and actors bring those explanations to life so that viewers can

Chapter 5. Lights, Camera ... Murder

take in the information and learn while perhaps being entertained. The flow of information moves from the screen to the viewer, and the social contract ends when the credits roll.

Today, especially since Netflix introduced the bingeable true crime documentary by dropping all ten episodes of *Making a Murderer*'s first season on December 18, 2015, the expectations of the documentary-audience relationship have changed. Although some more recent documentaries involve solved cases, such as 2019's *Conversations with a Killer: The Ted Bundy Tapes*, the response to *Making a Murderer* and other similar cases—including some podcasts discussed in Chapter 9—demonstrated the power of presenting audiences with cases that might appear closed, but are far more complicated than it first seems. "Often these [true crime] programs begin by asking the question: Who committed this crime? They then call the existing answers to those questions into doubt, showing how they are too simplistic"[22] and how the legal system has committed its own injustices with wrongful convictions. In short, the twenty-first-century documentary concerns itself with problems that it makes its viewers feel empowered to solve.

"On this view, crime junkies do not traffic in moral ambiguity but constitute responsible citizen sleuths in the making"[23] who tirelessly work to restore justice, solve unsolved cases, and make the world a safer place. Mistrust of the police and other members of the legal system is not new—see the letters sent to the editor during the Autumn of Terror in Chapter 1—but this idea that audiences can in fact effect change beyond expressing this dissatisfaction is a new component of the genre. In fact, the "after-life of the cases on which these true crime documentaries are based is swiftly becoming one of the genre's most thrilling features."[24] It is difficult to predict which cases will inspire audiences to such collective action that can lead to real change, but, when measured by this standard, the Ripper case is found lacking.

The murders of Polly Nichols, Annie Chapman, Liz Stride, Kate Eddowes, and Mary Jane Kelly are all unsolved, which seems to make them prime fodder for one of these new participant action documentaries, but there is no chance of viewers bringing the killer to justice. They might be able to take part in research, diving into the remaining evidence and over a century of theories, but no one will ever be brought to trial for these murders. At best viewers might be able to strengthen a case against one of the suspects or dredge up a new one, and at worst they could build a case against an innocent man who no longer has the chance to defend himself.

On the other hand, Laura Marsh observes that "now more than ever, this is how we respond to true crime: rather than dwelling on the nature of the crimes themselves or on loss, or pointing to problems with the justice system, people are swapping their own explanations of what happened,"[25] and this is a prime description of how we continue to share the Ripper narrative. Each piece of media about the Ripper, no matter the medium, deals with its own explanation of what happened. For Patricia Cornwell the answer is Walter Sickert; for Jeff Mudgett the answer is H.H. Holmes; and for some there is no answer but an array of suspects ranked by probability. Ripper narratives have long since passed the point of dealing with fear or mourning a loss, instead operating as a site of contested narratives where a single rediscovered piece of evidence merits reconstructed narratives as some use that new information to prop up their chosen suspect and others scramble to defend their choice in spite of it.

In this way, perhaps, Ripper narratives were ahead of their time when it came to documentaries encouraging viewers to make up their own minds. Because there was no trial, there is no single solution to the Ripper case and all retellings must, of necessity, be only a certain interpretation and not the ultimate truth. Indeed, this is why the story gets retold on *History's Greatest Mysteries* and has undergone so many variations even within the limitations of the documentary. Most who study the Ripper have learned, to their regret, that we cannot in fact answer the question of the Ripper's identity and thus must make do with our own lack of knowledge and inability to fulfill our desire for narrative closure. We are not even limited to a single suspect and a question of guilt, the "Is he or isn't he?" that fuels *Making a Murderer* and many of the podcasts under discussion in Chapter 9. With hundreds of possible suspects, it is difficult to find an agreement on the handful of the most probable in order to conduct a more in-depth investigation, and even then it would hardly look like the subreddits built up around other recent documentaries. There are no people left alive to interview and so many usual aspects of viewer participation, such as visiting the sites of the crimes, have already been repeated countless times.

The Ripper narrative is, perhaps, a disappointment when it comes to the true crime documentary. No matter how many episodes are devoted to the case, and no matter when the documentary is produced, there is no actual final solution. In order to reach such a firm conclusion, the narrative has to adapt further and become truly fictional.

CHAPTER 6

Once Upon a Time

Not everyone who engages with the Ripper story is necessarily concerned about the facts. This is a critique that has been leveled at various "Ripperologists" or so-called true crime books, but it certainly holds true when the Ripper enters the world of fiction. By switching the category from non-fiction to fiction, albeit with real-life references, authors open themselves up to broader opportunities in their storytelling.

Historical fiction has generic expectations in that authors cannot simply add, say, a dragon if it seems to be the best solution to writer's block, but it does allow them to explore these murders in ways nonfiction authors might not. In nonfiction, researchers look for sources from the time period to support their suppositions and need more than circumstantial evidence to ethically accuse someone of having been the Ripper. In fiction, authors can create their own suspects with no necessary correlation to real life, thereby avoiding accusing a real person of having committed serial murder and possibly libeling that person.

Nonfiction approaches to the Ripper frequently concern themselves with nobility or other recognized persons simply because there is a record of their existence and their movements. Attempts to name commoners or an average East End citizen as the Ripper run into issues of proving that person's existence or investigating that person's childhood and likelihood of having the proper personality ... or personality disorders. When opened up to fiction, the Ripper suspect's entire background can be created to fit the narrative, following the expectations provided by the experts in the FBI. There are still some limitations about what we would believe about the Ripper—he cannot be a well-adjusted person, for example—but fiction lets us explore the elusive concept of motive and fully explain what kind of person committed these murders, and why.

Fictionalization of the Ripper crimes began early, with J.F. Brewer's *The Curse Upon Mitre Square, A.D. 1530–1888* published in November 1888 and Margaret Harkness' *In Darkest London*, published in 1889.

Such stories were not limited to the English language, since "a Swedish short-story anthology entitled *Uppskäraren* ('The Ripper'), penned by one Adolf Paul,"[1] was published in 1892. These were just the first instances in a long line of Ripper stories investigating why contemporary society thought a man might have committed these crimes.

It is once again impossible to cover all representations of the Ripper since, even in fiction, he has inspired generations. Instead of moving from written fiction to filmed fiction, I instead separate my examples thematically. Although the figure of The Lodger—and the Avenger—originated in a short story by Marie Belloc Lowndes, she then expanded and adapted it into a novel, which transitioned to both the silent screen and the talkies. Sherlock Holmes has also had myriad encounters with Jack the Ripper, pitting the famous Victorian detective against the most infamous Victorian serial killer. The idea of the Ripper as a conspiracy theory involving both the Freemasons and the royal family has moved from print to graphic novel to screen, as well, continuing to tease our imaginations. Finally, we have not been content to let the Ripper rest only in Victorian London and have come to imagine him in our present, or his future. He is infinitely adaptable and can fit nearly every story we wish to tell.

Lodgers and Avengers

It is not just narratives of the real-life Ripper that allow the figure to change and evolve, but some fictional examples as well. When Marie Belloc Lowndes had her short story "The Lodger" published in *McClure's Magazine* in 1911, she began a new branch of Ripper narratives. Looking back on her work now, it has been observed that this was the moment when "Jack's handiwork was now legitimately regarded as entertainment"[2] and not education. Lowndes published her short story, and the expanded novelization in 1913, purely as fiction.

The Lodger is considered the first novelization of the Ripper murders because previous attempts lacked a true "plot."[3] The story follows Mr. and Mrs. Bunting, a former butler and former maid, attempting to keep up their dream of running a lodging house. Things look grim when a man named Mr. Sleuth decides to take a room. He asks not to be disturbed, although many disturbing events have been occurring and continue to occur: multiple brutal murders have been committed around the city of London, one coinciding with Mr. Sleuth's arrival and more being discovered the morning after Mr. Bunting accidentally brushed against Mr. Sleuth only to realize that the lodger was covered in blood.

The couple's worries peak when they realize their mysterious lodger has left in the company of Mr. Bunting's eighteen-year-old daughter, Daisy. Daisy is found safe, but Mr. Sleuth, who has been identified by experts as a "religious maniac," never returns to his room and the Avenger murders eventually stop.

It is notable that Lowndes made a change between the 1911 short story and the 1913 novel in that, "in the short story, he [the lodger] is Jack the Ripper,"[4] but, two years later, the only Jack mentioned in the novel is the executioner Jack Ketch. We see already the influence of passing time making it difficult to put the "real" Ripper into a contemporary tale. Already more than two decades have gone by since the murders, and the killer himself must have aged accordingly. Even if he was young and spry in 1888, it is difficult to imagine the same man, all these years later, still physically capable of committing so many murders in such a short amount of time. In the novel, then, the Lodger becomes the Avenger and is honestly the murderer, although no longer the Ripper.

Among the earliest adaptations of *The Lodger* was Hitchcock's silent movie released in the UK in 1927 as *The Lodger: A Story of the London Fog*. Moving a story from the page to the screen is generally a formula for changes in the plot and characters, and this was no exception. Here, though, it was in part the casting of Ivor Novello as the lodger, now named Jonathan Drew. Because of his established onscreen persona, "lodger and murderer could no longer be one and the same. A new subplot had therefore to be created to explain away his behaviour."[5] A romantic movie star could not be turned into a murderer, so Hitchcock adapted the script. Mr. and Mrs. Bunting still take in a lodger in the middle of a series of murders, but now the murderer only attacks blonde women and their daughter, Daisy, is a blonde dress model. Although she is in a relationship with police officer Joe Chandler, Daisy and the lodger quickly develop a relationship of their own.

Part of this change might be due to the new media format and not simply Novello's fame. Hitchcock argued that "a cinema audience finds it easier to identify with an innocent man who is wrongly accused than with a guilty man on the run,"[6] so that storytelling combined with Novello's pull as a romantic lead to change the lodger's background. He still must be suspect, leaving the house and returning after more murders are committed, and Joe, already jealous of the lodger's relationship with Daisy, discovers a bag locked in his room that contains photos, maps, and newspaper clippings all dedicated to the murders. It seems as though the police indeed found their man until Daisy asks Chandler and he explains that the first victim of the Avenger was his sister. He hopes to avenge her death against the Avenger. A mob falls on

Chandler, believing him to be the Avenger—the handcuffs he and Daisy tried to hide do not argue for his innocence—and only a newspaper boy announcing the capture of the true avenger saves Chandler's life. He and Daisy are thus free to be a happily married couple.

Something clearly seemed to work for Hitchcock and Novello, who revisited *The Lodger* in 1932 with sound this time. Unfortunately, this version was not received as warmly as the previous silent film. All the same, the murders—and the murderer—made their onscreen mark. Changing restrictions in Hollywood, including the abandonment of the Hays Code, increased directors' opportunities to show both sex and violence, two themes that have been attached to the Ripper murders since the beginning. The figure of the Lodger, who was adaptable to the stage and radio as well as film and who could be turned innocent when necessary and suggested as completing suicide if he were guilty, was no longer needed. Jack the Ripper had been hinted at long enough; "the next time he appeared on the big screen, it was in a starring role and under his own name."[7] With the rise of the slasher film, he could kill his victims in front of the camera and let the blood flow.

You Know My Methods, Watson

Sherlock Holmes and Jack the Ripper never met, in part because one is fictional and the other a real-life serial killer, but also because "Conan Doyle never actually wrote a story about the Whitechapel murders."[8] There is thus no canon interaction between the consulting detective, first introduced in 1887's *A Study in Scarlet*, and the "world's first serial killer." Even though they occupied print media at the same time, they were not connected ... unless, as Martin Willis suggests, "Conan Doyle partially reinvents Holmes in order to remove any possibility of explicit comparison with Jack the Ripper."[9]

Willis argues that the cold, calculating Holmes of *A Study in Scarlet* aligned far too closely with newspaper speculation about the sort of man who could be Jack the Ripper and thus Doyle modified his super sleuth to move him away from such comparisons. This is especially interesting because we have a long history of the idea that a detective clever enough to catch a serial killer must in some way be able to think like the serial killer, leading to such representations as Will Graham's overdeveloped sense of empathy in NBC's *Hannibal* (2013–2015). Indeed, this example of Graham also provides a reason for Doyle to have made that shift, since Graham ends up not only thinking like a killer on the wrong side of the law, but also becoming one. This does not mean, of course, that Holmes has ever been considered a warm and welcoming character, but Willis suggests the nature of his brilliance and calculation were massaged in order to more firmly mark him as being on the side of good.

Although Doyle did not introduce the pair, Holmes and the Ripper have since met in print, onscreen, and even in video games. It is the ultimate question of unstoppable force and immovable object: Holmes cannot fail to solve a case once it is put in front of him, but Jack the Ripper was never caught. Attempts to reconcile fiction's most famous detective with one of history's most well-known unsolved cases create interesting lines of tension.

As one example, 1965's *A Study in Terror* involves Holmes and Watson in the case when they receive a parcel in the mail that may have come from the killer. Unlike the real-life instance in which the chairman of the Whitechapel Vigilance Committee received a package purporting to be part of Catherine Eddowes' kidney, the one sent to Holmes is a case of surgical instruments with a scalpel—the likely murder weapon—missing. Nevertheless, it seems that someone is reaching out to the famed detective to engage him in the mystery, and the game is then afoot.

The movie resolves the tensions between Holmes' unmatched skills of deduction and the historically unsolved case by allowing Holmes to identify the Ripper only for the Ripper to die soon after. He is able to explain to Watson, and therefore the audience, the motive behind the Ripper murders and allow this narrative closure while also deciding not to pass this information on to the police, since the Ripper is dead. This allows for a touchpoint in reality because the police never did name the Ripper, while still allowing Doyle's detective to triumph over the mystery.

There is, however, a point in the narrative that directly subverts what we know happened in real life. Instead of attempting to reconcile fact and fiction, audiences see that one of the Canonical Five victims does not, in fact, die. Annie greets "Cathy" by name in the street, but viewers who do not know the names of the Canonical Five would not recognize it as being Catherine Eddowes, and those who do expect to see her killed, as well. Instead, Cathy walks safely offscreen. "Having Eddowes survive the knife of the Ripper defeats the object of using the correct names in the first place"[10] because audiences are given the real-life only to have the one solid fact known about her—that she was found murdered in Mitre Square—taken away. Her name is only known because she was connected in death to both the Ripper and the other murdered women, but that does not happen here.

In real life we are now aware that part of the serial killer narrative involves not always completing a murder even after the killer has set his sights on an intended victim. True crime author Ann Rule received myriad communications from such women after Ted Bundy was caught and she wrote *The Stranger Beside Me*. Her introductions to later editions of the book referenced these near-miss letters alongside those expressing the opinion that Bundy could have been rehabilitated. Rule rejected the writers of this second group out of hand, but she did believe a number who wrote the first.

What we do not know and can only speculate is the number of women in Whitechapel in the autumn of 1888 who narrowly avoided becoming a Ripper victim. John Bennett and Paul Begg have reached beyond the East End to collect stories for their book *Jack the Ripper: The Forgotten Victims*, but the brutalization of women in the East End was an everyday occurrence. Those who were physically accosted did not always report the incident to the police, and those who had narrow misses may not even have been aware of it at all. The women who wrote to Rule recognized their own escapes only after Bundy was caught and his photograph disseminated in the media. They may have gotten odd feelings about the man who spoke to them—or no feelings at all—but they only fully realized how lucky they were because he was caught. Had the Ripper been arrested, we might have those near-miss stories, but his anonymity means we do not.

Oddly, then, *A Study in Terror* introduces the idea of the woman who should have been a victim but is not aware of her lucky escape. Cathy walks the oddly empty Whitechapel streets but no danger comes out of the fog for her—just the annoyance of a policeman telling her she should be home so that she does not, in fact, become the next victim. She strolls off with a scoff. Savvy viewers would have already noticed that information about the Canonical Five has been skewed, since Annie is given Polly's famous last words about having a "jolly bonnet," but the movie Ripper still bypasses Cathy to kill a young woman, presumably Mary Kelly, in her upstairs room.

As fiction, this movie works to entertain, not educate. Viewers who come to watch because of their interest in Sherlock Holmes but who have no prior knowledge of the Ripper will not catch these inconsistencies with the real-world story. Those who do know the story of the Ripper, including the women's names, fates, and last known words, find the suspension of disbelief more difficult because of the many ways the movie directly references real life, broken up by this clear flaunting of the known facts.

A Study in Terror is hardly the only narrative where Sherlock Holmes is brought in to consult on the Ripper murders. He has now done so multiple times in multiple media formats with varying degrees of historical accuracy, if not varying degrees of success. One movie, *Murder by Decree* (1979), is even based on another commonly-repeated Ripper narrative so that Holmes tracks not only the Ripper but also the Freemasons. *Murder by Decree* even benefits from star power with Christopher Plummer taking on the role of the consulting detective.

Such stories bring us pleasure not only from a true crime story, but also because we have the familiar characters of Holmes, Watson, Lestrade, and the rest with their expected roles and recognizable lines. It is comforting to approach the Ripper as a Sherlock Holmes tale because we know that Holmes must solve it and that, even if he seems to die, he is not really dead. Fiction also provides us the pleasure of a solved Ripper case, complete with an understandable explanation for why, although Holmes knows the truth, he did not allow it to be shared with the world. It may be that the police did not know the identity of the Ripper, although they might have been involved in the conspiracy Holmes uncovers in *Murder by Decree* and that is discussed more fully in the next section, but Holmes, outside and generally above the police, knows the truth. He simply, in his wisdom, shares it with no one other than Watson, and viewers are lucky there was a camera present in that moment.

Freemasons from Hell

The story behind the great Freemason conspiracy began on the BBC in 1973 with a six-part procedural called *Jack the Ripper*. The show follows fictional detectives Barlow and Watt as they investigate the police files and available information about the killer. The series was adapted into the book *The Ripper File* by Elwin Jones and John Lloyd, published in 1975, and the final episode of the series and the last chapter of the book plant the seeds of the best-known Ripper conspiracy: this is where, after pages and pages of direct references to contemporary newspapers and police reports, Hobo Sickert is granted the chance to tell his story.[11] He explains Prince Eddy knew the artist Walter Sickert, and it was through Sickert that the prince met a lowly shopkeeper named Ann Elizabeth Crook. The pair fell in love, secretly married, and had a daughter, who was in part looked after by Mary Jane Kelly. Sickert's story implicates the coachman Netley and the Queen's physician Sir William Gull by name.

Barlow and Watt consider this story and find some circumstantial evidence to support it, but they do not end up agreeing with Sickert's theory. In fact, they do not come to a solid conclusion at all. Barlow points out that the files are in fact incomplete and tells his companion that "several documents had been removed"[12] before he was allowed to see them—not lost since 1888, but removed immediately before the files were handed over to him. Barlow thus concludes that someone in the Director of Public Prosecution's Office knows the identity of the Ripper and wants to ensure that this information does not become public.

This story from Hobo Sickert was meant to be a huge reveal that shocked and riled up the nation. Perhaps it did not have the immediate reaction that was hoped for, but Sickert's story did inspire Stephen Knight to write *Jack the Ripper: The Final Solution*—see discussion in Chapter 3—published in 1976. Knight took Sickert's story and expanded it into an entire book, including Sickert's own ancestor in the plot to murder the Canonical Five. Where Hobo, or Joseph, Sickert had only hinted at the full reasons behind the Ripper murders, Knight fleshed them out. Now Mary Jane Kelly is not just a witness to her friend's wedding and a nanny to her friend's child, but the one who enlisted her friends in a blackmail scheme against the crown—and thus got them killed.

This is indeed a conspiracy that goes all the way to the top as the Freemasons unite to protect the monarchy. If the heir apparent married a simple shop girl, and a Catholic at that, without the knowledge or blessing of his grandmother, and that marriage produced a child, then the entire line of descent could be thrown into question. Any arguments that the Queen would have had the power to annul that marriage and disinherit any child were squashed in order to make the situation seem all the more dire. For Knight's story to work, a single sex worker and her friends need to have the potential to topple the monarchy of one of the most powerful nations in the world.

Hobo Sickert, who was also Joseph Sickert, who was also Joseph Gorman, retracted his story after the publication of Knight's book, but the expanded story was already out there. It had many elements that made it worth telling, retelling, and remediating, and this conspiracy theory was not limited to the paranoid 1970s.

Jack the Ripper and *The Ripper File* relied heavily on evidence from 1888 in order to construct their narrative and present readers with as factual a story as possible. *Jack the Ripper: The Final Solution* was presented as factual, and indeed Knight found some circumstantial evidence to corroborate Sickert/Gorman's original story, but even with the solution provided in Knight's book, there was room for expansion. He may have "solved" the Ripper murders, but the story he constructed had enough gaps to inspire others to fill them by moving the narrative more firmly into the realm of fiction.

Chapter 6. Once Upon a Time

Alan Moore and Eddie Campbell took the Freemason conspiracy to its next iteration in the graphic novel *From Hell*, initially serialized from 1989 to 1998. The full collection was published in 1999 with the subtitle *Being a Melodrama in Sixteen Parts*. Once again the Ripper narrative became segmented, unrolling piece by piece the way it did in the original newspapers. Although graphic novels regularly struggle against public association with comic books, which are frequently seen as "lower" than proper literature, Moore includes an appendix of "Annotations to the Chapters"[13] showcasing the amount of research he put into this story. Campbell relies on photographs, when possible, to assist in his illustrations of historical figures.

It is not just the illustrated nature of this narrative that pushes it toward fiction, but the ways Moore turns events into a completed story. Every Ripper researcher is confronted with them: although we have certain pieces of information that seem to be irrefutable and must be included in each Ripper narrative, there are gaps between them. True crime certainly works to fill in those spaces and tell a solid narrative, but Moore approaches his work by accepting Knight's premise as fictional, giving himself more room to explore personalities and motivations as characters in his narrative and not necessarily real people who could serve as referents to determine whether his conclusions are "correct."

Moore unites the Freemasons with the police, explaining the latter's failure to identify the Ripper because they were in on the scheme from the beginning. Gull justifies his actions to himself by situating them as part of Freemason ritual. In this version of the narrative, Inspector Abberline triumphs and identifies the Ripper—with the help of psychic Robert James Lees, who is apparently the real deal instead of a fraud—and even gets a confession out of Gull. Unfortunately for Abberline and his legacy, this discovery was immediately hushed up by his superiors. Gull does not face a public trial, but he is sentenced by his Masonic brothers who have found him insane. Unfortunately this imprisonment does not hold him, since his spirit travels through time to inspire other serial killers and cause his assistant Netley's death. The Freemasons frame Montague John Druitt, one of the earliest Ripper suspects chosen solely because his suicide came shortly after Mary Jane Kelly's death.

Overall the graphic novel seeks to answer the enduring questions about the Ripper: how did he choose his victims? How did he kill his victims? Did he work alone? Was there a coverup? It also combines a number of theories from the Autumn of Terror, turning Gull into the mad doctor and incorporating a secret society. Psychics were also involved with the case from the beginning, although if Robert James

Lees properly identified the Ripper in real life, there is no record of it. There are enough twists and turns to the story to make it complicated enough to feel plausible, as is the tendency of conspiracy theories. It also provides us with that ever-elusive motive of the killer while turning the responsibility of the murders away from the man who wielded the knife and onto the final victim.

Here Mary Jane Kelly takes an active role in putting herself and her friends in the direct line of fire. She is not merely helping care for the child that others want eliminated so as to ensure a proper line of inheritance for the crown, but the mastermind behind a plan to blackmail the royal family. By enlisting three of her friends—Polly Nichols, Annie Chapman, and Elizabeth Stride—she signs their death warrants, as well. This shifts the narrative from a Ripper randomly choosing East End sex workers perhaps because of their anonymity or his hatred against those in the profession and turns it back to a Dr. Stanley sort of tale: the Ripper is truly seeking Mary Jane Kelly, who has wronged him in some way, and this version of Mary Jane Kelly has therefore also wronged her friends. The knowledge of Prince Eddy's secret marriage and child must be eliminated, and thus all of the women who know about it must die.

As in the story of the Lodger, we once again see a shift when the story moves from the page to the screen, brought about in part by the actors chosen to play some of the leading roles. In the 2001 film version directed by the Hughes Brothers, Johnny Depp plays Inspector Abberline and Heather Graham plays Mary Jane Kelly. Depp's Abberline is tragic, since his wife died in childbirth and his grief has led him to an opium addiction, but his choice of drug has also allowed him to get in touch with his psychic powers. Graham's Kelly is an innocent bystander who only wants to care for her friend's baby after that friend was mysteriously taken away, and she needs Abberline to show her a portrait of Prince Eddy and realize the identity of her friend's husband in order to understand why someone would be after the child. She is not a blackmailer, and both her beauty and her innocence allow Abberline to fall in love with her as they investigate the case and try to prevent further murders.

Because of the known course of history—and despite the changes already made to Abberline's character, who did not lose a wife in childbirth and who was married at the time of the murders—a murdered and mutilated body must be found in Mary Jane Kelly's room. There is no Joseph Barnett to identify her, since her only paramour in the movie is Abberline himself, and Abberline agrees that the murdered woman is indeed Kelly, although he realizes that the hair of the dead woman is the wrong color. Kelly has escaped with the child and even raises the baby as her own daughter, although this version of Abberline conceals his knowledge of her survival to protect everyone involved and dies of an opium overdose. "Abberline's death is a direct consequence of his promotion to protagonist in the film,"[14] since the added complication of his personal relationship with Kelly cannot end happily.

Despite the injection of romance into the story, it is still ultimately a tragedy: Prince Eddy is ripped away from Ann, who is forced to undergo a lobotomy so she can no longer tell her story, and Abberline knows he would risk the lives of both Mary Jane Kelly and the baby girl if he were to go to them. This Kelly is innocent of blackmail and persecuted only for trying to help her friend's baby, so she is allowed to survive and escape her life of sex work even if she cannot bring Abberline with her. She did not choose sex work as her preferred vocation but only out of desperation to survive, and her motherly devotion to her friend's child further protects her morality and allows her this happier ending.

Although this royal conspiracy began as a supposedly true confession by a man purporting to reveal his family's darkest secrets, the enduring form of this particular narrative has morphed into one of fiction with only a slight basis in fact. The supernatural components of both versions of *From Hell* indicate that, no matter how well-researched either version may or may not have been, it is not meant to be taken as truth. This is historical fiction instead of historical fact, although it uses the names of real people in depicting these events. Despite these obvious cues that the narrative is not meant to be nonfiction, audiences still experience a blurring between the two. Have they just engaged with truth that feels like fiction because it is indeed a real conspiracy? How much of the narrative was made up—and how much fantasy separates a true crime narrative from crime fiction?

Moore's appendix provides the opportunity for readers to answer some of these questions and follow his line of thinking about what elements were included and why, but those who read the graphic novel and skip the text-heavy Appendix I may come away thinking that, hallucinations or no hallucinations, this explanation for the Ripper is a plausible one, because they would not be aware that numerous strokes left Gull physically unable to do the activities ascribed to him. This information is deliberately left out in order to serve the narrative instead of undermining it, but does this mean the casual reader or viewer is meant to engage in research to help parse the reality from the fiction? Or does it simply add to the myth of the Ripper and continue to blur the lines between reality and fiction so that, from a public perspective, nothing is left of the story but the latter?

Time and Time Again

The more time passes, the further we find ourselves removed from the era of the Ripper. We are no longer curious outsiders who can make the trip to Whitechapel and walk the streets where these women lived and died, gazing upon the "Sisters of the Abyss" and getting an outsider's view of their lived experiences. Today, visitors can still venture to Whitechapel and gaze upon the locations where the women died, but they are called upon to use their imaginations to travel back into the past and "see" what was there in 1888 instead of what stands there now.

For a killer so strongly associated with his setting—the Victorian Era and a fog-shrouded Whitechapel—the Ripper could have quickly become obsolete. Instead, authors began "[t]ransplanting Jack the Ripper to other times and places"[15] as they reshaped and retold the old story. Just as the Lodger was slowly moved up from Victorian London to the "today" in which the story was written, these Rippers continued to move forward through time.

Robert Bloch first tackled the Ripper with his 1943 short story "Yours Truly, Jack the Ripper." This tale is set in Chicago in the writer's present day and follows our narrator, psychiatrist John Carmody, as he meets and engages with the English Sir Guy Hollis. The central issue is introduced immediately since, after ascertaining Carmody's identity, Hollis asks "have you ever heard of—Jack the Ripper?"[16] Bloch uses Carmody's vague recollection of the case to allow Hollis to explain the murders, not naming the victims but recognizably starting with Martha Tabram before moving onto the Canonical Five. Hollis includes a rhyme that was sent to the press and from which the story's title was taken, neatly summarizing the horrors of the case before revealing "Jack the Ripper is alive, in Chicago, and I'm out to find him."[17] While this understandably confuses Carmody in many ways, he now clearly understands why Hollis sought out a psychiatrist.

The two men go on to set their plans since, according to the schedule Hollis has charted, the Ripper will kill again in two days' time. When the Ripper does not appear to follow his own schedule, Hollis drunkenly explains that his interest in the case came because his own mother was one of the "drabs"[18] murdered by the Ripper, and that he inherited his quest from his father. Hollis' father was killed by the Ripper in the 1920s, and Hollis has since carried on the quest alone to avenge not only the women murdered in 1888, but all the people the Ripper has killed since then in order to keep himself young and apparently immortal. Even in his drunken state, Hollis convinces Carmody that he will not give up on his quest, causing Carmody to reach for a knife and, in the last line of the story, to urge the Englishman "Just call me—Jack."[19] Sixteen years before *Psycho*, Bloch nevertheless gives his readers a twist ending.

Here we already see some of the themes that will become enduring when stories take the Ripper out of his own time. He appears here in Chicago, another big city, and a big American city. Bloch predates the FBI's Behavioral Science Unit and its narrative of the serial killer based on "Golden Age"[20] killers such as Ted Bundy, but he still emphasizes that the Ripper is associated with big cities and not small towns or the country, and that these cities must be modern. London is too old-fashioned for these twentieth-century Rippers, who are infinitely adaptable to match the cunning they showed when they were not caught for their original crimes. After all, a killer who accelerated through the Autumn of Terror with increasing violence could hardly be expected to rest on his laurels just because one series of murders was complete.

This version of the Ripper is fantastic, but relies more on folk tale than science fiction. Like the so-called Blood Countess Elizabeth Báthory, this Ripper kills in order to maintain his youth. Báthory supposedly murdered and then bathed in the blood of young women to maintain her beauty while this Ripper, now known as John Carmody, uses his knife against apparently anyone. In 1888 it was "drabs," in 1929 it was Hollis' father, and now in 1943 it is Hollis himself. Presumably the Ripper can kill two birds with one stone and use each Hollis for his immortal ritual as well as removing the threat of those convinced he is still present.

Bloch does branch out into the fully science fictional with his 1967 *Star Trek: The Original Series* episode "Wolf in the Fold." Scotty is recovering from a blow to the head and somehow finds himself a suspect in a series of brutal murders on the planet Argelius II. Although all evidence continues to point to Scotty, an empathic ritual indicates that the true murderer goes under multiple names, and a search for some of those names brings up the Victorian serial killer Jack the Ripper. Kirk realizes that the real killer is an immortal, non-corporeal energy that has gone under various names at various times on various planets, including Jack the Ripper on Earth in 1888—much like the way *From Hell* (1999) depicts Gull as having a psychic influence over other serial killers long after his own death. Luckily our heroes manage to eject the murderous entity into space, saving the crew and rescuing Scotty from multiple murder charges.

This version of the Ripper story must fit into the established Star Trek universe, cast, and mode of storytelling. Anxiety is heightened when an established character is placed at risk of being—falsely, we hope—accused of murder, especially when he is put on trial for those same murders. Bloch adapted his original vampiric Ripper with this idea of immortal energy that, nevertheless, might be destroyed at the end of the episode, never to murder—or frame beloved engineers—again. Although this noncorporeal killer is known to have committed at least three series of murders, it is unclear whether framing an innocent party is part of its modus operandi, especially since no one went to trial for the Ripper murders. Although "Wolf in the Fold" was named seventy-sixth out of the top 100 Star Trek episodes of all time,[21] it has also been criticized as "predicated on the most tiresome sexist nonsense"[22] because of the theory that Scotty's murder spree was brought about because a woman previously hit him in the head and caused his concussion. It seems that, even as pure energy, the Ripper is misogynistic and brings out that quality in response to the murders.

Here we see the continued belief that a serial killer does not simply stop murdering. This was a common theme since 1888 when police and the press asked themselves why the Ripper seemed to have ended with the November 9 murder of Mary Jane Kelly. Some real-life ideas included the possibility that the killer was dead, arrested or now an inmate in an asylum, or a merchant seaman and had moved on. "Wolf in the Fold" simply takes this last premise to the next level, indicating that this ball of energy has indeed committed murders on other planets since 1888 and, like the FBI's perception of a serial killer, cannot simply cease. If Kirk and Spock have failed to neutralize the threat, it will go on under other names and kill again.

Karl Alexander introduced us to a different time-traveling Ripper in 1979 with his book *Time After Time*. Like "Yours Truly, Jack the Ripper," this killer is the same person who committed the Canonical Five murders—and more—in Victorian Whitechapel. Unlike Bloch's killer, Alexander's is not immortal. Physician Leslie John Stephenson (changed to "John Leslie Stevenson" for the following movie and television adaptations) is a regular man except, just as the police finally catch on that he is the killer, he realizes his friend H.G. Wells has invented a time machine and uses it to escape into contemporary San Francisco before he could be taken into custody. H. G., as the book refers to him, worries that the future manifests his personal vision of a peaceful utopia and quickly follows his erstwhile friend, hoping to save the defenseless and unsuspecting future from Stephenson's brutality.

Here we once again see the Ripper transplanted from Victorian London into a "modern" American city. Stephenson does not triumph in the same way John "Jack" Carmody does, but as the Ripper he finds himself far more prepared for this future than the forward-thinking

Chapter 6. Once Upon a Time   115

H.G. Wells. This is a theme carried into the 2017 ABC television series which, although it only broadcast five episodes, showcased Stevenson sent to contemporary New York City and quickly navigating this new culture, selling a watch as an antique and using the money to buy himself, among other things, an iPhone that he quickly masters while Wells quite literally stumbles around this overwhelming future. Despite the author's creative imagination, he has great difficulty coming to terms with this new reality and even finds himself distracted by a love interest as he pursues an unencumbered murderer. Even in 2017, Stevenson somehow navigates both the advantages and challenges of the future as he continues to murder, at least initially gaining the upper hand.

The book, television series, and more faithfully adapted 1980 movie all follow fiction's advantage over real life in that the Ripper can be properly identified, studied, and dispatched. The book opens by following an initially unnamed gentleman as he commits a crime, teasing an insight into the reason for his murders before drawing back to show readers that this must be his last crime because the police are now hot on his trail. Initially the change of focus to H.G. Wells feels like a distraction, but it is then revealed that one of the guests at H. G.'s house, present for his announcement that he has invented a real time machine, is his friend Stephenson. When the police come to search the house, they do not find their quarry, and H.G. soon realizes that no one in 1893 will find him. Although the time machine is right where he expected it to be, someone else has already taken it on a maiden voyage, quickly propelling the story from the past into the present where readers anticipate not only H. G.'s hunt for the Ripper but both men's interactions with, for them, an almost unimaginable future.

Unlike in "Yours Truly, Jack the Ripper" and "The Wolf in the Fold," audiences quickly learn alongside H.G. Wells what the killer's true name is. This shifts the story from a whodunit to a whydunit, allowing characters, storytellers, and audiences alike to explore questions about Stephenson's past, his motivations, and a proper fate for such a remorseless killer. Even here H.G. is foiled, or perhaps cheated out of his intention: although he wants Stephenson to return to the past and go on trial in 1893 to answer for his crimes, during the climax he instead ensures Stephenson is "permanently stuck outside of time."[23] The violent man who found himself to be so adaptable in this strange future is now alone, without any victims or an audience to discuss and publish his crimes. Although it was not his preference, Stephenson's own actions force H.G.'s hand and it does not matter if he likes how his hunt for his former friend ended. The important thing is that Stephenson is beyond contact, and therefore cannot reach—or harm—anyone else, no matter what decade or city they call home.

Ripper Evolutions

Onscreen, "Jack the Ripper has undergone no great revision in the 75 years between Hitchcock's *The Lodger* and the Hughes Brothers' *From Hell*."[24] The basis of the story must be the same: women must be murdered on the street, brutally and at high speed, spurring newspapers to write headlines that newsboys cry from the corners. The identity of the Ripper should be revealed, even if only to a small group that decides to keep this information a secret, and the Ripper himself needs to be neutralized. He can complete suicide, die as the result of an accident, or be locked up under another name—the method is not as important as the fact that he is rendered harmless in some way. Fiction reassures us what fact cannot: the Ripper was indeed identified and caught, even if it was not wise for those in the know to make this information public.

Films about the Ripper were allowed more freedom as Hollywood censorship deteriorated, and "filmmakers found themselves freer than they had ever been before to deal with the Ripper's crimes at source, and without having to resort to the euphemisms of fiction."[25] Early versions of the Ripper onscreen were called by other names, such as *The Lodger*'s serial-killing "Avenger," and the brutal murders were hinted at instead of shown. Early retellings sought to indicate the horror without showing the blood, even from cut throats, with the camera too close to fully make out what was happening, perhaps zoomed in on a dark figure flailing with a knife but no victim present before cutting to a closeup of a woman's screaming face and ending with an artfully posed woman lying on the cobbles. When other non–Ripper films pushed at the boundaries, such as Hitchcock's 1960 *Psycho* with its infamous shower scene and the clear shots of chocolate syrup running down the drain, they opened the doors for Ripper movies to be more explicit and present the real-life slasher with proper—or exaggerated—amounts of gore.

The Ripper does not just darken the screen but moves through novels and graphic novels, even facing off against Batman in 1989's "Gotham by Gaslight," which was adapted to an animated move in 2018, confronting a famous crime fighter outside of his contemporary fictional nemesis, Sherlock Holmes. When the detectives are fictional, they can be "better" than the real-life Victorian police and solve the case. Because these narratives are coded as fiction, they can easily ignore or emphasize known information about the murders, as well as introduce their own preferred backstories for the various real-life individuals now turned into fictional characters. Approaching the Ripper story as fiction opens up myriad possibilities for satisfying storytelling for the era in which the story is created.

As a subject, the Ripper is still fruitful for storytelling today. Twenty-first-century shows such as *Whitechapel* (2009–2013) and *Ripper Street* (2012–2016) showcase both methods of bringing the Ripper into the present and revisiting the Ripper in the Victorian era. Here the Ripper time travels but does not move out of the East End. Other recent adaptations bring the Ripper into fictional cities—*Gotham by Gaslight*—or real modern cities like New York in *Time After Time*. As a nemesis, the Ripper is eminently adaptable for contemporary conceptions of entertainment.

Katrina Jan, currently a doctoral researcher in the Department of English Literature at the University of Birmingham, shares that her research concerns Jack the Ripper and "how this historical figure has become a sexualised character in erotica and contemporary romance novels."[26] She presented her work during the University's 2023 Three Minute Thesis Finals[27] and earned the judges' runner-up prize[28] for her overview of how we have somehow turned the Ripper into a viable narrative for a romance novel. Although she has yet to come across a book in which the Ripper himself is the love interest, many versions have their heroine falling for a Ripper suspect who, at least, is proved innocent before the happily-ever-after ending. Jan relates this obsession with the bad—or abusive—love interest to such book series as E.L. James' *Fifty Shades* trilogy (2011–2012) with its focus on the BDSM relationship between Anastasia Steele and Christian Grey, and Caroline Kepnes' continuing *You* series (2014–) following stalker and serial killer Joe Goldberg through his various relationships. There is certainly room for romance stories concerning suspected or confirmed criminals, a fictional premise that has ties to real life in the women obsessed with Ted Bundy or who nearly married Charles Manson.

When we firmly move Jack the Ripper from fact into fiction, we have an archetypal character who still holds our fascination and can be placed at the center of a murder mystery story as easily in the twenty-first century as he was in the nineteenth. We know both so much and yet so little about the real Ripper that he was mythologized from the beginning and, as a criminal, still fits the mold of our interest today. As our understanding of serial killers has evolved, so has our representation of the Ripper, who has not been left behind due to our new knowledge but rather refined and reiterated.

Here the Ripper is still two-dimensional, projected on a screen or on the page of a book. We have, however, also brought the Ripper into three dimensions, albeit with different degrees of liveliness. We want more than just images of the Ripper—we would like to experience him in three dimensions and in real time.

Chapter 7

Reach Out and Touch Someone

There is a marked experiential difference between reading about an event and having the story occupy physical space. Even seeing photos of the murder locations at various points throughout history does not bring them to life. Only 13 Miller's Court, Mary Jane Kelly's room, was photographed in 1888 to document the gruesome extent of the way the Ripper mutilated her, and those photos have been circulated so extensively that the horror has nearly worn off. Other locations have been photographed for various books, documenting the changing landscapes, and the Victorian East End has been reproduced using CGI for *Jack the Ripper: CSI: Whitechapel* by Paul Begg and John Bennett, but still images and empty landscapes do not offer the sense of humanity and community that three-dimensional interaction with place and people can.

Even though panic spread beyond the East End, the sites of the Canonical Five murders are all very close together—close enough so that, from 1888 onward, interested parties could easily participate in walking tours and literally follow in the Ripper's footsteps. These tours can be led by guides in-person or via recording, or followed via Zoom from anywhere in the world, but people were coming to experience Whitechapel and its perceived gritty reality even before the murders. From slumming to viewing the murder sites, people have been interacting with the East End as spectacle for well over a century.

Since "evil that can be named and seen seems less malevolent, more manageable,"[1] attempts to put a human face on the Ripper and make the murders themselves more approachable have likewise been enacted since the murders. Some entrepreneurs quick to jump at the chance staged waxwork tableaus of the murder scenes, while others apparently took it upon themselves to playact as the Ripper himself not just through letters, but in person. By engaging with the space and creating stand-ins for the people involved, we have been negotiating finding meaning, discovering motive, and turning the crimes into something that allows us to have enough distance to consider such observation academic instead of horrific.

Turning the Ripper narrative into a performance on stage addresses many of these points all at once. The stage, after all, sets up a boundary between the actors and the audience, even when actors break this fourth wall and speak directly to them. Although actors might come into the audience to involve them or bring the action closer, as was especially popular in early twenty-first-century theater, none of the audience members will become a victim of the Ripper. If someone in one of the numbered seats does appear to die, it is an actor who has been planted there for the excitement of the reveal and the feeling of personally being involved without actually being at risk.

Through monologues, soliloquies, and song, characters onstage present their inner thoughts to the audience. Writers and directors can choose to reveal or conceal such interiority but, in cases such as representations of the Ripper, the techniques frequently help with the common questions of identity and motive. A stage Ripper who has a clear reason for choosing his victims and killing them as brutally as his real-life counterpart allows for narrative closure when real life has no such neat ending. There are, of course, far too many stage presentations of the Ripper narrative to be covered here, so I have chosen to focus on one of the earliest adaptations and explore some of the changes that have been made over the intervening decades as we continue to retell and remediate the Ripper story. But first, we return to the nineteenth century.

Slumming for Fun and Profit

Visitors coming from either abroad or greater London to explore the East End are not solely a post–Autumn of Terror occurrence. Although now separated from us by time as well as by geographical location, the East End was not familiar to anyone who lived elsewhere. Indeed, it was "a place as foreign to us now as it was to the average Victorian."[2] As we have already seen in both newspapers and letters to the editor, the Ripper murders brought news of the conditions in the East End to many who had no prior knowledge of them, and those who had already been working in social programs in the area felt the need to write letters themselves and explain what systems were already established.

Chapter 7. Reach Out and Touch Someone

The East End was treated largely as a fun experience for well-off young men who wished to have an experience they could mark as tantamount to visiting the supposed "wilds" of other continents without having to venture that far from home. It was "fashionable to go slumming on conducted tours of the toughest, roughest streets and taverns,"[3] and the Ripper murders only added to the apparent appeal of such a tour. These outsiders could dress the way they imagined East Enders to dress and spend a given amount of time attempting to live the lives they assumed East Enders lived, all the while knowing that they could return to their own positions of privilege should the trials prove to be more demeaning than appealing. The slummers, unlike the East End's inhabitants, always had the option of leaving.

Many of those who came to spend time in the East End looked upon it as a sort of vacation or perhaps a test of manhood, but some, like Jack London, went with a mission. London wrote about his experiences in the Abyss, as he called it, with the intention of "inform[ing] his readers of the cultural and social gulf he was aiming to overcome."[4] London, as well as those working for such groups as the church, went from his position of privilege into the poorer communities with the intention of informing others of the situation in order to induce them to use their privilege to contribute to social change.

Jack London, Beatrix Potter, and the others who did their best to disguise themselves as belonging in the East End so they could collect the stories and experiences of the true occupants had to be conscious of the fact that they "both held and described a privileged viewing position."[5] No matter how pure their intentions, they still entered the area with the intent of exploiting those they met in order to achieve their presumably socially-conscious goals. It might even be argued that those who presented themselves as clearly in positions of power, such as William Booth, founder of the mission that became the Salvation Army, were more honorable because they did not conceal their intentions. However, it has also been argued that Jack the Ripper did more for social reform than any system already in place, in large part because the murders brought attention to those systems as well as the current conditions within the East End.

Although it can hardly seem to have been a goal of the Ripper, the murders, combined with the newspaper coverage, did indeed allow not only greater London but also readers all over the world to explore the East End and discover the exact conditions facing the people there. The lack of streetlights, as mentioned in Chapter 1, was denounced even though the twisting and turning streets, along with the atmospheric conditions, meant that visibility within the East End was poor under the best of lighting conditions. Well-meaning suggestions, such as having police arrest any woman who was on the street after a certain hour, likewise showed a lack of understanding of the situation. It seemed that people wanted to help the women of the East End who seemed most at-risk from the Ripper, but they had no grasp of the realities of the situation and what, exactly, it was they were proposing. Many times such would-be philanthropists underestimated the population that needed such assistance or put restrictions on the offers of aid that highlighted, for example, the era's belief in alcoholism as a personal choice and a mark of poor character, or assumed all offers of help would be taken with goodwill. There was a distinct sense that only certain people were deserving of such aid and that anyone offering monetary assistance deserved to make such distinctions and determine that their money would only end up helping the "worthy" poor.

The East End faced not only issues of poverty, but of existing as a location in London that highlighted how the "metropolitan city [...] brought cultures into contact and negotiated their boundaries, generating an engagement with and a rethinking of difference and modernity."[6] There were language, cultural, and religious differences alongside class barriers, and the Autumn of Terror highlighted the antisemitism that was already prevalent. This meant both that a large segment of the tourist population was itself Jewish, but also that "exploring the East End emerged as an antipode to the prescribed tours of established travel guides,"[7] since it meant venturing off the beaten path and to the more "exotic" areas of the city. While the metropolis worked to homogenize its population through daily life and mass media, the East End was still different enough to appeal both to those who could see themselves in the area's population, and to those who viewed residents as Other.

Outsiders visiting the East End, then, were not uncommon prior to the Ripper murders, and it is a practice that has certainly not ceased since. After the murders, locals and tourists both came to view the murder sites, and these initial visits developed into their own industry.

Murder Tourism and Walking Tours

Although home to such a warren of streets and alleys, the East End is not geographically large. In fact, although "[y]ou would need to charter a bus to tour any other serial killer's murder sites[, ...] most of the Whitechapel murder sites can be toured in a single leisurely walk"[8]—and it is not only the authors of Ripper texts who have undertaken such a walk. As Paul Begg and John Bennett have pointed out, the locations of the Ripper murders are "accessible"[9] to the average tourist. There is no need to be capable of hiking wild trails, and the only indoor location of the Canonical Five murders, Mary Jane Kelly's rented room, was torn down in the 1920s. The Ripper was, after all, known for leaving his victims on display in the street, and the sites he chose were arranged within a small geographical area. Even then, visitors did not have to wait until Kelly's November 9, 1888, murder to come to Whitechapel because of the Ripper.

Now considered to be the first of the Canonical Five victims, Polly Nichols' August 31 murder was at the time linked to previous violent deaths in the area, including those of Martha Tabram on August 7, Emma Elizabeth Smith on April 4, and the newspaper-invented "Fairy Fay" sometime around Christmas 1887. Rather than the unrecognized first murder in a series to come, Polly Nichols was placed as the next in a line of murders, and therefore "morbid sightseers came in groups of two or three to gaze at the gaudy green gates of the workhouse mortuary,"[10] where her body had been taken, starting only a week after her death. Just as the murders themselves were news, the public places of those murders were places of note for sightseers to visit.

The papers played a large role in the visits of those earliest sightseers as one of their evolutions—including illustrations—meant they could publish maps of the area and the murder locations.[11] Rather than going on a "slumming" adventure, visitors could travel with the express purpose of seeing the sites where the women's bodies had been left on display. At times such visitors went not only to see the location, but then to "wander around in search of a souvenir to take home,"[12] since such trips were not merely worth taking, but worth telling others about. The places were so important that an item taken from it, even one that had nothing to do with the murder, was worth finding.

Aside from the changes to their structure and the technological advances that allowed them to publish such maps, the fact that papers chose to then do so indicates encouragement to readers to seek out those places. Those who purchased the papers "may visit the killing grounds in safety, enjoying a thrill, while protected by respectability. Prostitutes beware, but all others may pass."[13] Granted, these tourists, like the young men who wanted to go "slumming," had more control over their actions and locations than those who lived in the East End and may not have had a bed for the night. Tourists could carefully choose to venture out only in the daytime, in pairs or groups, and to be safely away from the East End before darkness fell and the Ripper might once again be on the prowl. Even then, visitors who retained their usual clothing might have had to worry about being robbed by roving gangs, but they would not have made themselves look like the poor sex workers who were being murdered.

Although these locations were outside, not all of them were easily reached and viewed from public property. This did not deter visitors and in fact inspired those who lived near the murder sites, such as "one enterprising resident of Hanbury Street [who] was charging visitors a penny to see the murder site next door."[14] Tourists were willing not only to travel to the East End in order to track down these locations, but also to pay for a better view into the yard where Annie Chapman had been killed. Both newspapers and conveniently-located citizens were able to profit off of the murder sites long after the crimes had occurred, the women's bodies removed, and the blood washed away.

It was not long before these informal written guides were replaced by guided tours, such as those "held by the Crimes Club (of which Arthur Conan Doyle was a member) at the start of the twentieth century,"[15] a lucrative business that continues today. How lucrative? There are so many tours to choose from that TourScanner ranks its top 20[16] to help visitors decide which one would be worth the money. Some of them are bus tours that include more than the East End locations, catering to those who might want more than "just" a murder tour. The Jack the Ripper Tour advertises itself as "The Original Terror Tour–Established 1982"[17] and even offers Zoom events on select nights, making any sort of travel, much less walking, unnecessary.

A more recent offering from Look Up London is the Feminist Jack the Ripper Tour. This updated twenty-first-century version is an "alternative Jack the Ripper walking tour [that] investigates the grim and unfair situations women had to face in the 19th Century"[18] rather than focusing on the crimes and identity of the killer himself. This approach is a response in part to cultural shifts such as the #MeToo movement and calls to shift the focus of true crime and representation of the murder victims in Hallie Rubenhold's 2019 *The Five: The Untold Lives of the Women Killed by Jack the Ripper* and my own 2018 *The Ripper's Victims in Print: The Rhetoric of Portrayals Since 1929*, and also responds to the resistance from citizens of the East End to the gore-centered Ripper tours.[19] The infamy of the murders has overshadowed not only Whitechapel's past but also its present, and the tours that walk strangers through the present-day locations of the Ripper's murders contribute to the idea that the area is "forever tainted by what took place there."[20] These tours, like much historical true crime, are couched as lessons on historical events, combined with the investigative challenge of an unsolved crime, and are frequently criticized for not giving the narrative the proper moral weight.

During Ripper tours and similar tours of historical events, "the guides often aim to transport their users back in time"[21] back to the era of the original events. It is impossible to visit the original murder sites themselves, since the last one fell to reconstruction in the 1960s,[22] but tour guides can paint verbal pictures of what the area looked like in 1888. They have to work to set the scene against a backdrop of electric lights, passing cars, and other signs of the twenty-first century, crossing barriers of not only class and culture but also the passing years. Even authors have attempted to create this mood in their written texts, telling their readers "Let me take you down. Catch the Underground to Aldgate East.... You are now on foot"[23] as they begin the journey back to the past. Indeed, there is such a sense of these crimes being rooted in *place* that the idea of walking through Whitechapel, with or without the aid of mental time travel, is inextricable from any narrative relating the murders.

Such walking tours allow visitors to put themselves in the Ripper's shoes and to contemplate, for example, the speed at which he must have moved from Berner Street to Mitre Square on September 30, 1888, the night of the Double Event when both Elizabeth Stride and Catherine Eddowes were murdered. Indeed, having been physically present in Whitechapel at these specific locations seems to lend weight to authors' arguments for their favorite suspect, leading them to inform readers authoritatively that "I have walked all the sites of the Ripper's crimes and timed all his routes"[24]—as though to do any less would detract from their claims. Visitors to London are certainly inundated with pleas to go on a Ripper tour, if they can sort through the number on offer and find one with a vacancy. Such tours are advertised alongside visits to the Tower of London, the various museums, and any number of West End shows and are now apparently simply a part of the tourist's experience of London, all but a requirement of a visit to the city.

These walking tours clearly continue to fill a space within our desire to experience the Ripper murders in a way that literally moves us through the very space he, and his victims, once occupied. The large and changing variety of these walks is a reflection of our "construction of performative memory,"[25] allowing us to participate in the remembrance of these events as groups rather than individuals, with guides who not only lead us along the walk but also are there to answer our questions and function as the experts—experts who, thanks to such a large selection of tours, are more likely to tell us the story the way we would like to hear it, depending on the tour's intended focus and the general mood it is meant to create.

Such tours also perform a specific function in our literal approach to the story, placing groups within the twenty-first-century physical locations of the crimes. It is impossible for guides to lead their groups to the actual locations, since they are long gone, but they can paint the picture of Whitechapel as it used to look then while standing in Whitechapel as it is now. This is the embodied representation of the book *CSI: Whitechapel* mentioned in Chapter 3, presenting spaces but also sanitized, empty spaces. To encounter representations of the murdered women and their butchered bodies, tourists need to look not on the streets of Whitechapel, but elsewhere.

Unresponsive Displays

As already seen in Chapter 1, the Ripper murders did not occur in a society that had no place for public consumption of violent crime. Even prior to the Autumn of Terror, "many Victorians derived their fix of sensation-horror from museum-like displays of waxen effigies and plaster casts of heinous murderers,"[26] and the Ripper murders simply provided the next subject for display. Regardless of literacy level, any citizen who could afford entry could "enjoy" the stories told by such exhibits, vicariously participating in attempts to solve the murder mystery even though "the figures of Jack [...] do not bring us any closer to revealing the identity of the killer or discovering the reality of this figure."[27] Wax figures of the murdered women, present from the earliest days of the case, encourage a distanced and almost clinical interaction between paying viewer and inert subject, calling for interaction and interpretation not present within textual forms alone.

There are reports that, shortly after Annie Chapman's murder on September 8, 1888, a "speculator had made a wax works representation"[28] of the scene. Those who were unable to enter one of the houses overlooking the backyard at 29 Hanbury Street and view the location of her murder could instead pay to view a representation of the murdered woman's body. Accuracy was not the highest concern; thrills and chills were rather the order of the day.

A display of one of the murdered women as she supposedly lay after her death avoids the issue of attempting to represent the Ripper himself who, after all, was never caught. This lack of identification, and the lack of a face to recreate, was the reason the Ripper himself was not immediately displayed in Madame Tussaud's Chamber of Horrors.[29] Despite the fact that "murderers were among Madame Tussaud's main attractions,"[30] it was up to the individual to create these original waxwork representations of the Ripper crimes. Indeed, it was more than a century[31] after the Autumn of Terror that Madame Tussaud's introduced its Ripper, informing visitors that their killer would look like suspect Aaron Kosminski,[32] In order to put the Ripper on display and adhere to their own longstanding rules of representation, they had to choose a suspect and make a declaration of guilt to present the crimes to the public.

Hastily cobbled together exhibits in the late 1880s were not so concerned with accuracy and were more focused on presenting audiences with the forms of the murdered women, far more visually striking and horrific than that of a man even in a top hat and cape, brandishing a knife. The moment caught was not of the murder itself, or even the moment directly preceding the murder; visitors instead looked upon the already-murdered women after the event was over and the murderer was gone. There was no impression that viewers could have intervened, either to warn a woman standing alone or to save her from an imminent attack by the male figure. She was already dead and on the ground, to be literally looked down upon as they examined her "wounds" and the resulting "blood."

David Schmid recognizes this clear separation between audience and represented victim, arguing that "[t]he presence of women at these shows suggests that they may have used these exhibits to distance themselves from the Ripper's victims, making themselves feel a little less vulnerable by underlining the fact that the Ripper had killed other ('fallen') women and not them."[33] This has been contradicted by others' arguments that, at the time, it seemed that all women were at risk and not simply the poorest sex workers,[34] but even then it seems that this lack of distinction would lend itself toward a further desire to separate the self from the murdered women. If there were no clear delineation of class or occupation in the public's eyes, then they would seek out other factors to categorize the murdered women as Others unrecognizable in themselves or the women in their lives. This has continued even up to the present time with the categorizing of the women into a homogeneous group of poor sex workers.

In such displays that "just" show the murdered women, the killer himself is highlighted by his absence. Even if he is not there *now*, he must have been present not too far in the past, especially considering the speed at which the women's bodies were found. The conceit of such waxwork displays is that the paying attendee has arrived in that gap between the killer's departure, rendering the audience safe, but prior to discovery and the arrival of the police, meaning that the viewer has the optimal chance to discover clues to the killer's identity before the scene is disturbed. Although Victorians were not as aware of forensic evidence as we are today, with even the ability to match fingerprints being in their future, such a scene still gives an aura of discovery and intimacy, as though the woman's death is known only to the viewer. The sense of calm is assisted by the fact that the unseen killer has left and is no longer a threat, and yet the body is indeed fake so that the viewer has no responsibility to check for continued life or find a policeman. Because they have paid to witness this moment, audiences have no responsibility to the figure of the woman other than to look their fill.

Lucyna Krawczyk-Żywko observes that sources she found of wax figures of the women in 1888 and 1889 reported that these figures were "reflecting and perverting reality"[35] in their representations of the murder victims. They allowed visitors to approach not a reality, but an isolated and at times warped representation of an actual event. Unlike newspaper reports, the wax figures allowed viewers a three-dimensional "scene" placed in front of them. Rather than text indicating the important pieces of information, this meant they could approach the wax figure themselves, make their own examinations, and come to their own conclusions.

These sorts of scenarios likely contributed to the negative response directed at the police who, after all, were able to interact on such a level with the actual murder scenes, and who had presumably undergone special training in order to attain their titles. If the average citizen, with spare coins but no such training, could come away from a wax figure purporting to be one of the murdered women with ideas for how to identify or capture the perpetrator, then how could the police continue to fail in their task? Such spectators may indeed have been among those writing letters to the editor making suggestions to law enforcement about how they should best go about their jobs.

Such displays were not, however, left in the 1880s. A far more recent display has been critiqued at the Jack the Ripper Museum, opened in 2015. Claire Hayward observed that "[t]he representation of women at the Jack the Ripper Museum is much the same as the waxwork of Catherine Eddowes: lifeless, wordless, passive."[36] It can be argued that *all* waxwork figures are lifeless, wordless, and passive, simply by definition, but the pose of the figure, as well as the real-life history ascribed to the person in question, can either emphasize or soften these tendencies. So many of the more famous personalities represented at, for example, Madame Tussaud's are positioned for visitors to stand alongside them as for a real-life photo opportunity, with the figure standing and looking toward the presumed photographer. Visitors might marvel at the amount of detail in the figure or the chance to feel as though they are standing next to the person being represented, but they are not cast in the role of a detective by the given setup.

If the waxwork figure is, instead, laid on the ground—or perhaps on a raised surface so viewers do not have to stoop so low to examine the figure's details—then the dynamic between figure and viewer is changed. A lifeless wax figure standing, with eyes open, is not the same sort of "lifeless" as a figure representing a murder victim after she has been killed. A wax figure itself invites the gaze in ways a living human being does not, as it would be rude to stare at minute details of a person's face, and the passivity inherent in the existence of such a figure already lends itself to close examination. When the figure is presented as a murder victim, especially of such a longstanding unsolved mystery, then that close examination is shifted from the realm of curiosity to one of fact-finding and education. Visitors are not merely participating in stargazing with a passive representation of famous faces, but are actively searching for clues that others have missed.

It is this passivity and the display of the mutilated bodies that has led Krawczyk-Żywko to conclude that these wax representations of the murdered women are "equivalent to the continuation of the selling of their exposed bodies to anyone willing to pay the admission price."[37] True crime itself has been described as inviting strangers not only into the private sphere but into ripped and torn bodies,[38] and these wax figures—especially those purporting to be accurate representations of murder victims—encourage a disconnected, clinical gaze from non-experts. They invite audiences to feel they have the right, and perhaps even the duty, to carefully catalog all visual evidence at their disposal, as though missing the tiniest detail would result in the killer walking free as opposed to being caught. The Ripper, of course, is long past being caught, and this further removal from the time period, location, and society of the murders adds to this distancing between victim and viewer even as physical interaction between them, at least as far as circling a three-dimensional figure, is encouraged.

Avenging Lulu

One of the Ripper's earliest stage appearances was not, in fact, as a main character. Jack emerges near the end of Frank Wedekind's Lulu arc, first written as the pair of *Erdgeist* (*Earth Spirit*) and *Die Büchse der Pandora* (*Pandora's Box*) in the early 1890s, "when to all intents and purposes, Jack the Ripper was still at large."[39] Lulu, our (anti-)heroine, strives to stay as young, perfect, and innocent as her portrait while collecting, and sometimes murdering, husbands. She ends up providing for the men in her life as a sex worker in London where her last client is the Ripper himself, who murders her and brings an end to her tragic story.

Wedekind himself played the Ripper in the original production, and his wife played Lulu, meaning he directed himself to kill his own wife onstage. This is complicated further due to the motif of "woman as a receptive surface for projected male desires,"[40] turning Wedekind's real-life wife into Lulu and then into his own fictional victim. Lulu herself was a complicated figure, often conflated with her two-dimensional portrait as men wanted her, and committed adultery with her, simply because of her beauty. The figure of Lulu was a malleable one, and the play has been adapted and restaged myriad times since Wedekind's death. Today the most common performance is a single play that completes her entire story arc, ending with her death at the Ripper's hands.

The Ripper was briefly removed from Lulu's story when Alan Berg composed his opera version in the 1930s, working to create a work that would pass Nazi censorship. Although he no longer had the Ripper and his knife, Berg's version of Lulu still required certain characters to die: "Jack the Ripper is erased altogether; Lulu is held responsible for the deaths of Schön, Geschwitz, and herself."[41] Once again a narrative reiterates the idea that the natural end of the sex worker is death, if not by another's hand, then by her own. If Lulu does not encounter the Ripper, then she must be her own Ripper.

Berg did not finish the opera, although he left behind notes on how it should be completed, including indications that certain cast members should play more than one role. Although Wedekind had not included any such double casting in his original, the theater director Erich Engel directed a version of Lulu in 1926 that used a small cast and this technique and, thereafter, "double casting became standard practice"[42] for very specific roles within Lulu's story, and Berg included this idea in his notes. For example, both Engel and Berg indicated that the role of the Ripper should be performed or sung by the same actor who played Dr. Schön. In fact, all three of Lulu's husbands in earlier scenes return during those set in London and become her clients when she turns to sex work.

Engel very deliberately chose the doubling of these roles in a move that resonated with many future directors of Lulu adaptations. Although critics largely rejected the doubling at the time of the original play adaptation, the association of Lulu's husbands with her clients has now become almost standard. Indeed, this association has caused Silvio José dos Santos to write the article "Marriage as Prostitution in Berg's Lulu." Although she is the central figure throughout all versions of her story, Lulu does not necessarily have much agency. She is controlled by the men in her life, first through marriage as they dictate her relationships to them because, or even despite, of her marriage vows, and in the end Lulu finally agrees to engage in sex work to support not just herself, but other men who do not have work. Her only moments of apparent freedom come after the deaths of her husbands, but Schön, for example, refuses to fully let her go until she murders him. By having Lulu drawn to Jack at the end of the story, she is enticed not only by the murderer and the idea of her own death, but also by his similarity to her murdered husband.

Despite his absence during Nazi Germany, Jack as a character and the murderer of Lulu continues to bring about Lulu's death and put an end to her evolving identities and attempts to be more than what the men in her life want from her. Some versions present her as helpless in the face of her life's trajectory, while others make Lulu "much more manipulative as is to give justification for her premature death,"[43] but in all versions she must die unnaturally before her time because she does indeed resort to sex work. Serial marriage in search of support and stability is not punishable by death, but sex work, outside of the marriage vows, is. Still Lulu, like the Ripper, rests uneasily and is always available for new adaptations and new meanings.

Breathing Life into the Legend

Even from the beginning in the autumn of 1888, the Ripper murders were not simply a story to be read about in the paper and engaged with on a purely written level. "No other murder case has so much emphasis on 'place' as the Ripper crimes,"[44] and people came from far and wide to look at the murder sites within hours of the bodies being discovered. Locals flocked to the now-infamous locations, including Catherine Eddowes' long-term boyfriend John Kelly going to Mitre Square. As he believed Eddowes had been in police custody all night, his viewing of the bloodstained flagstones was distanced and merely interesting until he realized whose blood it truly was.

Kelly was far from the only one to treat the murders as a simple diversion from everyday life. Although slumming had long been a standard pastime for young men from established backgrounds, the murders—and a desire to see all of the locations—prompted newspapers to publish "a tourist guide, through which the reader could examine and explore the seedy shadows of Whitechapel."[45] These maps directed visitors along the killer's path and indicated which out-of-the-way places were worthy of their attention, allowing outsiders to experience a thrill of pleasure without also needing to experience fear. Since they came during the daytime, and since they were in groups and not sex workers, they did not need to fear the Ripper's knife. Such danger was for other people, and these tourists would be gone before dark.

Not every visitor came purely for sightseeing. Some, spurred on by the recent realization of the true conditions of the East End, wanted to help the poor and moral-less, but, like so many who wrote letters to the editor, "often these philanthropic adventurers were entirely ignorant of the East End"[46] and the true extent of the need—and danger—present there. For those not living in Whitechapel, the stories of the living conditions and immorality that filtered through painted a picture of need, but not of the outreach already in place or what the East Enders themselves, as opposed to the outsider philanthropists, thought would actually help.

Aside from visiting as tourists and would-be rescuers, at least one man, Dr. William Holt, is meant to have "wandered through Whitechapel pretending to be the Ripper"[47] in a more immediate and interactive form of the letters supposedly written by the killer. Holt was soon accosted by a crowd intent on killing him and had to be rescued by the police. This was not the only instance in which a man identified by a mob as the Ripper found safety in a police station, but most accused were the victims of the pervasive fear and not their own actions inciting said fear.

Entrepreneurs who preferred to induce carefully-controlled fear while encouraging people to gaze upon the lifeless representations of the victims quickly created or modified wax figures to fit the bill. The accuracy of the injuries was not a concern as long as audiences could pay to see wax body parts daubed with red "blood." Since those whose windows looked out on the actual scenes of the crime found they could charge others for the chance to look out on the site, those without access to the actual locations made do with these stand-in victims. This was not merely a late Victorian idea but continues to be reproduced in tourist sites such as Madame Tussaud's and the London Dungeon as these wax figures continue to be "taken out of the context and original setting, accommodated to cater to the tastes of contemporary audiences."[48] After all, waxworks look like people but are not people, inviting the gaze but unable to gaze back or move to protect themselves from unwanted attention.

Bringing the Ripper into three-dimensional, active space was Wedekind's original *Die Büchse der Pandora*, starring Wedekind as Jack performing the final murder of the two-play arc and killing central character Lulu. While the original waxwork displays and Madame Tussaud's focused on representing the murdered women over the murderer, Madame Tussuad's because they have a strict rule of only working from real faces, these stage representations breathed life into Jack and gave him an active role—murdering—instead of the passive: having fled and presumably being in hiding after the murder. Indeed, the point of the variations of Lulu's stories is not about whether "Jack" is identified and brought to justice within the world of the story, but that Jack is a known murderer of sex workers and that Lulu deserves to meet him and die at his hands.

This was hardly the last time the Ripper trod the boards or even sang. For example, the Player's Theatre staged *Jack the Ripper: The Musical* in 1974,[49] Centastage Performance Group premiered *Jack the Ripper: The Whitechapel Musical* in 1997,[50] VJ Wilson released the album for his rock musical *1888 (Jack the Ripper: A Factual Account)* in 2005,[51] Actors Scene Unseen released the album of their musical *Jack—The Musical: The Ripper Pursued* in 2006,[52] the English National Opera staged *Jack the Ripper: The Women of Whitechapel* in 2019,[53] and Tory Doctor's self-described mega-musical *The Fallen: A Tale of Jack the Ripper* was given an online reading in 2020[54] to reach wider audiences. These are but a small sample of the Ripper onstage. All of these are real-world productions, although the Ripper has worked his way into fictional musicals, as well, such as the one apparently in-progress in the movie *This Is Spinal Tap*.[55] Not only have we accepted the Ripper narrative as one that should be retold, we have apparently determined that it should also be sung, in multiple venues and across multiple genres.

We are not content to confine the Ripper to the page where his story might be argued as educational over entertaining. Instead we want to inhabit a three-dimensional space with him, be it visiting the locations where he once stood and murdered, circling representations of his victims to study them in better light and for a longer period of time than he had with them, or to watch him perform, again and again, those same murderous acts. By putting the Ripper at center stage and giving him a literal voice, we allow him to explain himself to us and provide that ever-elusive motive that clarifies why a man would commit such crimes. On the stage, as a living, breathing actor, the Ripper conveys a sense of immediacy—this is happening in front of our eyes—that so many versions of the Ripper story try to present, despite the fact that these women were murdered over 130 years ago. But, perhaps most importantly, these productions give the Ripper a very human face, even if they do not present us with his "real" name.

We want to connect to the Ripper in some way, be it walking where he walked or following his train of thought through the murders. The opera *Jack the Ripper: The Women of Whitechapel* shows a timely shift of focus to the voices of the murdered women rather than that of the murderer, rising in tandem with Hallie Rubenhold's *The Five: The Untold Lives of the Women Killed by Jack the Ripper*, but it is an outlier. On the stage as well as in true crime, our focus is still on the killer: why did he do it? How does he tick? And now: can he explain himself in a catchy and memorable song?

Chapter 8

Raised Voices

When we tell crime stories, we do not just lay out a sequence of chronological events—we add in judgments and lessons the audience is meant to take away from the tale. There is a moral to the story that justifies the criminal's fate and, frequently, the victims' as well. Depending on the time period and the medium, the author can also add some other messages: reassurances that the reader will not herself become a serial killer's victim, for example, as seen in the majority of true crime books since the 1980s. But before we get to the author's message, we have to decide on the author him- or herself. Who, exactly, is the expert when it comes to crime narratives? Who is allowed to tell the stories?

Crime narratives are one of the earliest subjects presented in print media in what is now the United States. Back then, print was the sole means of disseminating a story beyond the local community. Word of mouth worked for a localized population, and the same people speaking those crime narratives to the locals were the ones then committing those speeches to print and selling them to be read over and over again not just by those within the community, but others in other communities. The first people to publish true crime in America were the Puritans.

The Minister Speaks

Starting in the 1600s, at least as far as preserved records go, Puritan ministers not only preached execution sermons, but also allowed their words to be typeset and then sold. Reading a printed sermon was considered the same as going to church and hearing one preached, and the fact that copies have been found re-bound after much handling shows that these documents were not simply purchased, read once, and discarded. The average person—execution sermons even caught on outside of Puritan communities—could engage with these texts repeatedly, and with full approval of their local church.

Just as we have to orient ourselves to life in the Victorian East End, we need to understand the social and cultural expectations here. Back in the day, Puritans lived in small communities where everyone knew everyone, and the rule was not law, but religion. People did not break the law—they committed sins. There was actually a very long list of sins for which the consequence was execution.

Having someone declared guilty of such a sin was disruptive to the community. It was highly likely that everyone knew the accused, so it was a very personal experience. Once the person had been accused of committing the sin and detained, the wait for the execution date could be months, but the accused did not have to waste those months. A "good" member of the community spent that time taking instruction from the ministers and making him- or herself right with God prior to the established day.

Either the Sunday before the execution or directly prior to it, the minister preached the execution sermon. A repentant accused would sit in the congregation with everyone else as they listened to the minister explain the situation: everyone in the community was a sinner, but this particular sinner had fallen down a slippery slope. It was a chance for the minister to list the "smaller" sins the accused had committed—sins shared by other members of the community—and to explain how the accused had fallen away from God … but also how the accused had used the last few months of their life to return to God.

The minister had a rather difficult job to do with one of these sermons. He had to reassure the community in multiple ways—that the accused was not in fact going to hell, and that it was possible to avoid the accused's fate—but also to strike enough fear into them so that they would not commit such sins themselves. Every single sin the accused had ever committed would be listed, to make the point that there are in fact no "small" sins, and the minister would be able to position himself at the center of the accused's return to the church.

Such a return, however, did not erase the sin. It simply meant that, once the sermon was over, the accused would walk—usually under their own power—to the scaffold, speak a few final words encouraging the community to not end up like them, and willingly face death. Part of returning to the church meant accepting the consequences of their sin and going bravely to their deaths, acknowledging that the Lord would happily receive them in heaven.

Because Puritans and other religious groups were living in small communities in an environment that they found hostile, every member of the community was necessary for the group's survival. It was a heavy blow when one of them was lost, religiously or through death, and the ritual of the sermon along with the execution was meant to reinforce the systems within the community. If the accused was not a community member—a number of "pirates" were executed without being publicly repentant—then the return to the church was not as necessary a part of the narrative, since those people were "Other" and not "one of our own." When the offense feels personal, the atonement is just as personal, and incredibly necessary. If a member of the community strays, then the community feels betrayed and needs solace and reassurance.

The minister provided not only these, but also the definitive narrative of what happened, and why, and how the average person should incorporate these things into their daily life. It was the minister's job not only to guide the sinner back to the Lord and carry out the proper consequences for the sin, but also to interpret these actions for the community at large and tell the accused's story. Although the accused was allowed to speak their last words—generally pre-approved—on the scaffold, the minister would stand with them, as well, and also have a chance to speak. Everything that took place during the ritual of execution was organized and sanctioned by the minister.

At least, it was all supposed to be.

Esther Rodgers Cuts In

Esther Rodgers never should have had a voice. She was a young, unmarried serving girl, so she did not even have a husband to speak for her. If there were any stories told about her life, they should not have been in her own words. But Rodgers, executed at age twenty-one for infanticide, refused to play by all the rules.

Bearing a child as an unmarried young woman would have been enough of an issue, but the father of Rodger's infant was a Black servant in the same household. Besides, Rodgers had already done this once and gotten away with it. When she was seventeen, she concealed a pregnancy, birthed a child, and left that household quickly enough that she had not even been suspected of the previous infanticide. With this second instance, however, she was caught and confessed to both. It was seen as a mark in her favor that she admitted apparently all of the sins on her soul, even when no one was able to make such an accusation against her.

The pamphlet published after Rodgers' execution is exceptional because the sermon itself does not take up the bulk of the contents. Yes, it mentions that she was visited by seven different ministers during her imprisonment,[1] but "much of the publication is given over to her conversion"[2] and not the sermon itself. In fact, while awaiting her execution, Rodgers was more likely to take her meals with various families in the town of Ipswich and claimed to have learned just as much from the average person as she did from the clergymen. This was already a deviation from many previously published narratives of sin and consequential death.

Rather than give in to the expected behavior, Rodgers refused to let her narrative be taken entirely out of her control. While she faltered on the way to the gallows, she steadied her resolve and completed the journey on foot, unassisted, before taking "the spotlight and steal[ing] the show"[3] from the community leaders. The walk to the gallows was itself part of the test, because she was harshly questioned by community members along the way. Prior to being accused of infanticide, Rodgers had not been a particularly religious person and, after all, she claimed to have taken instruction from regular people in the community instead of solely listening to the men in positions of power and expertise. Then, once she was up on the gallows, the pamphlet informs readers that Rodgers gave an emotional, stirring speech as she begged the listeners not to stray as she had strayed.

What is amazing is how well Rodgers took her story into her own hands even within the rigid structure of the execution ritual. All elements of the day were prescribed, from the delivery of the execution sermon, to the walk to the gallows, to her chance to speak a few final words, to the execution itself. The people in power were supposed to be the men: the minister preaching the sermon and the community members grilling her during her final walk. To properly play the role of the repentant condemned, Rodgers had to respond to those questions with the "correct" answers to reassure her community that she had indeed properly taken religious instruction and fully understood the prescribed doctrine.

The condemned was only given a few chances to speak, and expectations of what would be said were strict. She was indeed meant to have said a few final words, the sort of statement that would bolster the minister-centered and add support to the communal structures while accepting that her own execution was part of what kept those structures intact. She was *not* supposed to outshine the minister and have her own words be the focus of her execution.

The twenty-one-year-old woman who spoke from the gallows had never before been given such a platform, and she took it further than prisoners were meant to. Rodgers spoke passionately, reinforcing the idea that someone did not have to be a minister in order to be capable of religious teachings. Had she said something blasphemous or disturbing, her story would have taken a drastically different turn as the minister lamented the fact that she had not in fact learned proper religion, and her soul was at risk, after all. But Rodgers not only spoke well—she spoke accurately, adhering to her community's religious doctrine and personally reassuring those who knew her that these rules were right, and her impending execution was correct. The bare minimum would have been neither begging nor pleading for her life, but Rodgers looked death—and the ministers, and her community—in the face and spoke a better message than the trained men who regularly preached from pulpits.

The ministers had near total control because there was no separation of church and community. All community members belonged to the church, and they all relied on each other for survival. Anything that threatened the delicate balance of power had to be dealt with as quickly as possible, and then prevented from occurring again in the future.

With execution sermons, there was no question of motive. There did not need to be—the answer was original sin, which is in all of us. Nobody had to question *why* the accused committed such a sin, and the minister did not have to make that part of the narrative. It was simply accepted that everyone sinned, and that anyone could fall down that slippery slope to a sin that meant an execution.

These sermons also never had to argue over whether or not the accused actually committed the sin in question. "Good" citizens made their own confessions before their executions, and these were documented in the sermons for the benefit of the community at large. Those who refused to confess were seen as putting their eternal souls at risk, since the execution was coming whether or not they admitted to the crime and made amends beforehand, but no one spoke up against the minister and suggested that the accusation was wrong. With few exceptions, the minister held sole control over the narrative, and no one tried to argue with him about it. In fact, it seemed unthinkable that anyone might accuse the minister of being wrong. What he said was what had actually happened.

This did not last for very long.

How Do You Plead?

By the 1780s,[4] America had accepted the adversarial trial system. The Miranda Warning we all know was not established as a right until 1966, but the Bill of Rights grants defendants the right to counsel in the Sixth Amendment. Thanks to police procedurals and crime documentaries, even people who have never set foot inside a courtroom have a basic understanding of how an adversarial trial works: one side argues for innocence, the other for guilt, and a jury of the accused's peers has to decide if guilt has been proved beyond reasonable doubt.

This is a huge change from the era of the execution sermon.

For one thing, the accused was allowed to say "No, you're wrong. I didn't do it." Instead of being asked to confess not only to that crime (sin) but also to all past crimes (sins), the accused could plead not guilty. Even if the accused decides to confess, this usually comes in the form of a plea bargain rather than an outright full admission of guilt. The likely sentence is much less likely to be execution, but the accused can, in a sense, fight back.

This means that the accuser—the American criminal justice system instead of the minister—is not automatically granted the narrative. It opened up the possibility that charges laid against a person might, in fact be wrong ... or at least unprovable. After all, juries only have to agree that the case has been proved beyond a reasonable doubt, and not with one hundred percent certainty, which has led to so many of these recent documentaries and podcasts challenging legal outcomes.

Because witness testimony can be so unreliable, the adversarial trial resulted in a "growing reliance on forensic evidence"[5] as each side made its case. This system also created a *need* for those experts. No one needed certification in blood spatter analysis when it was expected that the accused would simply confess and not argue a competing narrative. The forensics in a case become the points around which each side has to build its story. The defense can bring in a competing expert to argue a different interpretation of the evidence, or offer an explanation for the evidence that does not involve the accused's guilt but, once introduced and accepted into the proceedings, the evidence cannot be ignored entirely. It has to be *explained*, just as we have seen happens with retellings of the Ripper narrative.

The reason behind the crime also needs to be explained. Original sin is no longer an acceptable motive. Fans of shows like *CSI* will know that a suspect needs to have three things: means, motive, and opportunity. Just because a chef had a knife and was alone in a kitchen with someone who ended up murdered does not mean the chef was the murderer—we want to understand the *reason* behind the crime. Motive became a large part of the story that each side has to argue in court.

All of this probably seems obvious today because we have all had decades to be offered all kinds of media about crime, trials, and criminal proceedings. We have engaged not only with true crime or newspapers, but also with shows "ripped from the headlines" or with "names changed to protect the innocent." There has been a blurring between news and entertainment that means the average person called upon for jury duty has expectations that real life no longer matches, to the point where this situation has been named "The CSI Effect." Yes, yes, we think we know how trials work, and how they do not work, and how evidence will be flashily displayed and explained, and lawyers from both sides even write books about their most famous cases to help the average person with this understanding.

But, back then, it was such a huge change that the media had to educate readers about this new approach to crime. Newspapers updated readers with news of what took place each day during a trial, and trial reports were written and sold after the trial concluded to explain each step. They laid out the evidence and then, in another change, asked the audience to actually do some of the work. It was no longer enough to simply listen to the minister or read the printed sermon and accept what had been said; now the audience was being asked to engage critical thinking and make their own conclusions about whether or not the outcome of the trial had been the correct one.

There is agency here that did not exist before because there is a space for arguing where it used to be a simple laying down of the law from a single expert. What the minister said was true and unquestioned, but what lawyers—and witnesses, and subject area experts—say is open for scrutiny. Ministers all stood in agreement, but these new experts and the two different lawyers disagree at every turn. What are we supposed to do when even the experts can manage to churn out two completely different stories?

We have not entirely figured this out yet.

Explain it to Me

The benefit of living in the twenty-first century is that we do not have to stand on gallows scaffolding in order to have a platform from which our voices can be heard. Granted, Esther Rodgers did not have to compete with other content-makers across the internet, but we are still living in an era of unprecedented access to each other. If we want to put something out there, places like Twitter/X, Instagram, Facebook, TikTok, and YouTube are all too eager to help us do it. We can even Google ways to get the most eyes on our photos, videos, or posts.

The positive is that basically anyone can go online and post anything.
The downside is, of course, that exact same thing.
The main channels—book publishing, documentaries, television series, etc.—involve lots of time, money, and production and marketing expertise. There is a lot of gatekeeping going into the content being

produced, which places a limitation on points of view being presented while certain voices, perspectives, and stories continue to be silenced, overlooked, and ignored. If an author or approach is not seen as marketable, then it will not be taken up for the long process of getting that person and those ideas into print or on film.

The rise of social media has done many things, and one of them has been allowing people direct access to an audience, if they can attract their attention with the proper hashtags and retain it through witty banter, artfully edited videos, and a smattering of facts. The access and technology are new, but the questions these content creators address are the same asked by the Puritan ministers from centuries ago: is the criminal Other, some sort of non- or inhuman creature beyond empathy, or are they one of us? And how do we incorporate these narratives into our daily lives, especially when we have more access to such narratives than ever before?

The rigid structure of the small religious community is gone. We no longer have any necessary connection to the community in which the crime took place so that even the "normal" people presented around the criminal can be seen as "Othered." Take, for example, the reactions to how the Avery family in general was presented in *Making a Murderer* voiced by people neither from, nor ever having visited, rural Wisconsin. It is difficult to process the complexities of a documentary that asks viewers to empathize with Steven Avery as a wrongly convicted murderer when his entire living situation and backstory seem so foreign, and these are representations of people in the twenty-first century. How in the world are we supposed to orient ourselves toward cases that happened in a foreign country prior to living memory if we struggle when the place is strange but the time is now?

This lack of universal structure, as well as a wider variety of "expert" voices, means that we do not all have to answer these questions in the same way. Like in the courtroom, we can argue over the narrative and make points supporting our various points of view. Unlike Esther Rodgers, we do not have to wait until the Powers That Be have turned the spotlight on us to be able to take a chance and speak our minds and, unlike the other women in her community, we no longer have to remain silent on the subject if we feel we have something important to say.

At times the resulting voices can sound like a cacophony as so many people fight for our time and attention, but those that can manage to get the ratings—those who prove to have staying power—tell us what we, as a society, want to hear these days, and the sorts of narrative approaches we are willing and eager to accept. In this on-demand world of podcasts and interactive forums, it is always time for true crime.

Chapter 9

I'm No Expert, But…

True crime narratives are apparently infinitely adaptable and enduringly interesting. They continue to expand and fill new spaces, finding new audiences and new authors. The advent of the internet has allowed many new possibilities for the production and consumption of true crime texts in ways that do not necessarily have to, or do not necessarily appear to, go through media production companies and jump through the required hoops for traditional publication or production. By lowering these barriers and opening up the dissemination of information, the internet has provided us with a new wealth of narratives, authors, and ways of storytelling.

We know that the "broadcasting of criminal investigations and trials is not a new phenomenon,"[1] but these new formats provide audiences with an increased feeling of intimacy. Creators are given the chance to critique dominant narratives, conduct interviews of their own, and in general provide "a sense of authentic insight into closed institutions"[2] to explore both the processes and their weaknesses. These narratives feel more personal as we read the words or listen to the voice of an individual—and have the opportunity to respond either directly to that person or discuss the information as a group. This sharing of information is not one-to-one or one-to-many, but many-to-many, and these interactions come with their own affordances and pitfalls.

It can be difficult to determine authors' ethos in online and digital formats. Although they might declare their backgrounds and mention that they are—or are not—in fact content experts, the presentation of the information can sway audiences to believe or doubt above and beyond any such background information. Entertaining and engaging storytelling can override audience caution even when, for example, anthropologists lament "shortcuts"[3] taken by *Serial*'s host Sarah Koenig that would not be allowed in academia. There is also perhaps some envy over the reach of certain media over others, including academic papers, as well as concerns about the spread of misinformation. Just because a work is popular does not mean that it is accurate.

Despite these changes and shifts in how true crime narratives are presented, to whom, and by whom, research "suggests that dominant narrative patterns that have proliferated the genre continue to drive podcast audiences"[4] among others—that is, the same tropes and generic expectations generally apply. However, we do see some standout examples of changes to the expected true crime narrative that follow the lines of documentaries such as *The Staircase* and *Making a Murderer*, questioning the legal system rather than reinforcing it. These narratives also modify the role of the audience further, inviting them not only to determine for themselves what the "true" story is but also to act in cases of injustice and fight for actual legal change, at least when it comes to the case under discussion.

Many-to-Many

One of the affordances of the internet is its offering of a many-to-many means of communication as opposed to the one-to-many broadcasts on television, such as the nightly news. Although it is perhaps an exaggeration to say that "on the internet, nobody knows you're a dog,"[5] the Web does open up the conversation for all sorts of people to take part. Individuals no longer have to be offered a platform and an in-person audience to share their views, but can create their own platforms or take part in those established by others with similar points of view.

Stephen P. Ryder, the executive editor of casebook.org, founded in 1996, connects this modern form of communication back to the Victorian era when he observes that letters to the editor are "the 1888 equivalent to a modern day internet message board."[6] During the Autumn of Terror many people wrote in to the newspapers to express their own feelings and opinions about the ongoing crimes, offering both criticism of and advice to the police, as seen in Chapter 1. Although papers required such letters to include names and addresses to be published in good faith, readers only had what those writers offered of their identities within the content of the letters. Some did indeed include their names to strengthen their ethos, while others offered tidbits of their personal experience to give weight to their suggestions. Still, readers had to be just as wary of what they read in print as we do online today when forums open the floor for anyone to share their opinion, if not their identity.

Casebook entered the fray after more than a century of investigation had already been completed, and "even in its early days, the website held the equivalent of 8,900 pages of text and over 450 photographs and illustrations."[7] It not only allows users to post to message boards, but also provides pages upon pages of information about the case available to anyone with an internet connection. This information includes both scans and transcripts of official documents, meaning that curious individuals do not need to travel to view the originals or strain their eyes attempting to decode handwriting. Collections of newspaper articles, letters to the editor, and other case-related documents have also been published in book form and modern fonts, likewise allowing wider access to the contemporary publications about the case.

"In recent years, amateur sleuths have taken to the internet to collect and share information surrounding cold cases,"[8] and websites like Casebook allow those interested in the Ripper to find each other. The very format of a website with accompanying message boards allows users to immediately ask their questions or pose their theories for likewise possible immediate responses, while still maintaining a record of all such conversations in a readily available, searchable format. "These online spaces allow communication to be multidirectional"[9] between users of all levels of expertise, allowing for both education of newcomers and deeper discussion among those who are already well-versed in the material on the Casebook main site. Like most message boards, users can also view the latest topics to see which are new, and trending topics to see which currently have the most discussion. At the time of this writing, the forums have over 12,000 topics, more than 554,000 posts, and over 100 active members.

Casebook's related podcast Rippercast, hosted by Jonathan Menges, has been putting out episodes since February 8, 2008.[10] The podcast has hundreds of episodes and has interviewed myriad guests, as well as sharing recasts of previously-recorded interviews and talks. It is advertised as a "free and loose discussion"[11] between those experts, generally centered around the Ripper but also overflowing into related topics of the Victorian era and beyond. Episodes range from half an hour to over two hours long, depending on the subject, formatting, and number of guests. Some episodes are presented by the Whitechapel Society and others are recordings of presentations from conferences related to the Ripper, offering them up for wider audiences than those who were able to attend in person.

One of the barriers to approaching the Ripper narrative beyond a single book or documentary is the vast amount of information and misinformation that has been amassed about the case. The fact that Casebook contains thousands upon thousands of book pages of information outside of the message boards means that newcomers have to be dedicated and established members need to be patient. Ripperologists have their own shorthand for specific important texts, easily bandying about phrases like "the Littlechild Letter" and "the Macnaghten Memoranda," the contents of which are available in the Casebook pages for those who know to look for them. The amount of information available on the website, on the message boards, and in the podcast, as well as the number of people involved in all facets, can be overwhelming and deterring for newcomers unsure of how to begin.

As seen in Chapter 4, even the presence of others who have studied the case for decades does not discourage novices from dismissing all the established information and striking out alone in the hopes that they will uncover the Ripper's true identity as long as they avoid preconceptions. This is a common feeling in twenty-first-century true crime, especially when it arrives in podcast form: "We all start to think that we, and not the experts and the lawyers, might know best."[12] Although the Ripper was never identified and never went to trial, so there were no lawyers and there is no verdict to be overturned, there are still issues when users from different backgrounds and with different perceptions of the case come across each other and try to make their own arguments. Establishing ethos online can be difficult, although certain users have been frequent guests on the podcasts and can prove longstanding connections to the subject through publications or talks. Those who are recognized as established Ripperologists occupy a central position online as well as in *real* life.

Rippercast is not the only podcast about Jack the Ripper, although it is the longest-running. *The Dark Histories Podcast*[13] covered the Ripper murders in the first five episodes of its first season, released daily in July 2017. Hallie Rubenhold hosted the first season of *Bad Women: The Ripper Retold*[14] in 2021, approaching the murders from the point of view of the women murdered, over fifteen episodes. These are all podcasts that take their history seriously, as opposed to those such as *Jackie the Ripper*,[15] a "darkly comic reimagining" in which men are murdered by a female serial killer. A search for podcasts about the Ripper provides multiple options for both fiction and nonfiction, although it seems that most serious podcasts that run for more than one season quickly move beyond the Ripper murders to find other cases or history of interest. Only *Rippercast* keeps exploring the same case year after year and episode after episode, digging deeper into lesser-known elements, players, and artifacts as they attempt to explore as much of the past as they can find.

There have, however, been some drastic changes and revelations in the recent history of true crime podcasting that have in turn had dramatic effects on the role audiences play in storytelling. Although recent, these have, however, already attracted academic attention and critique for the potential for further change in true crime overall and podcasts specifically.

Serial Killing

Any discussion of true crime podcasts these days must address 2014's surprise hit *Serial*.[16] Our host Sarah Koenig informs us that she is not a detective, and yet her purpose in covering her chosen story appears to be her own personal investigation of a murder for which someone was arrested, found guilty, and imprisoned. Koenig revisits the murder of eighteen-year-old Hae Min Lee and the sentencing of her former boyfriend, Adnan Syed, questioning whether Syed's conviction was truly justice. Throughout the twelve episodes of the podcast's first season, Koenig waffles in her belief over Syed's guilt, reenacts the proposed timeline of the day of the murder, and conducts interviews not only with Syed and others involved, but also those who had nothing to do with the crime. Indeed, part of her initial setup involves questioning a series of teenagers about what they did six weeks previously, another reenactment meant to show that it is entirely possible Syed could not remember the day of Lee's disappearance.

Serial's popularity exploded to tens of millions of downloads and attracted attention long before its external outcomes of continued legal developments for Syed, who has most recently appealed to the Maryland Supreme Court in his fight to overturn his life sentence.[17] Much of the appeal of *Serial*, as well as much of the critique leveled against it, applies to the more than thirteen decades of study of Jack the Ripper, although Ripperology has not yet been subjected to such dedicated academic study. Academic approaches to true crime in any of its forms are recent and slowly on the rise since, for decades, the two circles have avoided and largely dismissed each other. The popularity of *Serial* has helped lead to academic scrutiny and careful critique that has so far been lacking.

First, the fact that *Serial* is a podcast and therefore delivered in serial form with new episodes available weekly plays a large role in both its novelty and its connection to its true crime ancestry. Serial publication was in fact "a form that first realized its potency in the Victorian period,"[18] both through fiction from authors such as Charles Dickens and, as we have seen, through the serial news reports of current events. These slow releases of segments, piece by piece, situate the narrative in a specific orientation to the audience members, who know they have to wait for updates to come. In the case of the *Serial* podcast, a release schedule at least informed listeners of when they could expect the next installment. Those awaiting news updates during the Autumn of Terror did not know when they could expect to have them.

Stella Bruzzi observes that "a vital ingredient in the new true crime genre recipe is what we the audience/jurors/people on the street think about the facts and narrative presented for us,"[19] but this is an element we already saw during the Ripper murders. Then, audience members could not swarm to subreddits after an update, but they did engage in writing letters to the editor, offering their own interpretations and suggestions of how the police and the public should respond. During *Serial*, the release format and internet access allowed listeners to track down information for themselves before the next installment, performing their own investigation parallel to Koenig's. The podcast format "blurs the boundaries between journalistic non-fiction and narrative fiction,"[20] again an observation that can be made of newspaper reports from 1888. Newspapers were written to sell with less regard for accuracy than we see today, and frequently reporters held interviews with self-identified witnesses who had yet to inform the police of what they saw.

All reporting and recalling of real-life events inherently take on the form of a narrative, since we simply cannot talk about things in any other way. Reporters, just like Koenig, take the information they can find and do their best to construct a story that fits. During the Autumn of Terror, there was no solution. Koenig addresses a case that appears to be solved—and has been, from a legal point of view—but one where she questions that solution. Because of this questioning, *Serial* exemplifies the true crime podcast's ability to "inform, mirror, and transform cultural attitudes toward the law."[21] Koenig must guide us through the events of Lee's murder and Syed's resulting trials to show how such a verdict was reached while at the same time calling that verdict into doubt.

Again in regards to format, podcasts in the twenty-first century benefit from "open access settings and low barriers to entry for production and distribution,"[22] meaning that podcast hopefuls do not need to rely on heavy-hitting producers or an association with established programs in order to be created. Although Koenig did benefit from such assistance, with *Serial* being developed by the long-established *This American Life*, its success far exceeded anyone's expectations. Listeners can download episodes as they become available and then tune in while doing other tasks, such as driving or chores. This allows for an individual experience and control over when they engage—audiences do not have to all listen to a live broadcast at the same moment, grouped around a radio—as well as *how* they engage, and indeed has changed the expectations for audience relationships with true crime podcasts.

Serial "combined the solitary with the communal"[23] by providing these opportunities for individual listening with spaces for online discussion and investigation. Each podcast episode's official website includes scans of official documents and other material referenced within that episode, much in the same way *Casebook* and other sources about the Ripper include reproductions of the most important documents in the case. Audience discussion on, for example, Reddit was not directly connected to the podcast's website, which does not link to any interactive discussion boards, although this, too, quickly grew beyond expectations. Listeners took to the internet not only to discuss evidence, but also to dox those involved in the case, uncovering their social media pages and sharing addresses and other contact information. Although such activity is against the site's content policy,[24] at times the information would be up for quite a while before one of Reddit's moderators removed it. Those who volunteered to be interviewed for the podcast, as well as those who refused or who were only marginally associated with the case, found their privacy invaded beyond their consent.

Despite Koenig's acknowledgment that she is not a detective, *Serial* participates in the new trend of podcasts inducing listeners to "undergo a process of 'jurification'"[25] as part of their engagement. By providing such easy access to the documentation she discusses in each episode, and also by publicly performing her own uncertainty of Syed's guilt, Koenig as our host invites us to further investigate and form our own opinions. We are not meant to simply receive a recitation of events as the truth, but, "as listeners we become involved in the events and how we felt about the evidence was genuinely important."[26] As members of the podcast's jury, it is our duty to produce our own verdict concerning the case. Since we are not jurors in the legal sense, however, we *are* allowed to conduct our own investigations and to let our emotions sway our final opinion. We are not limited by the constraints of the law and the legal system, although we are invited to critique it from the outside.

This podcast, unlike a news report, invites its audience to interact and indicates that such interaction will impact future episodes and future discussions in the same way that shows like *America's Most Wanted* included running tallies of how many criminals were apprehended thanks to viewer tips. Part of the serial release of these episodes, outside of preventing listeners in 2014 from bingeing all of them at once, meant that Koenig *could* respond to earlier audience reactions in later episodes. Audience members were not just listeners, but could play a role in how Koenig's presentation of the narrative unrolled. Ultimately participants felt that they had an impact on the American legal system overall, since Syed was released from prison in September 2022. The case is not over, but, without the podcast, presumably Syed would still be serving out his life sentence.

This audience involvement does, however, come with its own ethical and moral concerns. When a show like *Serial* both declares that its host is not a detective and then follows her as she completes the work of a detective, and when a narrative already blurs the line between fact and fiction before the implementation of other techniques, we find ourselves needing to address the intersection of crime stories and real life.

Just the Facts

The dominant form of true crime that rose to prominence in the 1980s and has been challenged by shows such as *Serial* and *Making a Murderer* comes in the form of a whydunit instead of a whodunit. The "who" has already been determined through an arrest, a trial, and a guilty sentence. The guilty party is already known before the audience engages with the book or documentary, and they only do so to learn *why* a person would commit such crimes. Even if the narrative of the criminal's capture is a long and twisted one, in the end, law enforcement triumphed and the criminal is behind bars. The audience members are safe in their consumption of true crime media because the criminal, especially a serial killer, is not crouched outside their house, ready to make them the next victim. The interesting part of these stories is the criminal's background, childhood, and major life events that turned them from an innocent babe into a prison inmate.

Even shows such as *America's Most Wanted*, discussed in Chapter 5, did not undermine the established systems. Many crime narratives, both fact and fiction, have been produced with the approval and support of various law enforcement members, the way the FBI worked with actors in *The Silence of the Lambs* (1991) to ensure that characters such as the head of the FBI's Behavioral Science Unit represented the position favorably. Only rarely were unsolved cases presented, especially in full-length book form, and even shows like *Unsolved Mysteries* (1987) included stories of aliens or supernatural beings alongside segments of realistic missing people. Shorter segments were allowed to be unsolved, but longer investments followed the lives of convicted criminals with few exceptions.

Especially since the centenary of the Autumn of Terror in 1988,

Jack the Ripper has long been one of those exceptions. The passage of time not only means that the killer is dead, but that the East End of 1888 is a foreign land none of us have entered. We cannot go "slumming" in an attempt to experience life as one of the poor, or volunteer with any of the social services meant to help those houseless and those without a steady income. While we can participate in a tour of the murder sites as they look today, and many do, we have to imagine the conditions as they were back then. Although there are many indications that East Enders felt true sympathy for the murdered women, they were quickly deindividualized so that the Ripper killed "prostitutes" who had made a series of poor decisions that landed themselves in his path. Their backstories blended and homogenized, making them all alcoholics who had chosen to leave their husbands and children before likewise choosing sex work as their preferred form of income. In short, it was not just the Ripper who became a figure of myth early on in history, but his victims, as well.

This is an issue that has recently been centered not only in my own *The Ripper's Victims in Print: The Rhetoric of Portrayals Since 1929* (2018) but also in Hallie Rubenhold's 2019 winner of the Baillie Gifford Prize for Non-fiction, *The Five: The Untold Lives of the Women Killed by Jack the Ripper.* My own book conducted a survey of the words and phrases used to describe the Canonical Five women *as* women, rather than as corpses and evidence, and concluded that both myth-making and minimization have long occurred when discussing them. The focus has been on their deaths and what their bodies can tell us about their murderer, as Bruce Robinson candidly observed: "As far as this narrative is concerned, Catherine Eddowes' life lasted about thirty-five minutes: from the time she left the police lock-up to the time the Ripper killed her."[27] Because it is assumed that the Ripper did not know his victims, their only interaction came at the end of the women's lives, and this is the only time period that needs to be searched for such clues. The women's presumed occupation only matters as an explanation for why they were out on the street at the given hour, and their husbands or long-term boyfriends are generally given the chance to excuse themselves for no longer being together.

Rubenhold intensely researched the women's lives before they ended up in the East End, placing not their deaths but their lives in historical context. Unlike Robinson, she is concerned with far more than the last half hour of their lives and approaches the commonly-repeated elements of their stories from a position of critique. Part of the uproar surrounding her book comes from her assertion that only two of the Canonical Five can be proved to have engaged in sex work, but there is no evidence that any of the Five went out on the last night of her life to sell sex. *The Five* likewise does not consider oft-repeated eyewitness reports to be reliable, no matter how frequently those words have been reprinted. Through both rejecting frequently-reprinted information and suggesting new interpretations of the known facts, Rubenhold found herself facing not only a wide audience of readers newly interested in the crimes, but also resistance from the Ripperologists.

This blurring of the lines between real people and fictional characters is a trait of the true crime genre in general, but in the case of the Ripper narrative, we have decades upon decades of evidence of cultural approaches to crime, criminals, and victims. These repetitions demonstrate not only the current era's expectations, but also trade presses' expectations of what will continue to sell. Publishing is likewise a slow process, whereas individuals can set up, record, and release podcast episodes much more quickly. If we are to look for change, it is in these newer, more accessible technologies and not, perhaps, in the long history of book publication.

In all true crime, audiences are presented with information that purports to be true. Not every member of the audience simply accepts what is stated. In a podcast, for example, "the real world is our referent, and the listener must decide to what degree the storyworld corresponds to it."[28] In essence, the podcast is doing the same work as both the defense and the prosecution during a trial: taking the evidence and constructing a plausible story around it. Each side in an adversarial trial must work with the same established points, connecting them in believable ways to argue for either guilt or innocence. The jury then decides whether the prosecution has presented them a story that withstands reasonable doubt.

It is not a jury's job to construct a story on their own, but those of us engaging with cases outside of a courtroom generally do so because "[c]lues and their serial renderings are what compel us ... to continue the inquiries to which we devote ourselves"[29]—we look into things because we are interested in putting the pieces together to reach the outcome. In historic true crime, this means following along the intrepid detective's steps and taking pleasure in understanding the process. For a book like *Helter Skelter* (1974), this allows the prosecutor of a famous—or infamous—case to lay out all the pieces, whether or not they made it into the courtroom. Although it seems commonly accepted today that Charles Manson was the mastermind behind his Family and their crimes, in the 1970s there was a need for Vincent Bugliosi to clearly explain himself and his reasoning behind the charges. After all, there was no evidence that Manson himself had killed anyone, so his first-degree murder convictions needed further explanation.

Despite Bugliosi's involvement not only in the prosecution but the investigation of the case, his book—still the best-selling true crime book today—is only his perspective on events. When it comes to crimes committed in the past, law enforcement officials, authors, and curious onlookers must confront the fact that "recovery is impossible. They have only fragments and *versions* of events, not a reliable history,"[30] and arguments of guilt and innocence happen because of these versions. Bugliosi's book might be the most commonly accepted way of connecting the established events in the Manson Family murders, but it is not the only way. Like the Ripper, the Manson case saw a surge in publications, this time at the half-century mark and after Manson's death. Once again we are faced with confronting a crime committed in a time and place now foreign to us so that motivations and actions might seem inexplicable.

What *Serial* does is question a story that apparently already had an established ending. By the time Sarah Koenig began her podcast, Syed had been sentenced over a decade previously. Although Syed's first trial ended in a mistrial, he was convicted in February 2000 to life plus thirty years. It seemed that the story was over and could be told in historic true crime fashion as an investigation into Syed's past and events that led him to the murder of his ex-girlfriend. Instead, Koenig summarized the legal events to get them out of the way so she could begin questioning the outcome with her audience along for the journey.

Having already been through his trial, Syed demonstrated an understanding that his fate depends upon "'true information' or evidence ... that is shaped by presentation and interpretation."[31] As presented and interpreted in the courtroom, this apparent truth led to his conviction. As presented in the podcast, there is a chance that his conviction might be overturned if the story is told properly. As echoed in *Making a Murderer*, post-conviction appeals are incredibly difficult to launch successfully, since the legal system must place faith in itself and the original outcome. Doubt is not welcome here, just as it is not welcome in historical true crime. *Serial*, however, makes full use of doubt.

(Not) Guilty?

Many listeners found season 1 of *Serial* to be unsatisfying. Because episodes were released one at a time, listeners were both prevented from bingeing the first season and encouraged to spend their time considering the latest episode and all it had uncovered. Despite her admission to her audience that she is not a detective, Koenig invites her listeners to accompany her as she reexamines evidence, even recreating the prosecution's proposed timeline of events. Koenig does not merely recount past events but actively engages with them, thereby encouraging her listeners to the do the same. She wonders, she worries, she waffles ... and then, "after all these weeks of telling us the story, Koenig does not reveal a definitive finding that her investigation has uncovered."[32] Although there is a final episode to the season, there is not a satisfying ending.

This dissatisfaction with Koenig's open-ended finale comes in part because of both the format and the title of the podcast. "When we talk about seriality, we are concerned with endings (how a story wraps up), and when we are concerned with endings, we are concerned with narrative and desire"[33]—indeed, in the desire to experience what we consider to be a complete narrative. We want to be able to sort events into a beginning, a middle, and—most important—an end. This is, after all, what crime narratives have been doing for centuries: explaining to readers why the outcome is what it is, and why we should be satisfied with that outcome. Whether we engage with execution sermons, "A Narrative of the Life of William Beadle," or *Helter Skelter*, we expect a very specific format for our true crime. The criminal was caught, and his private sphere has been dissected for us to examine. We know not only who did it, but also why he did it and how the "good guys" caught him in the end. It is reassuring, because surely the good guys will take what they have learned and be faster next time.

Serial is not reassuring. There are clues that this is the series' intention from the beginning, because "Koenig's style is to draw out inconsistencies and doubt"[34] as she examines the story. She herself cannot settle comfortably into a narrative of guilt or innocence, and she passes that discomfort on to her audience. Certainly Adnan Syed is not comfortable, either with the legal outcome or entirely with Koenig and her personal goals. No matter what Koenig hopes to prove, she is still using his story to gain listeners and grow her platform. Syed and Koenig even disagree over whether two people in their positions can be friends, much less know each other completely. Syed is aware of the power disparity in ways that Koenig either ignores or overlooks.

In this new approach to true crime, "hearing the narrator coming to grips with the unknowability of the case is as much a part of the journey for listeners as solving the case"[35]—but, as an early instance of this new approach, *Serial* faces audience backlash. For centuries we have been conditioned to a certain kind of crime narrative with its own tropes and generic expectations, including conclusive outcomes and faith in the justice system. The narrator operates from a place of authority and informs audience members of the singular narrative truth. Once the adversarial trial became the established method of determining guilt, this narrator passes on the narrative that won and became the established truth. We cannot have doubt in our legal system and its established forms of authority. If we start questioning trial outcomes, where do we stop?

Legal boundaries are not the only ones that come into question with *Serial*'s approach. Along with other recent podcasts, *Serial* has a "perceived potential to provide expressive justice to the victims"[36] that is not shared by other true crime formats. We have already seen that the victims have recently been a subject of contention within the Ripper narrative as authors argue over whether the murdered women have been properly represented; whether they should get credit for preserving the women's names no matter what their representation has been; if everything that needs to be said about them has already been said; and whether critique is even warranted because the true crime genre has traditionally focused on the criminal and ignored the victims. Such podcasts do allow for stories to be told in new ways and break from such traditions, leaving space for them to both question the legal proceedings and also focus on the victims. However, this second possibility "is further complicated in true crime podcasts by the power imbalance between narrator and victim-survivor"[37] and can be overshadowed if a podcast decides to focus on the former. A podcast like *Serial* season 1 focuses on whether or not its subject did indeed commit the crimes for which he was sentenced and not on the murder victim outside of whether her story can be used to support a narrative of guilt or innocence for the man found guilty of her murder.

Such podcasts, like the Ripper narrative, are limited based on the information they can uncover and what surviving friends and family members are willing to share. These sorts of shows are praised for giving possibly wrongly-convicted people the chance to speak and tell their own stories, but murder victims are no longer around to speak about themselves. If they have left diaries, journals, or videos, these can be used in an attempt to determine who these people were before their names made headlines, but even then we run up against moral and ethical questions. Many of these documents were private and written or recorded with the expectation that no one else would see them without express permission of the author. After death, our private documents can now become public and publicly consumed as podcasters or Reddit bring them to public attention and allow strangers to consume those words and make judgments not only about the content, but also about the person who wrote them.

When someone like Adnan Syed talks to someone like Sarah Koenig, there is already a marked difference of power and control in the construction of a narrative where its subject is still alive and has at least some ability to shape what becomes public. When the subject of a narrative has died, somehow that violent death means her life and actions are not only available for public scrutiny, but also that it is our duty to examine her identity and choices to agree upon her shortcomings that led to her death. With such a history of victim representation in true crime, it is hardly surprising that victims' loved ones prefer not to surrender their voices to the creators of such narratives in order to have their words twisted or misinterpreted based on the narrator's intention. Within the Ripper story, we can see how the women's words, reported by those who knew them, have been picked apart, mocked, and derogatorily declared as lies when, for example, Liz Stride told people her husband and children died in the sinking of the pleasure ship the *Princess Alice* or Mary Jane Kelly told her boyfriend that she once went to France with a gentleman but did not like that life, so she left him and returned to England. Such tales are derisively dismissed, frequently without an empathetic analysis of why someone of her class, gender, and position might choose to tell them. The same issue is now translated into teenagers' diaries where the person leading the interpretation might be the same gender as the victim, but removed from her age and not sharing the same race and culture.

Such perspectives matter because, once again, "it is not always clear that audiences assiduously differentiate between the real and the imaginary,"[38] or between the bare facts and their interpretation. We cannot relate events without turning them into narratives, but the framework applied to those narratives comes from within the storyteller and not from the events themselves. Syed has the advantage of conversations with Koenig in order to attempt to clarify his point of view, but Hae Min Lee does not. Any of her words that Koenig finds are static, and the work of interpretation lies with Koenig, whom listeners must trust to present information properly. Discussion and arguments over that interpretation can occur on subreddits devoted to the case, but *Serial* itself presents Koenig's point of view as the official narrative. She frequently performs doubt over her interpretation of Syed's guilt, culminating in the first season's lack of conclusion, but hers is still the recognizable voice and the voice of authority.

This blurring between real life and narrative happens because, "[e]ven if a podcast depicts events that actually happened, we are immersed in a carefully crafted storyworld all the same."[39] Koenig shares the narrative of Lee's murder and Syed's arrest and then even moves through the storyworld when she and a friend test the possible timeline and path Syed had to travel to commit the murder. Koenig must reference the real world when it comes to evidence presented in court and then scanned and shared on the podcast's website and, since "her project is journalistic at heart"[40] she incorporates interviews and first-person reports from witnesses and those involved with the case before comparing them to each other and to these real-world references. Doubt, Koenig's stock in trade, comes when these narratives clash with each other or with the provided documentation. When these disagreements happen, one—or both—of the storytellers must be lying ... or perhaps the documented evidence is faulty. It is then up to Koenig to provide suggestions for how her listeners should interpret the evidence, the stories, and the discrepancies.

Koenig and her perspective are therefore integral to stories crafted throughout *Serial*'s seasons since her identity and background—with the emphasized element of "not a detective" and other unnamed facets that nevertheless color her interpretation—shape the narrative she presents to her listeners. Clearly there was something in the way *Serial*'s first season was presented that captured the attention of a large audience, and many members were not content to simply sit and wait for the next week's installment. They sought other listeners and collaborated on research into the real places, events, and people discussed in the podcast, creating dangerous situations when listeners overstepped their bounds, doxxing people involved in the case beyond even those who had consented to be interviewed for the podcast. Once again the danger of the true crime narrative came in this blurring of real life and fiction so that audience members became caught up in the idea of a mystery to be solved without considering the real-world consequences to the people they treat as fictional characters.

Clearly there are a lot of parallels between the podcast format pioneered by *Serial* and the continued narrative approach to the Ripper and the Canonical Five. However, are the Ripper murders a solid narrative choice for such serial podcasts rather than one-off episodes discussing the case?

Listening for Justice

Although the Ripper narrative has been incredibly popular with full-length nonfiction books and has been covered in single episodes or multi-episode arcs in various historical or true crime podcasts, and although much of the critique surrounding *Serial*'s first season can—and perhaps should—be applied to these Ripper retellings, the Ripper narrative does not fit well with this new podcasting style. *Serial*, like *Making a Murderer*, does more than just question a legal verdict. It encourages audience participation and support in calling for a review of a legal case with the possibility of such audience participation bringing about actual change for the proposed wrongly-convicted subject. The podcaster is in charge of "sharing someone's story, particularly an unacknowledged story,"[41] and inviting listeners to pursue an investigation of their own. These stories are no longer a one-way communication meant to educate a listening audience and be done, but rather a means of informing the audience of an injustice and passing on the responsibility of rectifying it.

We are now learning how "true crime podcasts can act as a medium for informal justice, and how it might work in tandem with or impede the process of formal justice."[42] Podcasts not only question completed trials and sentences that have already been handed down, but can also work along the lines of shows like *America's Most Wanted* and ask audiences for help in identifying and taking suspects into custody. In fact, the Newport Beach Police Department set about "producing a podcast in hopes of engaging the public in its search for one of the country's most-wanted fugitives,"[43] making a podcast that was not created by outsiders working in tandem with the police, but one produced by the police themselves. Granted, this approach brought up new questions of ethics and legality, but it shows that the podcast format has been recognized as a useful tool of informally deputizing listeners and asking for their assistance. This approach is an interesting balance because such podcasts generally critique law enforcement for not being able to identify or arrest the proper suspect, and it remains to be seen if other police departments will also take up the process of producing podcasts for the same purpose.

The issue with true crime podcasts is the same that has always dogged the true crime genre: "listeners primarily regard TCPs as entertaining, compelling and exciting"[44] rather than educational. Even when asked to review the evidence and draw their own conclusions, relating the information in the podcast to what they know of the real world and real life, the lines between real world and fiction blur. People become characters and events become plot as audiences turn into "amateur investigators"[45] who, like Sarah Koenig, are not trained as detectives but can pretend to be one from the comfort of their own home, assisted by others like them in online forums. There are, of course, multiple online forums dedicated to Jack the Ripper, but podcasts such as *Serial* benefit from a narrower focus in which the question centers on a single suspect and whether or not he is guilty. When it comes to the Ripper, the list of suspects ever accused runs into the hundreds, and even the list of theoretically possible suspects hits double-digits.

Although arguments can be, and clearly have been, made for certain suspects and their guilt, the Ripper narrative lacks the possibility of justice. The Autumn of Terror happened more than 130 years ago so, no matter which suspect is chosen, he—or she, or they—is long dead. No one went on trial for being Jack the Ripper, so there is no need to clear someone's name as being wrongfully convicted, and there is no possibility of putting a suspect on trial. No one will ever serve out a sentence for being Jack the Ripper. Retelling the story of these murders is not about justice. Recruiting audiences to investigate the surviving documents will not lead to legal action.

A podcast, like a written true crime narrative, "promises to bring order out of chaos"[46] in its telling. Someone has spent a great deal of time first researching a case and then constructing a story around it, so we expect to come away with a complete narrative arc. There will be a specific beginning, a middle with rising action, a climax, and an end—none of which are inherent in lived experience, but which must arise when we tell about that lived experience. For podcasts such as *Serial*'s first season, the beginning and ending are easier to find than when it comes to the Ripper, since they focus on a specific single instance of murder, continue through the suspect's trial, and cover the sentencing. There is a legal narrative that can be recounted as "truth" or as suspect, and witness statements and documentation can be compared to this given narrative to make arguments for which one is actually "real." Did the jury get it right or were they somehow mislead? If the second is true, what can audiences do to rectify the situation?

There is still room for experimentation within the world of true crime podcasts. Gracie Bain, a doctoral student at the University of Arkansas, is creating a podcast as her PhD dissertation. At the time of this writing, *Ripperature: Building the Myth*[47] exists solely as a trailer episode, so it remains to be seen how Bain approaches both her subject and the podcast format. The fact that the University of Arkansas has approved a podcast as a dissertation says a great deal about academia's changing approaches to both crime narratives and the podcast format, and indicates that, in so many ways, despite the challenges, we are not done with the Ripper narrative or adapting it to new technologies and formats.

Although Ripper narratives can certainly argue with previous versions and declare them to be problematic, full of holes, or patently untrue, there is nothing audiences can do aside from come up with their own narrative. Despite new headlines, claims, and technological advances, there is no way to currently prove a suspect was indeed the Ripper. In the end, identifying the Ripper is a battle of stories as we search for the one that seems most plausible: the same way that podcasters like Sarah Koenig search for the most plausible narrative in their search for the "truth" behind guilt and innocence.

Conclusion: Connect the Dots

Robert Bloch was not far off the mark when he turned Jack the Ripper into a sort of vampire. Like the living dead, this serial killer will not simply lie down and die. He keeps emerging in new forms, new media, and new stories. It seems we simply cannot let him go. "Fear inspires a search for meaning, while mystery virtually assures that none will be found,"[1] although we are too fascinated—or perhaps too stubborn—to stop looking.

The Ripper is now a foundational story, touted as the world's first and credited with creating "celebrity serial killer culture."[2] The killer did not create this, though. We did.

We were the ones who first put the crimes in the headlines and then changed the very format of those newspapers as a reaction to the audience response to those stories. We published maps of the murder sites and then traveled to view them. We revived the story even after the police closed the file, protected the information we had, and kept an eye out for more. As technology advanced, we used it to share evidence, theories, and suspects. We no longer have to catch the attention of a major publisher or producer in order to air our views on the killer in text, audio, or film. Anyone can—and many do—continue to engage with the murderer and the murders, breathing life back into the old story with updated psychological approaches and scientific techniques. Some of us have even had the apparent temerity to suggest that the Ripper's victims were people, too.

With no one arrested, much less tried, for the murders during the Autumn of Terror, "[t]here is no clear demarcation that allows the fear to end and the healing to begin."[3] We have, then, traded on this fear for over a century, allowing audiences to experience it as a delightful frisson from the safety of their homes. Even those who go to walk the Whitechapel tours do so knowing that the killer is no longer out there—and, if he were, we would still feel a certain level of safety and smug satisfaction in not being "his type." We have kept that aspect of pleasant fear and superiority over the police who failed to catch him, and we have cultivated a distinct distance between ourselves and the murdered women.

We can say things like "The real truth behind the Ripper crimes is not so much that we'll never know as that it doesn't matter,"[4] except our actions fail to support such a noble sentiment. Clearly it *does* matter, or else we would have dropped this story long ago and let another rise in its place. Jack the Ripper has become a mind game, a sort of Murdle[5] we might be able to solve if we only had one more clue. We both deride those so certain of the Ripper's identity when we do not agree with them and keep on looking just in case, returning to the same puzzle over and over instead of putting it down and picking up something new. Even now new books are announced declaring new suspects who, although not as laughable as some past suggestions, cannot be proved above and beyond the other top half dozen or so most likely candidates. All the work we have done to weed out the top contenders may now be undone as others do their best to bring more names to the table, once again crowding the list and giving us renewed debate.

"As a myth-maker, Jack the Ripper has shown himself to be without rival among criminals,"[6] although again: *we* are the ones making the myth. The series of murders that we connected as having been enacted by the same person, including some and discarding others, was simply a number of events until we made them something else. We connected them, first as a media event, and broadcast the name "Jack the Ripper," also to sell papers, and so many others started getting involved with letters to the editor, suggestions to the police, and letters where the writers playacted as the murderer. There were so many murders and so much violence occurring in the East End—see, for example, Florence Fenwick Miller's WOMAN KILLING NO MURDER discussed in Chapter 1—and most of it was ignored, even by those who heard someone calling out the very word "Murder!" Newspapers did not cover these stories, because they did not sell, but when they published about the Whitechapel murders and connected them to each other, circulation improved so drastically that the entire look of the newspapers, including the ads and the number of letters to the editor summarized instead of included, changed.

The Ripper, if there was a single murderer for all Canonical Five victims, killed them and slipped away into obscurity, often represented dramatically by the thick London fog. He finished his bloody work, as it has so often been termed, and managed to do so without ever being identified. Since the "Dear Boss" letter likely came from a reporter, the actual murderer played only a very small role in the creation of the myth that we have nurtured, and continue to nurture, more than a century after the initial events. Our impact on the Ripper narrative—changing understandings of violent criminals, new research into the events and culture of Victorian England, new technologies, new fears—has been far greater than the Ripper's role in his own story. The Ripper is, now more than ever, only what we make him.

The Setting

The Ripper is so connected to the "place of his murders"[7] that tourists continue to flock to Whitechapel to participate in tours of the murder sites. When movies want to show us the Ripper stalking his victims, he has to do so through a thick fog or else the atmosphere is off. It helps if he can remain in 1888 and have his glinting eyes visible between the brim of his top hat and the raised collar of his cloak. Brought to the modern day, we still prefer him in suits as a gentlemanly sort of killer who reminds us of time gone by.

This nostalgia, if we might call it that, is for an era none of us remembers. Since the Autumn of Terror occurred over 130 years ago, the murders are no longer in living memory, and neither is the East End in 1888. We might flock there today and take our pick among the tours depending on whether we want to focus on the murderer, the murdered women, or only make Whitechapel a tiny part of the history we consume, but it is not a true glimpse into the lives either the Ripper or the women lived. If Londoners at the time did not venture into the East End, and indeed were shocked at the conditions revealed by the newspapers' intense focus on the murders, then it is so much harder for us to understand what life was really like then.

The East End was indeed set apart from London proper, occupied by the poor, the immigrants, and those who were deliberately separated from the "better classes" of society. This included the stigma of profession, such as butcher or tanner, and that of religious prejudice. A large number of the East End's immigrants were also Jewish, and the Ripper murders highlighted the already-present antisemitism and xenophobia. If the Ripper did indeed turn out to be an Englishman, then he must have been a *mad* Englishman, because no *real* Englishman would even be capable of committing such crimes. This Othering of the killer's perceived identity was strong in 1888 and we continue to feel it in murder cases today.

More of a challenge for twenty-first-century readers is the

understanding of what the police force looked like in 1888. Indeed, many Ripperologists champion the police and argue that they did all they could at the time, only to be met with backlash that the police should have been able to catch the Ripper ... unless a conspiracy theory was afoot. Audiences need to understand that the Metropolitan Police as an organization was less than sixty years old at the time of the Ripper murders,[8] and that the expectations of individual officers differs greatly from what we know today. The letters to the editor seen in Chapter 1 remind us that police officers could only serve if they were above a certain height, and "[u]ntil the Police Act of 1890 the tradition was to recruit men from the country in the hope that they would be physically tougher than Londoners and untainted by London ways."[9] Further, the purpose of the Metropolitan Police back then was to *prevent* crimes, not *solve* them. This explains why police walked their beats using measured steps and could be so easily timed, and why certain officers were rooted to one spot for the length of their shift. When men discovered Annie Chapman's body, for example, the first officer they found refused to leave his post because of strict orders not to do so. Those orders were critiqued at the time, so it is not difficult to understand why today's readers would likewise express disdain for this practice.

Today we have been trained by myriad media forms on what to expect from law enforcement, be they FBI, CSI, NCIS, or any number of other acronyms. Some of these media presentations are created with the full cooperation of law enforcement, such as *America's Most Wanted* or even *The Silence of the Lambs*, while other fictional versions exaggerate the mental and technological abilities of such people. Indeed, it is rare to read about or watch a film or show concerning a "good guy" who does not, in fact, capture the "bad guy" in the end. We want to engage with the Sherlock Holmeses, Hercule Poirots, and Adrian Monks of the world: they might not officially be policemen themselves, but they clearly work on the side of the law and never fail to solve the case. Even when Holmes comes up against the Ripper and chooses not to make his identification public, he can still solve one of the world's most famous criminal mysteries.

In part because these famous consulting detectives are not themselves police, we are also used to the idea of men—and some women—outside of uniform collecting clues and following the evidence. In the Victorian era, dominant thought was that "plain-clothed detectives were an infringement upon their civil liberties"[10] and would be able to act as spies by, for example, sitting in a pub and remaining unidentifiable as they listened to the conversations around them. Victorians *wanted* their officers to be recognizable, although even this was not a

Conclusion: Connect the Dots

solution to all problems. They also "always feared that uniformed constables with the power to prohibit soliciting might harass or blackmail innocent women,"[11] and this was a fear that proved true—there are records of women being stopped on suspicion of being sex workers and having to struggle to show that they were, in fact, "respectable" women. The power wielded by the police in the late nineteenth century was still being negotiated and, although so many men accused of being the Ripper fled to the nearest police station to escape mobs, women were not quick to turn to officers for assistance.

This was not helped by the fact that "there were still parts of the East End a uniformed bobby would not go for fear of being murdered by the inhabitants."[12] The greater world may have learned that the streets of Whitechapel were not properly lit, but they are also not laid out in a grid, making it easy for people to get lost or to be within a short distance of each other and still be unable to see each other. While this all bolsters the argument that the Ripper must have been familiar with the area himself, it makes things difficult for a policeman who was not. Further, an official uniform was not merely a sign that those around him should hold their tongues and not reveal any questionable activity, but a call to action for gangs or groups to show him exactly what they thought of the organization in its entirety.

Those who lived in the East End were not just society's outcasts, but desperate. For them, "Unemployment was not merely unfortunate. It was literally lethal."[13] Having a steady job was generally out of reach for those whose lives had brought them here, although within the stories of the Ripper's victims we do see attempts to work as maids or charwomen, or to sell handicrafts, for a steady income. While some maintained their relationships through these changes in earnings, we also see how Joseph Barnett left Mary Kelly in part because he lost his own job as a porter and had to resort to day labor. It has been suggested that she returned to sex work in order to make up these lost wages and that Barnett in part felt unmanned by this choice, which played into his decision to seek lodging away from her room. He could not support them but also could not "allow" her to sell sex and support them herself.

Just as we struggle with properly setting the scene of Whitechapel 1888 because our culture and society are so far removed from that experience, we also struggle with allowing more than the Ripper himself to have complex emotions and an internal life. We must put all of this information together piece by piece, struggling against missing data. When it comes to a preferred Ripper suspect, we charge boldly ahead and make assumptions at will, as long as those assumptions fall into the current understanding of what makes a person turn into a serial killer.

At other times, however, we are far too hesitant to fill in the gaps and leave so many other figures in this narrative as two-dimensional paper dolls with no agency of their own.

Supporting Characters

A serial killer only achieves this label by killing multiple other human beings. The number has recently changed to be two instead of three. If we accept that the Ripper is responsible for at least four of the Canonical Five victims, then he still qualifies. We have also seen that the FBI examines victims of violent crimes to determine whether their lifestyles as well as the crimes themselves are considered high-risk or low-risk in order to build their profile of the unknown subject suspected to be their killer. This involves a level of categorization and finding similarities that has long been a part of the crime narrative.

"Characteristics of the victims can also affect a community's reaction to a serial killer"[14] and, early on in the Autumn of Terror, it was determined that these victims were connected not just by their location and the brutality of the mutilations, but by their occupation as sex workers. Although newspapers did spread the news all over the city, the country, and the world, and many readers felt fear because of the reports, there was still a noted separation between the identity of the murder victims and that of the readers. If this separation did not exist, then no one would have felt safe venturing on a walking tour of the murder sites, and we know that many people flocked to the locations after each murder. In the daylight, at least, and in crowds, it was exciting and not terrifying to try to catch a glimpse of blood on the cobbles.

These locations and the dates of the murders are points of evidence that any narrative of the crimes must cover, because they are fixed elements of the case. Varying amounts of detail are known about each murder, due to missing official documents and having to sort through purported witness testimony, but these deaths must be accounted for. Even if an author wants to argue that Elizabeth Stride was not killed by the Ripper, her name must still be mentioned. The Canonical Five have long been cemented in public consciousness as "the" victims of Jack the Ripper.

Part of this grouping comes in the assertion that "all five of the Ripper's victims were prostitutes, or 'sisters of the abyss,' as the Victorians preferred to call them."[15] Othering the murdered women and grouping them together with a recognizable classification helps form the narrative of the murders because, while it might not provide a motive for the crimes, it seems to offer some explanation. The killer specifically targets sex workers, which means anyone who is not a sex worker does not have to worry about their own safety. It also assists in the part of the story that asks how a man could continue to commit such murders when they were already making headlines because sex workers willingly and continually take strangers to secluded locations in order to ply their trade. Their murders thus become even more their fault as they have not only chosen sex work as their means of income but also participate in such risky activity despite the fear of murder.

Collecting these women into such a limited group also functions "as an aesthetic strategy for managing certain kinds of sexual, social, and political anxieties"[16] by using the tale of the murders to chastise women for stepping outside of moral bounds. It allows for the continued assertion that the natural end of the sex worker is death and serves as a warning to other women not to engage in such work, threatening them with this possible outcome if they leave their husbands and children. Lumping the murdered women together and erasing individual characteristics therefore both offers a sense of safety to audience members who do not identify with the given category and also functions as a deterrent for readers who might be tempted to act in ways deemed unacceptable to society.

This concurrent action of Othering the murder victims and erasing their individuality to focus on the group identity is part of what allows us "to ignore not only the pain but also the indignities suffered by Nichols, Chapman, Stride, Eddowes, and Kelly after death."[17] Part of this representation can be attributed to social expectations concerning "polite" conversations and to film censors for downplaying the violence of the murders and the horror of the women's last moments. We (still) do not like considering the physicality of death, both in the effort put forth by the killer to end a life and the struggle of the victim to live. When Patricia Cornwell points out that Mary Jane Kelly did not necessarily die quickly and painlessly from the wound to her throat but may have been aware of the other injuries and their physical effects before she lost consciousness and died,[18] it comes as a jarring observation that seems to have no place in true crime accounts. Readers are allowed a buffer between themselves and the murder victims and are not asked to empathize with their lives, much less the long moments of their deaths.

This distancing and victim blaming go so far that some have argued "it is common to find witnesses playing down the faults of Jack the Ripper's victims. And so we must read between the lines"[19] in order to properly paint them as women who perhaps not merely deserved, but asked for, death. They are framed as *choosing* to become alcoholics, to leave their husbands and children, and to become sex workers all as though these events happened when they cheerfully and freely opted for these things, waving away all potential consequences. It is not presented as a struggle when they continue to take clients for sex work during the Autumn of Terror, and indeed, their emotions and personalities rarely factor into any accounts of their lives. If a witness tries to say that the murdered woman in question did her best to avoid selling sex, then that testimony must be discounted—even if such critique is not leveled against other witnesses who purport to have seen the killer. Aside from this, these kind witnesses must be looked down upon for interfering with our belated investigation and not treated with understanding for being in mourning.

If we remove these women from the socio-historical context and only focus on the information available from the time of their murders, then they become more useful for storytellers with an agenda. While some narratives argue that it is the apparently simple attribute of being a sex worker that attracted their deaths, others construct more elaborate tales around their chosen Ripper and his motive. If little is known, or cared to be known, about the women, then they become blank slates, available for any backstory that will support the larger narrative arc. This is the main reason why Mary Jane Kelly has played such a pivotal role in many of these stories: there is the least documentation about her, so she can be whoever the authors need her to be and there is no historical record to prove this wrong.

True crime encourages audiences to look at the story as a case full of evidence and therefore through a pseudo-scientific lens. We are all invited to become forensic investigators and examine every last detail so we can piece together clues and solve the mystery, preferably in agreement with the author of the narrative. With this established relationship between author, text, and audience, we have been trained to distance ourselves from the humanity of the victims as well as the killer and to treat crime narratives not only as fiction but also as logic puzzles to strengthen our brains and prove our intelligence. All of this flattens the representation of the murder victims into objects instead of people, and the purpose of including these objects in the narrative is to provide evidence for the identity of their killer.

Audience Participation

This long-established role of the audience has recently undergone some more dramatic changes. At first, crime narratives were created to inform readers of what happened, presenting them with an authoritative storyline that was above reproach. The author—generally a minister—and his subject agreed on guilt and the sequence of events being described, and no one else would question it. Audiences either listened to the original sermon or bought and read the printed versions, learning about events and taking in words which they were not originally there to experience. The execution sermons educated readers about events that took place and offered warnings and cautions about making the same decisions and committing the same sorts of sins as their subjects. There was no room to question whether this was the truth, since author and subject were in agreement on that point, and no reason to ask about motive since it was always "original sin."

The adversarial trial system that arose in both America and England meant that the general public had to be educated in the format and proceedings. Execution sermons were not necessarily only preached by Puritans, but they did come from religious members of authority and thus contained religious teachings and ideals. The repentant sinner always confessed and was a full participant in the pre-execution rehabilitation, but also always went to the scaffold because they understood that the consequences were just. There was no room for doubt, and no room for complaints. This changed, because the "adversary criminal trial is a regulated storytelling contest"[20] and it centers around questions of doubt.

Where there was initially a single authority voicing a single narrative, there were now two sides forming stories around the same pieces of evidence. One side crafts a tale of guilt and the other a tale of innocence, forced to work with the same pieces of evidence and explain their existence in a way that makes narrative sense. The prosecution's story must present the accused's guilt beyond reasonable doubt, as determined by a jury of the accused's peers. If the defense can present an equally plausible counter-narrative, then the jury is instructed to find the accused not guilty.

In the twenty-first century, even those who have not experienced a trial themselves are familiar with the structure and proceedings from film, television, and books. Granted, the slickly-presented courtrooms are not an accurate representation of real-life trials, and there are complaints about how "the CSI effect" impacts jurors and their expectations for how thrilling a trial will be, but both fiction and nonfiction accounts are readily available in multiple media for us to consume. These stories generally prime audiences to side with certain characters and thus have strong opinions about which version is truth and which is a lie. In, for example, *CSI*, audience sympathies are directed to the recurring characters and their job to uncover forensic evidence in order to land convictions. If the usual gang declares that the evidence points to a specific character as the criminal, we agree with them, in part because we have come to trust their characters over the course of the season or the series and in part because the show uses specific film techniques to allow us to uncover and interpret the evidence alongside these characters. It seems that nothing is hidden from us and that anyone arguing against our favorite lab techs is the one concealing something or twisting it to make the story work.

In the eighteenth century, Americans were faced with a major transition to the system that seems so commonplace today. Juries and the general public were presented with two competing stories, each coming from a presumably expert author, and now asked to choose which one was the correct one—that is, which one most closely aligned with the truth. Instead of printed sermons authored by ministers, readers had daily newspaper reports that covered the most recent events at trial and then, when the trial was over, trial reports that likewise covered both sides of the argument. This is also the time when more experts were demanded and therefore created to testify about evidence, increasing the visibility of specific branches of science as they came to be used repeatedly in such trials. As technology advanced, new experts and areas of expertise were introduced, and audiences had to be convinced over and over again that they were trustworthy.

Today's audiences are so used to hearing about DNA testing, blood typing, and fingerprinting that the issue during trials is more toward pointing out the limitations of these procedures than arguing for their use. We tend to forget how recent DNA evidence is—first used in a criminal trial in England in 1986[21]—but even fingerprints were not used in court until the trial of Thomas Jennings in 1911.[22] Although the theories and technologies were known prior to these first legal uses, each was still questioned when brought forth as evidence. For fingerprinting and DNA specifically, experts faced the further challenge of needing a database of records in order to compare evidence to them, rather than being able to, for example, declare a blood type of a sample. It is not simply a question of convincing other experts that every individual human has different fingerprints or that the DNA test is accurate enough to trust when sending people to the electric chair, but convincing the jury and the average citizen, as well.

These competing narratives of guilt and innocence introduced the idea that there *could* be more than one explanation for the given evidence and, as we can see in the newspapers during the Autumn of Terror, people learned that they, too, could question the proceedings.

Letters to the editor allowed newspaper readers to air their opinions, grievances, and arguments publicly in a medium that gave them the chance to be heard. Individuals not appearing in court and therefore free from having to provide their own credentials for scrutiny could challenge established experts, including the Metropolitan Police, with their own possibly less-educated opinions and have them appear in print exactly as the newspaper reports were, lending them credibility by appearance and association.

During the Autumn of Terror, "all the unknowns in these murders created a thousand and one openings for imaginations to riot,"[23] and the general public jumped to participate. Aside from writing letters to the editor, they mobbed strangers accused of being the Ripper, went into Whitechapel disguised as either the Ripper or a potential victim, and wrote letters proclaiming to be the killer himself. The Victorian reading and writing public raised this audience participation to new levels, at times heedless of the danger they presented themselves or others and without consideration for whether their actions were legal. If the police were unable to catch the criminal, then why should the public refrain from defending themselves or those they saw as more vulnerable? Some wrote letters to stir up public emotion, and others took a weapon into the East End.

Given the technologies at the time, newspaper readers in 1888 united in the ways they could with like-minded others upset with not only the murders but also the way they were being treated by the police. Over a century before *Making a Murder* and *Serial*, without even a trial to soothe them, they came together in the papers to voice opinions, call for radical change, and critique what had already been done. They did not have access to Reddit or scanned official documents, but the seeds of this twenty-first century new level of audience engagement were already planted. Crime was not just something to read about passively, but an event that demanded some sort of personal response—in this case, to help solve it.

More recent moves toward this greater level of participation in true crime narratives call for audience intervention in cases of apparent wrongful conviction. These narratives have the benefit of a trial, complete with all attendant evidence, in constructing their own retelling of events, as well as interviews with the possibly wrongly-convicted parties. They also warrant a sense of urgency no longer seen in the Ripper story because it seems possible, if not likely, that these convictions can be overturned with the help of viewers or listeners who can then feel that they have been a part of correcting a major injustice. The system, despite its experts and supposed checks and balances, got it wrong, but the passion of the people can ensure that true justice prevails.

The public response during the Autumn of Terror certainly fits this level of passion. There will always be well-meaning people whose ideas are not realistic or who, having just come upon a problem, seek to jump right in and solve it without first orienting themselves toward what has already been done. As we have seen, this includes recent authors of Ripper books who have deliberately turned their backs on over a century of work in order to pursue what they hope will be the truth, perhaps not realizing that they signal more of their amateur status to their readers than they would like. Other creators specifically call for their audiences to leap into action following the aggravating tale they have just told, encouraging them to complete research on their own or asking them to sign petitions, write letters, and show public support for the wrongly accused.

Justice is no longer limited to the courtroom and has become interactive with a wave of documentaries and podcasts in the early twenty-first century, and though it remains to be seen whether this new, collaborative style will continue to be used or hold sway, we do know that the Ripper story does not lend itself to this approach. In order for the kinds of stories told on *America's Most Wanted* to capture our attention in longer and/or serial formats, we want to know that there is indeed some action that can be taken in the name of doing the right thing. Calling for, or even securing, the release of apparently wrongly convicted people can be a thankless task and will only be repeated if we continue to see signs of success. These men and their lawyers are fighting a losing battle, and although there is some satisfaction in siding with David against Goliath, the length of time it takes to complete these appeals can wear audiences down. Without that personal stake in the outcome, these people become just another name to mention when friends start comparing true crime knowledge.

There are, however, already well-established websites with forums and message boards dedicated to the Ripper. Casebook.org, for example, performs some of the work of the podcast *Serial* in presenting readers with scans and transcriptions of old documents, along with helpful explanations when necessary information is no longer common knowledge. Other authors, some associated directly with Casebook, have compiled and reprinted documents from 1888 so interested readers can easily read them, collected in one place, rather than needing to travel the world to view the originals. The resources are, and have been, preserved as much as possible, although the outcome cannot be the same as *Serial*. No matter how much we engage with the Ripper mystery, until some intrepid audience member creates a time machine, our ability to influence the legal outcome is restricted. Even if we do somehow manage to name the Ripper conclusively, he will always already be dead and beyond the reach of any legal system.

The Star of the Show

This is not, of course, to suggest that we will ever leave the Ripper alone. He is far too malleable, and far too mysterious, for that. The Ripper is, and has been, a "convenient boogeyman"[24] for reflecting the contemporary fears and concerns of the society in which his story is (re)told. The facts, as we have seen, are few and far between, creating a constellation that can be interpreted in many different ways as we make or break connections based on new understandings of serial killing, violent crime, and psychology. There is little to stand in the way of incorporating this knowledge into the Ripper story, since, at its base, it covers so little.

Our changing understanding of violent criminals, not only assisted but also thrust forward by the FBI and its Behavioral Analysis Unit, offers the general public a cookie-cutter biography for the sort of men who would violently kill multiple strange women. Prior to psychological profiling in its newly refined and widely publicized state, various people from various times struggled to explain one of the most important missing pieces of the Ripper murders: the motive. As motive is inextricably tied up in identity, this is not a surprise. If we knew *who* the Ripper was, then we could have long ago worked out *why* the Ripper was. The foundational work completed by John Douglas, Robert Ressler, and Ann Burgess had the goal of collecting stories from already-arrested violent criminals in order to determine the commonalities in their backgrounds. These commonalities became the accepted story of how a serial killer is created, and now Ripper authors have far more than small pieces of evidence to work with in creating their stories. They have this step by step—and fully authorized—generic backstory for the average serial killer.

The important factor here is that this backstory has been presented to the wider public by the FBI, positioned as experts. Those who are trained and paid to know what they are talking about have informed us of these basics, including an absent father; a domineering mother; and the triad of arson, animal cruelty, and bed-wetting past the usual age. Thanks in no small part to the characters of Clarice Starling and Jack Crawford in the award-winning *The Silence of the Lambs*, the BAU (then the Behavioral Science Unit) and the practice of psychological profiling became household knowledge. This has even gone to the extreme in the fact that many now wrongly believe that "psychological profiler" is a specific job within the FBI rather than a task that falls under various job titles. We all somehow just know what a serial killer is, and that you want the FBI and its profilers to help you catch one. That is how successful the FBI has been at establishing expertise and disseminating at least pieces of its knowledge.

Even before we had the FBI or the term "serial killer," people fought to understand the Ripper through both motive and identity. Since they did not have the language surrounding serial killers, much less an understanding of a half-dozen classifications thereof, authors worked with what they knew ... and what they knew readers coming from their own time and society would accept. This is a critical distinction: each individual Ripper suspect is not the product merely of the author's personal background and beliefs, although they do play a role, but also the result of that author's cultural and social upbringing. None of us exists in a vacuum, and the dissemination of stories only works when others find those stories interesting and worth repeating. When I say that our Ripper stories reflect us far more than they do the Ripper, I mean that as a literally communal "us" in a certain time and place.

We know, for example, that specific theories have been published as a mere blip on the radar, while others have been published, refined, repeated, and remediated. An example of the first is the idea that the Ripper was in fact two gay men working together for whatever reason— as an odd extension of their relationship, a reaction to a breakup, or because they both happened to know Prince Eddy and wished to secure his inheritance—because, although mildly interesting for a while and especially in the wake of the AIDS epidemic when fear of the disease was conflated with fear of the marginalized gay population, it could not be supported by continued evidence. Straight men can certainly be understood to violently murder women, and this idea has apparently never been questioned. Even in 1888, the Ripper was automatically assumed to be a man, and it was only as the Autumn of Terror dragged on, the police failed to catch him, and he managed to find more victims from among the women supposedly most on their guard that other theories were put forth.

Even as a man, though, the Ripper must still be Other. He "came to personify Victorian fears of imminent change"[25] in regards not only to class but also to profession, reactions to perceived insanity, religion, and national origin. The Ripper could not be British although, if he were, he had to be mad. Perhaps he was a doctor who preyed on the lowest class of women, but he was still also likely a mad doctor. Or he was Jewish, or a Jewish foreigner, or some other means of identification that removed him from the dominant culture and pushed him into a marginalized identity that could safely be seen as distanced and very much Other. We do not like to think that someone capable of these murders would be an ordinary boy next door.

We have seen this idea get complicated and change not only as time passed but also as technology introduced the idea of film versions of the Ripper narrative. When Ivor Novello was cast in Hitchcock's 1927 *The Lodger: A Story of the London Fog* in the title role, Marie Belloc Lowndes' original narrative had to be changed because this romantic film star could not turn out to be the murderous Avenger. He could still be mysterious and fall under suspicion, although in the film this comes in part because of the love triangle between the Lodger, Daisy, and her policeman boyfriend, but he could not turn out to be the killer himself. Instead, this Lodger needed a happily romantic ending purely because of the actor's reputation.

This line of thinking has not gone unchallenged in the decades since. In 1986, heartthrob Mark Harmon—who also won *People*'s title of "sexiest man alive" that year—played serial killer Ted Bundy in the television miniseries *The Deliberate Stranger*. Although warned that such a role could end his career, Harmon was clearly not adversely affected by this choice. More recently former Disney Channel child stars Zac Efron and Ross Lynch have played Bundy and Jeffrey Dahmer respectively, in *Extremely Wicked, Shockingly Evil and Vile* (2019) and *My Friend Dahmer* (2017). Where once it was unthinkable to cast likable actors in the role of such a murderer, our stance has evolved so that it seems playing a serial killer can be an indication that an actor is no longer a child star and is ready to be seen as an adult.

What we also see, and have seen from the beginning, is this constant placement of the killer in the spotlight while other people and their lives are so much set dressing. We put serial killers like the Ripper at center stage and then, through both fact and fiction, ask him to speak ... and explain himself. Othered and therefore at a safe distance, he is positioned to help us understand how he came to be the sort of person who would commit these crimes. Even with the FBI's basic framework, we still seek specifics. At which moment did this apparently normal child become a killer? Is it nature, nurture, or a combination of both? Are there things we can do as good parents to ensure that our own children never make it up on that stage, either as killer or victim?

These questions come cloaked in an air of scientific discovery. Psychology is a soft science, but still a science, with methods of testing and academic rigor behind the results. (Douglas and Ressler were not trained in academic research, but Ann Burgess was.) Because of the rise of experts and areas of expertise in response to the adversarial trial system, and the publication of court proceedings in daily newspapers, trial reports, and book-length accounts, we as a media-consuming public have been taught not only to respect such experts, but also to follow their ways of relating to crimes, violence, evidence, and victims. The professional language and orientations that help such trained experts in their day-to-day interactions with violent crime are publicly used as a framework to approach not only the criminals, but also the victims, and has been reflected in true crime as a fascination with the serial killer and a desire to learn everything possible about him and his life, in tandem with the presentation of his victims as mere pieces of evidence only useful in identifying the serial killer.

In true crime as well as much crime fiction, murder victims are encountered as already dead, or in the last minutes of their lives and therefore only during their encounter with the killer. Since the publication of the Beadle narrative in 1783, crime stories have opened with the body discovery scene, meaning that the victims are already dead before the story begins. In the case of a serial killer such as Jack the Ripper, some of the victims might still be alive on the first page if the narrative goes in chronological order and does not begin at the end only to jump back to the first murder, but readers know that, at the time of their reading, all of the victims are dead. If they are to speak directly to the readers at all, it is only through what they wrote when they were alive, unaware that a violent end would suddenly thrust them—or at least their corpses—into the headlines.

When we select a Ripper suspect, and especially when we do so in the course of a fictional narrative rather than constraining ourselves to nonfiction, we give him a literal voice that he can use to explain himself to us. We have spent so long trying to identify him and tease out his motive that new research and new cultural expectations surrounding violent crime help us fill in the blanks and deepen our understanding of the sort of person who might do these things, so of course we will use this knowledge to answer all of our burning questions about this longstanding mystery. We craft the figure of the Ripper, give him another name, and then allow him a monologue—internal or external—or perhaps grant him a soliloquy or solo where he pours his (apparent) heart and soul out to a rapt audience who just want to understand him. Not only that, but our Rippers, especially the fictional ones, crave our understanding. They are so often poor, lost souls—or Abrahamsen's "victims of victims"[26]—who can be both explicable and empathetic if only we take the time to get to know them.

These apparently understandable, if not entirely acceptable, motives change with the times, as "Jack the Ripper has been, and looks destined to remain, whatever writers, songsters and film-makers wish him to be."[27] We do keep returning to certain motives, such as revenge, at times casting the murdered women as co-conspirators or merely manipulative wenches who apparently deserve death even more than the average sex worker. Other motives are picked up for a while, tried out, and then left behind, just as some proposed identities of the Ripper are now mentioned merely as novelties. "Look how silly we were back then, thinking this person could have been the Ripper," we chuckle, without considering whether today's most likely suspects might be tomorrow's embarrassment.

What these continuing stories about the Ripper show, then, is how we as a culture have grown and changed in our understanding of violent crime and serial killers, and also how we have not. The recent uproar surrounding the suggestion that we have not in fact represented the murdered women *as* women and have done both them and us harm in this oversight is just one example of the ways we cling to old ideas and old stories. While it is true that *selling* variations on a narrative is dependent on an audience willing to buy, those in charge of the purse strings are not always fully in tune with changes in audience desire. It remains to be seen whether such calls for transformation in true crime narratives and our culturally-taught framing of serial killers' victims will continue to result in changes in the production of such narratives, or whether the previously-dominant voices will drown out these critiques and return us to these stories where the serial killer remains on a pedestal, brightly lit as an object of fascination, and his victims linger in the shadows except for any scraps of evidence that support the identification of the killer.

Ripper Reflections

So much of writing crime narratives is filling in the gaps between what is known—or what can be known—and a complete narrative arc that includes a backstory, a three-dimensional main character, and action sequences that show the killer committing the crimes. Depending on the sensibilities and the censorship of the time, this last might not be communicated in detail, but audiences still know that the killer *is* the killer. He has been, as a number of Ripper titles indicate, revealed.

Whether these storytellers are from England or North America, it seems we have little issue accepting that a man might kill women the way Jack the Ripper murdered his victims. This is the most often repeated explanation, no matter the decade. Perhaps he needs to be mad or foreign, but we can easily craft narratives around a man wielding a knife and attacking the bodies of women. It is more difficult for us to imagine a woman using a knife against other women—or perhaps anyone, since the FBI's input on female serial killers tends toward smothering and poisoning—although the idea pops up every so often, perhaps for shock value. We have also tried to make the Ripper either a pair or group of men and although this latter has permeated various narratives and media, it is commonly accepted as fiction instead of fact. The Ripper has been British royalty, honored physicians, recognized painters, Jewish, foreign, lawyers, merchant seamen, men shortly to be locked up in asylums ... but is there any possible identity we have not tried on him?

Although a man and wife have separately been accused of having been the Ripper—Sir John Williams and his wife Lizzie—no married or heterosexual couple has been suggested. We do know of such killer couples who worked together to murder or who used the female half of the pair to lure victims in for her partner, such as Paul Bernardo and Karla Homolka, Ian Brady and Myra Hindley, and Fred and Rosemary West, but we have not shifted these killer couples back to the Victorian era. When women murdered at this time, they made use of increased access to poisons through medications and household products, as seen in the case where Florence Maybrick was convicted of killing her husband, Ripper suspect James Maybrick. This is the main argument against the idea of the Ripper being a woman working alone, but it could be explained by a woman approaching other women on the street and luring them to where the Ripper was waiting. Still, perhaps this is one supposition too far.

We have argued for older Rippers who, after more research, have been proved too infirm to actually have committed the crimes, but we balk at choosing Rippers who are too young. The FBI tells us that serial killers generally begin their murders in their mid- to late-twenties, and we have not strayed below this range. These are the crimes—and this is the rage—of a man, not a boy.

The fact that so many Ripper narratives arguing for a lone male killer have been written and forwarded by men reinforces the possibility that men are indeed capable of such violence, since men themselves easily believe one of their number could have done it. No one, of any gender, has to stretch their imagination to make this explanation work and this, too, is a reflection on us and our society. What is the difference between "Yes, *a* man could have done this, but no one I know" and recognizing the violence "other" men enact in their daily lives?

In our interactions with the Ripper, we have continually distanced ourselves from all involved, murderer and murdered alike. Time has also passed since the Autumn of Terror, further removing us from the social, cultural, and economic conditions experienced by the men and women who make up our stories. The tale of the Ripper had already spread across the globe in the Victorian era and has continued to be revived with new technologies and new means of telling it, bolstered by new accounts of new criminals, and refined with the rise of experts and the public dissemination of their knowledge. We have not let the Ripper go, not only because we keep battling the gaps in the evidence to finally solve this mystery once and for all, but also because, when we look at the Ripper, we find ourselves endlessly fascinated by what we see … and by what we end up reflecting back at ourselves in the name of solving an apparently unsolvable crime.

Chapter Notes

Introduction

1. Leonard Matters, *The Mystery of Jack the Ripper* (London: W.H. Allen, 1929, reprinted 1948), 16.
2. Elizabeth Hurren, "Dissecting Jack-the-Ripper: An Anatomy of Murder in the Metropolis," *Crime, History & Societies* 20, no. 2 (2016): 5–30, 8.
3. Paul Begg and John Bennett, *Jack the Ripper: CSI: Whitechapel* (London: André Deutsch, 2012), 5.
4. Charles Booth, "Charles Booth's London: Poverty maps and police notebooks," n.p., https://booth.lse.ac.uk/map/12/-0.2838/51.5018/100/0.
5. Paul Roland, *The Crimes of Jack the Ripper* (Edison: Chartwell Books, 2006), 19.
6. Donald Rumbelow, *The Complete Jack the Ripper* (Boston: New York Graphic Society, 1975), 12.
7. Paul Begg and John Bennett, *Jack the Ripper: The Forgotten Victims* (New Haven: Yale University Press, 2013), 1.
8. Nils Roemer, "London and the East End as Spectacles of Urban Tourism," *Jewish Quarterly Review* 99, no. 3 (Summer 2009): 416–434, 417. DOI: https://doi.org/10.1353/jqr.0.0053.
9. Philip Sugden, *The Complete History of Jack the Ripper* (London: Robinson, 2006), 359.
10. Patricia Cornwell, *Ripper: The Secret Life of Walter Sickert* (Seattle: Thomas & Mercer, 2017), 15.
11. Jean Overton Fuller, *Sickert & The Ripper Crimes: The 1888 Ripper Murders and the Artist Walter Richard Sickert* (Oxford: Mandrake, 1990, new revised edition 2003), 223.
12. Paul Begg, *Jack the Ripper: The Facts* (London: Anova Books, 2006), 52.
13. Sugden, 46.
14. Hallie Rubenhold, *The Five: The Untold Lives of the Women Killed by Jack the Ripper* (Boston: Houghton Mifflin Harcourt, 2019), 70.
15. Rubenhold, 97.
16. Paul Begg, *Jack the Ripper: The Definitive History* (London: Pearson Education, 2003), 188.
17. Stewart P. Evans and Donald Rumbelow, *Jack the Ripper: Scotland Yard Investigates* (Gloucestershire: Sutton, 2006), 177.
18. Martin Fido, *The Crimes, Detection and Death of Jack the Ripper* (London: Weidenfeld and Nicolson, 1987), 15.
19. Trevor Marriott, *Jack the Ripper: The 21st Century Investigation* (London: John Blake, 2005), 5–7.
20. Sugden, 23.
21. Evans and Rumbelow, 208–09.
22. Paul Begg, *Jack the Ripper: The Uncensored Facts* (London: Robson Books, 1988), 317.
23. Mark Seltzer, *True Crime: Observations on Violence and Modernity* (New York: Routledge, 2006), 35.

Chapter 1

1. Andrew Cook, *Jack the Ripper* (Gloucestershire: Amberly, 2010), 8.
2. David C. Fisher, *Killer Among Us: Public Reactions to Serial Murder* (Westport: Praeger, 1997), 209.
3. Christopher A. Casey, "Common Misperceptions: The Press and Victorian Views of Crime," *Journal of Interdiscipli-*

nary History 41, no. 3 (Winter 2011): 367–91, 374. Parentheses in original.

4. Begg and Bennett, *Forgotten Victims*, 16.

5. L. Perry Curtis, Jr., *Jack the Ripper and the London Press* (New Haven: Yale University Press, 2011), 49.

6. Sudgen, 310.

7. Curtis, 59.

8. Paul Begg and John Bennett, *The Complete and Essential Jack the Ripper* (London: Penguin, 2013), 87.

9. Curtis, 95.

10. Richard Wallace, *Jack the Ripper, "Light-hearted Friend"* (Melrose: Gemini Press, 1996), 34.

11. Casey, 380.

12. A. Luxx Mishou, "Murder for a Penny: Jack the Ripper and the Structural Impact of Sensational Reporting," *The Wilkie Collins Journal* 16 (2019), n.p.

13. Begg in Alexander Chisholm, Christopher-Michael DiGrazia, and Dave Yost, *The News from Whitechapel: Jack the Ripper in* The Daily Telegraph (Jefferson: McFarland, 2002), 3.

14. Mishou, n.p.

15. Fisher, 209.

16. Sugden, 75.

17. Alexander Kelly, *Jack the Ripper: A Bibliography and Review of the Literature* (London: Association of Assistant Librarians S.E.D., 1973), 21. Capitalization from the original.

18. Donald McCormick, *The Identity of Jack the Ripper* (London: Jarrolds, 1959), 80.

19. Edwin T. Woodhall, *Jack the Ripper or When London Walked in Terror* (London: Mellifont, 1937, limited facsimilie edition P & D Riley, 1997), 23.

20. Sugden, 118.

21. Shirley Harrison, *Jack the Ripper: The American Connection. Includes the Diaries of James Maybrick* (London: Blake, 2003), 116.

22. Robin Odell, *Jack the Ripper in Fact and Fiction: New and Revised Edition* (Oxford: Mandrake, 2008), 52.

23. Curtis, 15.

24. Chisholm, DiGrazia, and Yost, 155.

25. Spiro Dimolianis, *Jack the Ripper and Black Magic: Victorian Conspiracy Theories, Secret Societies and the Supernatural Mystique of the Whitechapel Murders* (Jefferson: McFarland, 2011), 15.

26. Fisher, 28.

27. Mishou, n.p.

28. Begg and Bennett, *Complete and Essential*, 4.

29. Chisholm, DiGrazia, and Yost, 36.

30. Cornwell, *Secret Life*, 123.

31. Begg, *Uncensored Facts*, 87.

32. Chisholm, DiGrazia, and Yost, 229.

33. Stephen P. Ryder, ed., *Public Reactions to Jack the Ripper: Letters to the Editor August–December 1888* (Madison: Inklings, 2006), 1.

34. Patricia Cornwell, *Portrait of a Killer: Jack the Ripper—Case Closed* (New York: Berkley, 2008), 337.

35. Curtis, 239.

36. Robin Odell, *Ripperology: A Study of the World's First Serial Killer as a Literary Phenomenon* (Kent: Kent State University Press, 2006), 27.

37. Ryder, 13.

38. Ryder, 26.

39. Sugden, 135.

40. Ryder, 91.

41. Ryder, 186.

42. McCormick, 44.

43. Ryder, 1.

44. Ryder, 82–84.

45. Ryder, 121.

46. Ryder, 49.

47. Ryder, 190.

48. Ryder, 107.

49. Ryder, 10.

50. Ryder, 153.

51. Ryder, 143.

52. Ryder, 175.

53. Chisholm, DiGrazia, and Yost, 141.

54. Begg and Bennett, *Complete and Essential*, 59.

55. Curtis, 141.

56. Paul Woods and Gavin Baddeley, *Saucy Jack: The Elusive Ripper* (Hersham: Ian Allan, 2009), 93.

57. Curtis, 155–56.

58. Odell, *Fact and Fiction*, 84.

59. Begg and Bennett, *Complete and Essential*, 113.

60. Woods and Baddeley, 49.

61. Odell, *Fact and Fiction*, 82.

62. Stewart P. Evans and Keith Skinner, *Jack the Ripper: Letters from Hell* (London: Sutton, 2005), 17.

63. David Bullock, *The Man Who Would Be Jack: The Hunt for the Real Ripper* (London: Robson Press, 2012), 21.

64. David Schmid, *Natural Born Celebrities: Serial Killers in American Culture* (Chicago: University of Chicago Press, 2005), 14. Parentheses in original.
65. Begg and Bennett, *Complete and Essential*, 31.
66. Fido, 11.
67. Martin Howells and Keith Skinner, *The Ripper Legacy: The Life & Death of Jack the Ripper* (London: Sidgewick & Jackson, 1987), 8.

Chapter 2

1. Walter Dew, *I Caught Crippen* (London: Blackie & Son, 1938), 148.
2. Evans and Rumbelow, 252.
3. Robert Anderson, *The Lighter Side of My Official Life* (London: Hodder and Stoughton, 1910), 137.
4. George Plimpton, "The Story Behind a Nonfiction Novel," *The New York Times*, January 16, 1966, https://archive.nytimes.com/www.nytimes.com/books/97/12/28/home/capote-interview.html.
5. Peter Vronsky, *Sons of Cain: A History of Serial Killers from the Stone Age to the Present* (New York: Berkley, 2018), 295.
6. John Douglas, "UNSUB: Jack the Ripper," FBI Records: The Vault, https://vault.fbi.gov/Jack%20the%20Ripper.
7. Post Staff Report, "They Don't Know Jack," *New York Post*, May 15, 2011, https://nypost.com/2011/05/15/they-dont-know-jack/.
8. Douglas, "UNSUB," 1.
9. Douglas, "UNSUB," 2.
10. Douglas, "UNSUB," 7.
11. Mark Seltzer, *True Crime: Observations on Violence and Modernity* (New York: Routledge, 2006), 35.

Chapter 3

1. Odell, *Ripperology*, 79.
2. Dimolianis, 133.
3. William Beadle, *Jack the Ripper: Anatomy of a Myth* (Brighton: Wat Tyler Books, 1995), 99.
4. Denis Meikle, *Jack the Ripper: The Murders and the Movies* (London: Reynolds & Hern, 2002), 74.
5. Tom Cullen, *Autumn of Terror: Jack the Ripper, His Crimes and Times* (London: The Bodley Head, 1965), 206.
6. Matters, 113.
7. Matters, 134.
8. Woodhall, 53.
9. T.E.A. Stowell, "Jack the Ripper—A Solution?" *The Criminologist* 5, no. 18 (1970): 40–51.
10. T.E.A. Stowell, "Jack the Ripper," *The Times*, Issue 58018, column F (November 4, 1970), 9.
11. Ian Barnard, "The Racialization of Sexuality: The Queer Case of Jeffrey Dahmer," *Thamyris Overcoming Boundaries: Ethnicity, Gender and Sexuality* 7, no. 1–2 (2000): 67–97, 69.
12. Colin Wilson and Robin Odell, *Jack the Ripper: Summing Up and Verdict* (London: Bantam, 1987), 211.
13. David Abrahamsen, M.D., F.A.C.Pn., *Murder & Madness: The Secret Life of Jack the Ripper* (New York: Donald I. Fine, 1992), 202.
14. Bruce Galloway, *Prejudice and Pride: Discrimination Against Gay People in Modern Britain* (London: Routledge & Kegan Paul, 1983), 67.
15. Russell Edwards, *Naming Jack the Ripper* (Guilford: Lyons Press, 2014), 4.
16. AFP, "Jack the Ripper Identified Says Patricia Cornwell," *The Age*, November 12, 2002, n.p.
17. Odell, *Fact and Fiction*, viii.
18. Odell, *Fact and Fiction*, ix.
19. Shirley Harrison, 29.
20. Kelly, 25.
21. Odell, *Fact and Fiction*, vii.
22. Stephen Knight, *Jack the Ripper: The Final Solution* (London: Book Club Associates, 1976), 47.

Chapter 4

1. Wilson in Kelly, 14.
2. Wilson and Odell, xi.
3. Woods and Baddeley, 124.
4. Stephen P. Ryder, ed., "Ripperana," Casebook.org, https://www.casebook.org/ripper_media/book_reviews/periodicals/ripperana.html.
5. *Ripperologist Magazine*, http://www.ripperologist.co.uk/.
6. Sugden, 7.
7. Beadle, 81.
8. Woods and Baddeley, 261.

9. AFP, n.p.
10. Meikle, 142.
11. Odell, *Ripperology*, 199.
12. Sugden, 3.
13. Howells and Skinner, 29.
14. Odell, *Ripperology*, 191.
15. Odell, *Ripperology*, 88.
16. Odell, *Fact and Fiction*, xiii.
17. Odell, *Fact and Fiction*, xxi.
18. Sugden, xxiv.
19. Woodhall, 3.
20. Begg and Bennett, *Complete and Essential*, 125.
21. Begg and Bennett, *Complete and Essential*, 157.
22. Rumbelow, 13. Parentheses in the original.
23. Begg and Bennett, *Complete and Essential*, 160.
24. Cullen, 50.
25. Paul H. Feldman, *Jack the Ripper: The Final Chapter* (London: Virgin Books, 2005), xiii.
26. Edwards, 12.
27. Bruce Robinson, *They All Love Jack: Busting the Ripper* (New York: HarperCollins, 2015), 265.
28. Cornwell, *Portrait*, 68.
29. Robinson, 359.
30. Shirley Harrison, 22.
31. Marriott, 3.
32. Cornwell, *Secret Life*, 13.
33. Feldman, 19.
34. James Tully, *The Real Jack the Ripper: The Secret of Prisoner 1167* (London: Magpie Books, 2005), xi.
35. Begg, *Uncensored Facts*, 11.
36. Odell, *Ripperology*, 166.
37. Fuller, 206.
38. M.J. Trow, *The Many Faces of Jack the Ripper* (Chichester: Summersdale, 1997), 106.
39. Robinson, 99.
40. Howells and Skinner, xiii.
41. Odell, *Fact and Fiction*, xxi.

Chapter 5

1. Paul Kaplan and Daniel LaChance, *Crimesploitation: Crime, Punishment, and Pleasure on Reality Television* (Stanford: Stanford University Press, 2022), 4.
2. Wilson and Odell, 189.
3. Stella Bruzzi, "Making a Genre: The Case of the Contemporary True Crime Documentary," *Law and Humanities* 10, no. 2 (2016): 249–80, 255.
4. Ethan Stoneman and Joseph Packer, "Reel Cruelty: Voyeurism and Extra-Judicial Punishment in True-Crime Documentaries," *Crime Media Culture* 17, no. 3 (2021): 401–19, 405.
5. Bruzzi, 270.
6. Elizabeth Walters, "Netflix Originals: The Evolution of True Crime Television," *The Velvet Light Trap* 88 (2021): 25–37, 26.
7. Stoneman and Packer, 401.
8. Bruzzi, 271.
9. Stoneman and Packer, 407.
10. Walters, 29.
11. Walters, 30.
12. Laura Marsh, "Murder, They Wrote," *Dissent* 63, no. 2 (2016): 6–11, 8.
13. Stoneman and Packer, 403.
14. Bruzzi, 249.
15. Kaplan and LaChance, 22.
16. Marsh, 9.
17. Marsh, 11.
18. Bruzzi, 253.
19. Erica Haugtvedt, "The Ethics of Serialized True Crime: Fictionality in *Serial* Season One," in Ellen McCracken, ed., *The Serial Podcast and Storytelling in the Digital Age* (London: Routledge, 2017), 9.
20. Bruzzi, 258.
21. Walters, 34.
22. Kaplan and LaChance, 106.
23. Stoneman and Packer, 402.
24. Bruzzi, 277.
25. Marsh, 7–8.

Chapter 6

1. Woods and Baddeley, 67.
2. M.J. Trow, *Jack the Ripper: Quest for a Killer* (Barnsley: True Crime, 2009), 20.
3. Meikle, 40.
4. Meikle, 46.
5. Meikle, 50.
6. Rumbelow, 234.
7. Meikle, 64.
8. Woods and Baddeley, 35.
9. Martin Willis, "Jack the Ripper, Sherlock Holms and the Narrative of Detection," in Alexandra Warwick and Martin Willis, eds., *Jack the Ripper: Media Culture History* (Manchester: Manchester University Press, 2007), 148.
10. Meikle, 95.

11. Elwyn Jones and John Lloyd, *The Ripper File* (London: Future Publications, 1975), 189–91.
12. Jones and Lloyd, 201.
13. Alan Moore and Eddie Campbell, *From Hell* (San Diego: Top Shelf Productions, 1999), "Appendix" 1.
14. Meikle, 195.
15. Meikle, 137.
16. Robert Bloch, "Yours Truly, Jack the Ripper," in Allan Barnard, ed., *The Harlot Killer: The Story of Jack the Ripper in Fact and Fiction* (New York: Dodd, Mead, & Company, 1953), 224.
17. Bloch in Barnard, 228.
18. Bloch in Barnard, 247.
19. Bloch in Barnard, 248.
20. Vronsky, 295.
21. Charlie Jane Anders, "The Top 100 *Star Trek* Episodes of All Time!" October 2, 2014, n.p.
22. Keith R.A. DeCandido, *Star Trek: The Original Series* Rewatch: "Wolf in the Fold," December 8, 2015, n.p.
23. Karl Alexander, *Time After Time* (New York: Tom Doherty Associates, 1979), 350.
24. Meikle, 8.
25. Meikle, 73.
26. "Katrina Jan," University of Birmingham, n.p.
27. Katrina Jan, "The Sexualization of Jack the Ripper," University of Birmingham. 3 Minute Thesis Finals, 2023.
28. "Three Minute Thesis 2023," University of Birmingham, posted May 23, 2023.

Chapter 7

1. Lucyna Krawczyk-Żywko, "On Waxworks Considered as One of the Hyperreal Arts: Exhibiting Jack the Ripper and His Victims," *Humanities* 7, no. 54 (2018): 1.
2. Rumbelow, 30.
3. Roemer, 420.
4. Roemer, 418.
5. Roemer, 419.
6. Roemer, 416.
7. Roemer, 429.
8. Tom Wescott, *The Bank Holiday Murders: The True Story of the First Whitechapel Murders* (Crime Confidential Press, 2014), 2.
9. Begg and Bennett, *Complete and Essential*, 271.
10. Sugden, 59.
11. Mishou, n.p.
12. Curtis, 69.
13. Mishou, n.p.
14. Curtis, 123.
15. Laura M. F. Bertens, "Tracing Memories: The Guided Trail as an Aid to Cultural Memory in Artworks by Janet Cardiff," in Daniel Svensson, Katarina Saltzman, and Sverker Sörlin, eds., *Pathways: Exploring the Routes of a Movement Heritage* (Winwick: White Horse Press, 2022), 171. Parentheses in original.
16. TourScanner, "Jack the Ripper Tours in London," n.p.
17. "Jack the Ripper Tour: A Walk Worth Investigating," n.p.
18. Look Up London, "The Feminist Jack the Ripper Tour," n.p.
19. Claire Hayward, "Waxwords and Wordless Women," *The Public Historian* 39, no. 2 (2017): 51–57, 52.
20. Fisher, 19.
21. Bertens, 176.
22. Trow, *Quest*, 23.
23. Trow, *Many Faces*, 15.
24. Edwards, 38.
25. Bertens, 181.
26. Curtis, 78.
27. Krawczyk-Żywko, 2.
28. Sam'l E. Hudson, *"Leather Apron," or, The horrors of Whitechapel, London, 1888* (Philadelphia: Town Printing House, 1888), 14.
29. Schmid, 36; Krawczyk-Żywko, 2.
30. Woods and Baddeley, 19.
31. Curtis, 79.
32. MadameTussauds.com, "Chamber of Horrors," n.p.
33. Schmid, 35.
34. Wilson and Odell, 55.
35. Krawczyk-Żywko, 4.
36. Hayward, 57.
37. Krawczyk-Żywko, 3.
38. Mark Seltzer, *Serial Killers: Death and Life in America's Wound Culture* (New York: Routledge, 1998), 1.
39. Meikle, 33.
40. S.E. Jackson, "Whose Lulu Is It Anyway? Performing through Dramaturgies of Excess," *Theatre Journal* 72, no. 1 (2020): 21–37, 35.
41. Margaret Notley, "Berg's Propaganda Pieces: The 'Platonic Idea' of Lulu,"

The Journal of Musicology 25, no. 2 (2008): 95–142, 139.

42. Bryan R. Simms, "Berg's 'Lulu' and Theatre of the 1920s," *Cambridge Opera Journal* 2, no. 2 (1994): 147–58, 151.

43. Karin Littau, "Refractions of the Feminine: The Monstrous Transformations of Lulu," *MLN* 110, no. 4 (1995): 888–912, 904.

44. Begg and Bennett, *Complete and Essential*, 265.

45. Mishou, n.p.

46. Roemer, 423.

47. Curtis, 194.

48. Krawczyk-Żywko, 9.

49. Woods and Baddeley, 75.

50. *Jack the Ripper: The Whitechapel Musical*, n.p.

51. V.J. Wilson, "1888 (Jack the Ripper—A Factual Account)," n.p.

52. Actors Scene Unseen, "*Jack—The Musical: The Ripper Pursued*," n.p.

53. Dan Meyer, "Read Reviews for the World Premiere of Iain Bell's *Jack The Ripper: The Women of Whitechapel*," April 1, 2019, n.p.

54. "Allan Cozzubbo Academy of Dancing Alumni Data," n.p.

55. Woods and Baddeley, 76.

Chapter 8

1. Daniel A. Cohen, *Pillars of Salt, Monuments of Grace: New England Crime Literature and the Origins of American Popular Culture, 1674–1860* (Oxford: Oxford University Press, 1993), 61.

2. Kristin Boudreau, "Early American Criminal Narratives and the Problem of Public Sentiments," *Early American Literature* 32, no. 3 (1997): 249–69, 258.

3. Cohen, *Pillars*, 64.

4. Randolph N. Jonakait, "The Rise of the American Adversary System: America Before England," *Widener Law Review* 14, no. 2 (2009): 323–56, 328.

5. Daniel A. Cohen, "The Beautiful Female Murder Victim: Literary Genres and Courtship Practices in the Origins of a Cultural Motif, 1590–1850," (*Journal of Social History* 31, no. 2 (1997): 277–306, 281.

Chapter 9

1. Lili Pâquet, "Seeking Justice Elsewhere: Informal and Formal Justice in the True Crime Podcasts *Trace* and *The Teacher's Pet*," *Crime Media Culture* 17, no. 3 (2021): 421–37, 423.

2. Laura Vitis, "'My Favourite Genre Is Missing People': Exploring How Listeners Experience True Crime Podcasts in Australia," *International Journal for Crime, Justice and Social Democracy*, advance online publication, 4.

3. Mariam Durrani, Kevin Gotkin, and Corrina Laughlin, "*Serial*, Seriality, and the Possibilities for the Podcast Format," *American Anthropologist* 117, no. 3 (2015): 593–96, 595.

4. Vitis, 6.

5. Peter Steiner, *The New Yorker*, July 5, 1993.

6. Ryder, 1.

7. Begg and Bennett, *Complete and Essential*, 195.

8. Jason Tashea, "Serial Sleuths," *ABA Journal* 105, no. 1 (January–February 2019): 16–17, 17.

9. Pâquet, 428.

10. *Rippercast—Your Podcast on the Jack the Ripper Murders*, "Sudden Death: Robert Donston Stephenson," February 8, 2008, n.p.

11. *Rippercast—Your Podcast on the Jack the Ripper Murders*, "Rippercast—Jack the Ripper," n.p.

12. Bruzzi, 274.

13. "The Dark Histories Podcast," n.p., https://www.darkhistories.com/.

14. "Bad Women: The Ripper Retold," n.p., https://www.pushkin.fm/podcasts/bad-women-the-ripper-retold.

15. "Jackie the Ripper," n.p., https://player.fm/series/jackie-the-ripper.

16. "Serial," n.p., https://serialpodcast.org.

17. Michelle Watson, "Adnan Syed Asks Maryland Supreme Court to Review Lower Court's Ruling That Reversed His Vacated Murder Conviction," May 24, 2003, n.p., https://www.cnn.com/2023/05/24/us/adnan-syed-conviction-maryland-supreme-court-review/index.html.

18. Haugtvedt in McCracken, 8.

19. Bruzzi, 274.

20. Vitis, 2.

21. Pâquet, 421.
22. Vitis, 2.
23. Ellen McCracken, "The *Serial* Commodity: Rhetoric, Recombination, and Indeterminacy in the Digital Age," in Ellen McCracken, ed., *The* Serial *Podcast and Storytelling in the Digital Age*, 54.
24. "Reddit Content Policy," n.p.
25. Pâquet, 425.
26. Bruzzi, 272.
27. Robinson, 162.
28. Jillian DeMair, "Sounds Authentic: The Acoustic Construction of *Serial*'s Storyworld," in Ellen McCracken, ed., *The* Serial *Podcast and Storytelling in the Digital Age*, 24.
29. Durrani, Gotkin, and Laughlin, 596.
30. Haugtvedt in McCracken, 16.
31. Sandra Kumamoto Stanley, "'What We Know': Convicting Narratives in *NPR's Serial*," in Ellen McCracken, ed., *The* Serial *Podcast and Storytelling in the Digital Age*, 77.
32. McCracken in McCracken, 64.
33. Ryan Engley, "The Impossible Ethics of *Serial*: Sarah Koenig, Foucault, Lacan," in Ellen McCracken, ed., *The* Serial *Podcast and Storytelling in the Digital Age*, 88.
34. Bruzzi, 273.
35. Amanda Keeler, "Listening to the Aftermath of Crime: True Crime Podcasts," in Jeremy Wade Morris and Eric Hoyt, eds., *Saving New Sounds: Podcast Preservation and Historiography* (Ann Arbor: University of Michigan Press, 2021), 124–34, 126.
36. Vitis, 9.
37. Pâquet, 429.
38. Haugtvedt in McCracken, 10.
39. DeMair in McCracken, 24.
40. Durrani, Gotkin, and Laughlin, 594.
41. Vitis, 10.
42. Pâquet, 422.
43. Tashea, 17.
44. Vitis, 4.
45. Durrani, Gotkin, and Laughlin, 593.
46. Pâquet, 427.
47. Gracie McBain, "Ripperature: Building the Myth," n.p.

Conclusion

1. Fisher, 207.
2. Schmid, 52.
3. Fisher, 14.
4. Woods and Baddeley, 265.
5. G.T. Karber, murdle.com.
6. Cullen, 246.
7. Schmid, 49.
8. Begg, *Uncensored Facts*, 15.
9. Trow, *Many Faces*, 97.
10. Wescott, 90.
11. Fido, 127.
12. Hinton, 6–7.
13. Trow, *Many Faces*, 31.
14. Fisher, 15.
15. Cullen, 14.
16. Tatar, 6.
17. Curtis, 264.
18. Cornwell, *Portrait*, 443.
19. Begg and Bennett, *Forgotten*, 50.
20. Goodpaster, 120.
21. Panneerchelvam and Norazmi, 22.
22. Acree, n.p.
23. Curtis, 9.
24. Meikle, 129.
25. Dimolianis, 149.
26. Abrahamsen, 202.
27. Sugden, 117.

Bibliography

Abrahamsen, David, M.D., F.A.C.Pn. *Murder & Madness: The Secret Life of Jack the Ripper.* New York: Donald I. Fine, 1992.

Acree, Mark A. "People v. Jennings: A Significant Case in American Fingerprint History." n.d. https://murderpedia.org/male.J/j/jenning-thomas.htm#:~:text=His%20fingerprint%20card%20was%20on,murder%20on%20February%201%2C%201911.

Actors Scene Unseen. *"Jack—The Musical: The Ripper Pursued."* https://www.amazon.com/Jack-Musical-Actors-Scene-Unseen/dp/B00147PZ12.

AFP. "Jack the Ripper Identified Says Patricia Cornwell." *The Age*, November 12, 2002. https://www.theage.com.au/entertainment/books/jack-the-ripper-identified-says-patricia-cornwell-20021112-gdus3s.html.

Alexander, Antonia. *The Fifth Victim: Mary Kelly Was Murdered by Jack the Ripper. Now Her Great-Great-Granddaughter Reveals the True Story of What Really Happened.* London: John Blake, 2013.

Alexander, Karl. *Time After Time.* New York: Tom Doherty Associates, 1979.

"Allan Cozzubbo Academy of Dancing Alumni Data." https://www.allancozzubboacademyofdancing.com/student-alumni-data.php.

Anders, Charlie Jane. "The Top 100 *Star Trek* Episodes of All Time!" October 2, 2014. https://gizmodo.com/the-top-100-star-trek-episodes-of-all-time-1641565699.

Anderson, Robert. *The Lighter Side of My Official Life.* London: Hodder and Stoughton, 1910.

Augustyn, Brian, and Mike Mignola. *Gotham by Gaslight.* Burbank: DC Comics, 1989.

"Bad Women: The Ripper Retold." n.p. https://www.pushkin.fm/podcasts/bad-women-the-ripper-retold.

Bain, Gracie. "Ripperature: Building the Myth." https://open.spotify.com/show/3Wrk8iWkOI60bVzOBdTtbV?si=1200858f1e594877&nd=1.

Barnard, Allan, editor. *The Harlot Killer: The Story of Jack the Ripper in Fact and Fiction.* New York: Dodd, Mead, & Company, 1953.

Barnard, Ian. "The Racialization of Sexuality: The Queer Case of Jeffrey Dahmer." *Thamyris Overcoming Boundaries: Ethnicity, Gender and Sexuality* 7, no. 1–2 (2000): 67–97. Print. https://digitalcommons.chapman.edu/cgi/viewcontent.cgi?article=1018&context=english_books.

Beadle, William. *Jack the Ripper: Anatomy of a Myth.* Brighton: Wat Tyler Books, 1995.

Begg, Paul. *Jack the Ripper: The Definitive History.* London: Pearson Education, 2003.

_____. *Jack the Ripper: The Facts.* London: Anova Books, 2006.

_____. *Jack the Ripper: The Uncensored Facts.* London: Robson Books, 1988.

Begg, Paul, and John Bennett. *The Complete and Essential Jack the Ripper.* London: Penguin, 2013.

_____. *Jack the Ripper: CSI: Whitechapel.* London: André Deutsch, 2012.

_____. *Jack the Ripper: The Forgotten Victims.* New Haven: Yale University Press, 2013.

Berlinger, Joe, dir. *Conversations with a*

Killer: The Ted Bundy Tapes. Elastic, Gigantic Studios, Outpost Digital, and RadicalMedia, 2019.

Bertens, Laura M.F. "Tracing Memories: The Guided Trail as an Aid to Cultural Memory in Artworks by Janet Cardiff." *Pathways: Exploring the Routes of a Movement Heritage*. Daniel Svensson, Katarina Saltzman, and Sverker Sörlin, eds. Winwick: White Horse Press, 2022. Stable URL: jstor.org/stable/j.ctv2p5zn1t.15.

Bloch, Robert. *Psycho*. New York: Simon & Schuster, 1959.

_____, writer. "Wolf in the Fold." *Star Trek: The Original Series*. Season 2, Episode 14. December 22, 1967.

Booth, Charles. "Charles Booth's London: Poverty maps and police notebooks." https://booth.lse.ac.uk/map/12/-0.2838/51.5018/100/0.

Boudreau, Kristin. "Early American Criminal Narratives and the Problem of Public Sentiments." *Early American Literature* 32, no. 3 (1997): 249–69.

Brewer, John Francis. *The Curse Upon Mitre Square: A.D. 1530–1888*. London: Simpkin, Marshall and Co., 1888.

Bruzzi, Stella. "Making a Genre: The Case of the Contemporary True Crime Documentary." *Law and Humanities* 10, no. 2 (2016): 249–80.

Bullock, David. *The Man Who Would Be Jack: The Hunt for the Real Ripper*. London: Robson Press, 2012.

Bushwick, Sylvie, supervising producer. *American Ripper*. The History Channel, 2017.

Casey, Christopher A. "Common Misperceptions: The Press and Victorian Views of Crime." *Journal of Interdisciplinary History* 4, no. 3 (Winter 2011): 367–91.

Chisholm, Alexander, Christopher-Michael DiGrazia, and Dave Yost. *The News from Whitechapel: Jack the Ripper in* The Daily Telegraph. Jefferson: McFarland, 2002.

Clark, Bob, dir. *Murder by Decree*. AVCO Embassy Pictures, 1979.

Cohen, Daniel A. "The Beautiful Female Murder Victim: Literary Genres and Courtship Practices in the Origins of a Cultural Motif, 1590–1850." *Journal of Social History* 31, no. 2 (1997): 277–306.

_____. *Pillars of Salt, Monuments of Grace: New England Crime Literature and the Origins of American Popular Culture, 1674–1860*. Oxford: Oxford University Press, 1993.

Conan Doyle, Arthur. *A Study in Scarlet*. London: Ward, Lock, 1887.

Cook, Andrew. *Jack the Ripper*. Stroud: Amberly, 2010.

Cornwell, Patricia. *Portrait of a Killer: Jack the Ripper—Case Closed*. New York: Berkley, 2008.

_____. *Ripper: The Secret Life of Walter Sickert*. Seattle: Thomas & Mercer, 2017.

Court, Ben, and Caroline Ip, writers. *Whitechapel*. Carnival Films, 2009–2013.

Cullen, Tom. *Autumn of Terror: Jack the Ripper, His Crimes and Times*. London: The Bodley Head, 1965.

Curtis, L. Perry, Jr. *Jack the Ripper and the London Press*. New Haven: Yale University Press, 2001.

"The Dark Histories Podcast." https://www.darkhistories.com/.

DeCandido, Keith R.A. "*Star Trek: The Original Series* Rewatch: 'Wolf in the Fold.'" December 8, 2015. https://www.tor.com/2015/12/08/star-trek-the-original-series-rewatch-wolf-in-the-fold/.

Demme, Jonathan, dir. *The Silence of the Lambs*. Strong Heart Productions, 1991.

Dew, Walter. *I Caught Crippen*. London: Blackie & Son, 1938.

Dimolianis, Spiro. *Jack the Ripper and Black Magic: Victorian Conspiracy Theories, Secret Societies and the Supernatural Mystique of the Whitechapel Murders*. Jefferson: McFarland, 2011.

dos Santos, Silvio José. "Ascription of Identity: The Bild Motif and the Character of Lulu." *The Journal of Musicology* 21, no. 2 (Spring 2004): 267–308.

_____. "Marriage as Prostitution in Berg's Lulu." *The Journal of Musicology* 25, no. 2 (Spring 2008): 143–82.

Douglas, Arthur. *Will the Real Jack the Ripper*. Chorley: Countryside Publications, 1979.

Douglas, John. "UNSUB: Jack the Ripper." FBI Records: The Vault. https://vault.fbi.gov/Jack%20the%20Ripper.

Durrani, Mariam, Kevin Gotkin, and Corrina Laughlin. "*Serial*, Seriality, and the Possibilities for the Podcast Format." *American Anthropologist* 117, no. 3 (September 2015): 593–96.

Edwards, Russell. *Naming Jack the Ripper.* Guilford: Lyons Press, 2014.

Evans, Stewart, and Paul Gainey. *Jack the Ripper: First American Serial Killer.* New York: Kodansha International, 1996.

Evans, Stewart P., and Donald Rumbelow. *Jack the Ripper: Scotland Yard Investigates.* Gloucestershire: Sutton, 2006.

Evans, Stewart P., and Keith Skinner. *Jack the Ripper: Letters from Hell.* London: Sutton, 2005.

Fairclough, Melvyn. *The Ripper & The Royals.* London: Duckworth, 1991.

Farson, Daniel. *Jack the Ripper.* London: Michael Joseph, 1972.

Feldman, Paul H. *Jack the Ripper: The Final Chapter.* London: Virgin Books, 2005.

Fido, Martin. *The Crimes, Detection and Death of Jack the Ripper.* London: Weidenfeld and Nicolson, 1987.

Fishburne, Laurence, host. *History's Greatest Mysteries.* The History Channel, 2000–present.

Fisher, David C. *Killer Among Us: Public Reactions to Serial Murder.* Westport: Praeger, 1997.

Fuller, Bryan, developer. *Hannibal.* NBC, 2013–2015.

Fuller, Jean Overton. *Sickert & the Ripper Crimes: The 1888 Ripper Murders and the Artist Walter Richard Sickert.* Oxford: Mandrake, 1990. New revised edition, 2003.

Galloway, Bruce. *Prejudice and Pride: Discrimination Against Gay People in Modern Britain.* London: Routledge & Kegan Paul, 1983.

Goodpaster, Gary. "On the Theory of American Adversary Criminal Trial." *Journal of Criminal Law and Criminology* 78, no. 1 (1987): 118–54.

Gordon, R. Michael. *Alias Jack the Ripper: Beyond the Usual Whitechapel Suspects.* Jefferson: McFarland, 2001.

_____. *The American Murders of Jack the Ripper: Tantalizing Evidence of the Gruesome American Interlude of the Prime Ripper Suspect.* Guilford: The Lyons Press, 2005.

Harkness, Margaret. *In Darkest London.* Cambridge: Germinal Productions/Black Apollo Press, 2009.

Harris, Melvin. *The Ripper File.* London: W.H. Allen, 1989.

_____. *The True Face of Jack the Ripper.* London: Michael O'Mara Books, 1994.

Harrison, Michael. *Clarence: Was He Jack the Ripper?* New York: Drake, 1974.

Harrison, Paul. *Jack the Ripper: The Mystery Solved.* London: Robert Hale, 1991.

Harrison, Shirley. *Jack the Ripper: The American Connection. Includes the Diaries of James Maybrick.* London: Blake Publishing, 2003.

Hayward, Claire. "Waxworks and Wordless Women." *The Public Historian* 39, no. 2 (May 2017): 51–57.

Hill, James, dir. *A Study in Terror.* Columbia Pictures, 1965.

Hinton, Bob. *From Hell...: The Jack the Ripper Mystery.* Abertillery: Old Bakehouse, 1998. Reprint 2005.

Hitchcock, Alfred, dir. *The Lodger: A Story of the London Fog.* Gainsborough Pictures, 1927.

_____, dir. *Psycho.* Shamley Productions, 1960.

House, Robert. *Jack the Ripper and the Case for Scotland Yard's Prime Suspect.* Hoboken: Wiley, 2011.

Howells, Martin, and Keith Skinner. *The Ripper Legacy: The Life & Death of Jack the Ripper.* London: Sidgwick & Jackson, 1987.

Hudson, Sam'l E. *"Leather Apron," or, The horrors of Whitechapel, London, 1888.* Philadelphia: Town Printing House, 1888.

Hughes, Albert, and Allen Hughes, dirs. *From Hell.* Underworld Pictures, 2001.

Hurren, Elizabeth. "Dissecting Jack-the-Ripper: An Anatomy of Murder in the Metropolis." *Crime, History & Societies* 20, no. 2 (2016): 5–30.

Jack the Ripper: The Whitechapel Musical. https://www.jacktheripper musical.net/.

"Jack the Ripper Tour: A Walk Worth Investigating." https://www.jack-the-ripper-tour.com/.

"Jackie the Ripper." n.p. https://player.fm/series/jackie-the-ripper.

Jackson, S.E. "Whose Lulu Is It Anyway? Performing through Dramaturgies of Excess." *Theatre Journal* 72, no. 1 (March 2020): 21–37.

James, E.L. *Fifty Shades of Grey.* New York: Vintage, 2011.

Jan, Katrina. "The Sexualisation of Jack the Ripper." University of Birmingham, 3 Minute Thesis Finals, 2023. https://www.youtube.com/watch?v=YLQDsdEBytM.

Jonakait, Randolph N. "The Rise of the American Adversary System: America Before England." *Widener Law Review* 14, no. 2 (2009): 323–56.

Jones, Elwyn, and John Lloyd. *The Ripper File.* London: Futura Publications, 1975.

Kaplan, Paul, and Daniel LaChance. *Crimesploitation: Crime, Punishment, and Pleasure on Reality Television.* Stanford: Stanford University Press, 2022.

Karber, G.T. "Murdle." https://murdle.com/.

"Katrina Jan." University of Birmingham. https://www.birmingham.ac.uk/schools/edacs/departments/english/research/postgraduateresearch/profiles/jan-katrina.aspx.

Keeler, Amanda. "Listening to the Aftermath of Crime: True Crime Podcasts." *Saving New Sounds: Podcast Preservation and Historiography.* Jeremy Wade Morris and Eric Hoyt, eds. Ann Arbor: University of Michigan Press, 2021. 124–134.

Kelly, Alexander. *Jack the Ripper: A Bibliography and Review of the Literature.* London: Association of Assistant Librarians, S.E.D., 1973.

Kepnes, Caroline. *You: A Novel.* New York: Atria/Emily Bestler Books, 2014.

Knight, Stephen. *Jack the Ripper: The Final Solution.* London: Book Club Associates, 1976.

Krawczyk-Żywko, Lucyna. "On Waxworks Considered as One of the Hyperreal Arts: Exhibiting Jack the Ripper and His Victims." *Humanities* 7, no. 55 (2018). doi:10.3390/h7020054.

Linder, Michael, and Stephen Chao, creators. *America's Most Wanted.* 20th Century Fox Television, 1988–2010.

Littau, Karin. "Refractions of the Feminine: The Monstrous Transformations of Lulu." *MLN* 110, no. 4 (September 1995): 888–912. Comparative Literature Issue.

Liu, Sam, dir. *Gotham by Gaslight.* Warner Bros. Animation and DC Entertainment, 2018.

Look Up London. "The Feminist Jack the Ripper Tour." https://lookup.london/walking-tours/feminist-jack-the-ripper-walk/.

Louhelainen, Jari, and David Miller. "Forensic Investigation of a Shawl Linked to the 'Jack the Ripper' Murders." *Journal of Forensic Sciences* 65, no. 1 (2020): 295–303. https://doi.org/10.1111/1556-4029.14038.

MadameTussauds.com. "Chamber of Horrors." https://www.madametussauds.com/london/whats-inside/experiences/chamber-of-horrors/chamber-of-horrors-information-page.

Marriott, Trevor. *Jack the Ripper: The 21st Century Investigation.* London: John Blake, 2007.

Marsh, Laura. "Murder, They Wrote." *Dissent* 63, no. 2 (2016): 6–11.

Martin, Troy Kennedy, and Elwyn Jones, creators. *Jack the Ripper.* BBC1, 1973.

Matters, Leonard. *The Mystery of Jack the Ripper.* London: W.H. Allen, 1929. Reprint 1948.

Maxouris, Christina, and Sara Smart. "Maryland Court Reinstates Murder Conviction of 'Serial' Subject Adnan Syed." CNN, March 29, 2023. https://www.cnn.com/2023/03/28/us/adnan-syed-conviction-reinstated-maryland/index.html.

McCormick, Donald. *The Identity of Jack the Ripper.* London: Jarrolds, 1959.

McCracken, Ellen, editor. *The Serial Podcast and Storytelling in the Digital Age.* London: Routledge, 2017.

Meikle, Denis. *Jack the Ripper: The Murders and the Movies.* London: Reynolds & Hern, 2002.

Meyer, Dan. "Read Reviews for the World Premiere of Iain Bell's *Jack The Ripper: The Women of Whitechapel.*" April 1, 2019. https://playbill.com/article/read-reviews-for-the-world-premiere-of-iain-bells-jack-the-ripper-the-women-of-whitechapel.

Mishou, A. Luxx. "Murder for a Penny: Jack the Ripper and the Structural Impact of Sensational Reporting." *The Wilkie Collins Journal* 16 (2019). Stable URL: jstor.org/stable/10.2307/26996133.

Mitchell, Stephen Mix, and John Marsh. *A narrative of the life of William Beadle, of Wetherfield, in the State of Connecticut. Containing I. The particulars of the "horrid massacre" of himself and family. II. Extracts from the Rev. Mr. Marsh's sermon at the Funeral of his wife and children.* 1783. http://name.umdl.umich.edu/N14090.0001.001.

Moore, Alan, and Eddie Campbell. *From Hell.* San Diego: Top Shelf Productions, 1999.

Morris, John. *Jack the Ripper: The Hand of a Woman.* Bridgend: Seren, 2012.

Notley, Margaret. "Berg's Propaganda Pieces: The 'Platonic Idea' of Lulu." *The Journal of Musicology* 25, no. 2 (Spring 2008): 95–142.

Odell, Robin. *Jack the Ripper in Fact and Fiction: New and Revised Edition.* Oxford: Mandrake, 2008.

———. *Ripperology: A Study of the World's First Serial Killer and a Literary Phenomenon.* Kent: Kent State University Press, 2006.

Pâquet, Lili. "Seeking Justice Elsewhere: Informal and Formal Justice in the True Crime Podcasts *Trace* and *The Teacher's Pet.*" *Crime Media Culture* 17, no. 3 (2021): 421–37. DOI: 10.1177/1741659020954260.

Paul, Adolf. *Uppskäraren.* Grönlund: Åbo, 1892.

"Philip Sugden—obituary." https://www.telegraph.co.uk/news/obituaries/10836835/Philip-Sugden-obituary.html.

Plimmer, John. *The Whitechapel Murders—Solved?* Thirsk: House of Stratus, 2003.

Plimpton, George. "The Story Behind a Nonfiction Novel." *The New York Times*, January 16, 1966. https://archive.nytimes.com/. www.nytimes.com/books/97/12/28/home/capote-interview.html.

Post Staff Report. "They Don't Know Jack." *New York Post*, May 15, 2011. https://nypost.com/2011/05/15/they-dont-know-jack/.

"Reddit Content Policy." https://www.redditinc.com/policies/content-policy#:~:text=Instigating%20harassment%2C%20for%20example%20by,of%20someone%20without%20their%20consent.

Ricciardi, Laura, and Moira Demos, dirs. *Making a Murderer.* Synthesis Films, 2015–2018.

Rippercast—Your Podcast on the Jack the Ripper Murders. "Rippercast—Jack the Ripper." https://podcasts.apple.com/us/podcast/rippercast-your-podcast-on-the-jack-the-ripper-murders/id301395708.

———. "Sudden Death: Robert Donston Stephenson." February 8, 2008. https://podcasts.apple.com/us/podcast/sudden-death-robert-donston-stephenson/id301395708?i=1000391343765.

Ripperologist Magazine. http://www.ripperologist.co.uk/.

Robinson, Bruce. *They All Love Jack: Busting the Ripper.* New York: HarperCollins, 2015.

Roemer, Nils. "London and the East End as Spectacles of Urban Tourism." *Jewish Quarterly Review* 99, no. 3 (Summer 2009): 416–34. DOI: https://doi.org/10.1353/jqr.0.0053/.

Roland, Paul. *The Crimes of Jack the Ripper.* Edison: Chartwell Books, 2006.

Rubenhold, Hallie. *The Five: The Untold Lives of the Women Killed by Jack the Ripper.* Boston: Houghton Mifflin Harcourt, 2019.

Rule, Ann. *The Stranger Beside Me.* New York: W.W. Norton, 1980.

Rumbelow, Donald. *The Complete Jack the Ripper.* Boston: New York Graphic Society, 1975.

Ryder, Stephen P., editor. *Public Reactions to Jack the Ripper: Letters to the Editor: August–December 1888.* Madison: Inklings Press, 2006.

Ryder, Stephen P., editor. "Ripperana." *Casebook.org.* https://www.casebook.org/ripper_media/book_reviews/periodicals/ripperana.html.

Schmid, David. *Natural Born Celebrities: Serial Killers in American Culture.* Chicago: University of Chicago Press, 2005.

Seltzer, Mark. *Serial Killers: Death and Life in America's Wound Culture.* New York: Routledge: 1998.

———. *True Crime: Observations on Violence and Modernity.* New York: Routledge, 2006.

Serial. https://serialpodcast.org.

Sharkey, Terence. *Jack the Ripper: 100 Years of Investigation.* London: War Lock, 1987.

Shelden, Neal Stubbings. *The Victims of Jack the Ripper*. Knoxville: Inklings, 2007.

Simms, Bryan R. "Berg's 'Lulu' and Theatre of the 1920s." *Cambridge Opera Journal* 2, no. 2 (1994): 147–58.

Spiering, Frank. *Prince Jack: The True Story of Jack the Ripper*. New York: Doubleday & Company, 1978.

Steiner, Peter. "On the Internet, Nobody Knows You're a Dog." *The New Yorker*, July 5, 1993.

Stoneman, Ethan, and Joseph Packer. "Reel Cruelty: Voyeurism and Extra-Judicial Punishment in True-Crime Documentaries." *Crime Media Culture* 17, no. 3 (2021): 401–19.

Stowell, T.E.A. "Jack the Ripper—A Solution?" *The Criminologist* 5 (November 1970): 40–51.

Stowell, T.E.A. "Jack the Ripper." *The Times* Issue 58018, column F (November 9, 1970): 9.

Sugden, Philip. *The Complete History of Jack the Ripper*. London: Robinson, 2006.

Tashea, Jason. "Serial Sleuths." *ABA Journal* 105, no. 1 (January–February 2019): 16–17. https://www.jstor.org/stable/10.2307/26913058.

Tatar, Maria. *Lustmord: Sexual Murder in Weimar Germany*. Princeton: Princeton University Press, 1995.

"Three Minute Thesis 2023." University of Birmingham. Posted May 23, 2023. https://intranet.birmingham.ac.uk/student/graduateschool/news/public/three-minute-thesis-2023.aspx.

TourScanner. "Jack the Ripper Tours in London." https://tourscanner.com/s/london/i/jack-the-ripper-tours.

Trow, M.J. *Jack the Ripper: Quest for a Killer*. Barnsley: True Crime, 2009.

———. *The Many Faces of Jack the Ripper*. Chichester: Summersdale, 1997.

Tully, James. *The Real Jack the Ripper: The Secret of Prisoner 1167*. London: Magpie Books, 2005.

Vitis, Laura. "'My Favourite Genre Is Missing People': Exploring How Listeners Experience True Crime Podcasts in Australia." *International Journal for Crime, Justice and Social Democracy*, advance online publication. https://doi.org/10.5204/ijcjsd.2362.

Vronsky, Peter. *Sons of Cain: A History of Serial Killers from the Stone Age to the Present*. New York: Berkley, 2018.

Wallace, Richard. *Jack the Ripper "Lighthearted Friend."* Melrose: Gemini Press, 1996.

Walters, Elizabeth. "Netflix Originals: The Evolution of True Crime Television." *The Velvet Light Trap* 88 (2021): 25–37.

Warlow, Richard, creator. *Ripper Street*. Tiger Aspect Productions, Lookout Point, 2012–2016.

Warwick, Alexandra, and Martin Willis, editors. *Jack the Ripper: Media Culture History*. Manchester: Manchester University Press, 2007.

Watson, Michelle. "Adnan Syed Asks Maryland Supreme Court to Review Lower Court's Ruling That Reversed His Vacated Murder Conviction." CNN, May 24, 2003. https://www.cnn.com/2023/05/24/us/adnan-syed-conviction-maryland-supreme-court-review/index.html.

Wescott, Tom. *The Bank Holiday Murders: The True Story of the First Whitechapel Murders*. Crime Confidential Press, 2014.

Wilding, John. *Jack the Ripper Revealed*. London: Constable, 1993.

Williams, Paul. *Jack the Ripper Suspects: The Definitive Guide and Encyclopedia*. Toronto: Vronsy Parker Publications, 2018.

Williams, Tony, with Humphrey Price. *Uncle Jack: The True Identity of Jack the Ripper—Britain's Most Notorious Murderer—Revealed at Last*. London: Orion Books, 2005.

Wilson, Colin, and Robin Odell. *Jack the Ripper: Summing up and verdict*. London: Bantam Press, 1987.

Wilson, V. J. "1888 (Jack the Ripper—A Factual Account)." https://music.apple.com/us/album/1888-jack-the-ripper-a-factual-account/199319963.

Wolf, A.P. *Jack the Myth: A New Look at the Ripper*. London: Robert Hale, 1993.

Woodhall, Edwin T. *Jack the Ripper or When London Walked in Terror*. London: Mellifont, 1937. Limited facsimile edition P & D Riley.,1997.

Woods, Paul, and Gavin Baddeley. *Saucy Jack: The Elusive Ripper*. Hersham: Ian Allan, 2009.

Index

Abberline, Frederick 18, 42, 45, 109, 110, 111
Abrahamsen, David 65–66, 176
Actors Scene Unseen 133
adversarial trial system 20, 94, 96, 139–140, 152, 155, 169, 176
AIDS *see* HIV/AIDS
alcoholism 3, 7, 8, 9, 27, 56, 65, 122, 167
Aldgate East 125
Alexander, Karl 114–116
American Ripper 96
America's Most Wanted 92, 94–95, 149, 150, 158, 164, 172
Anderson, Sir Robert 44–45, 49
antisemitism 26, 28, 39, 122, 163
Autumn of Terror 1, 2, 4, 6, 15, 18, 19, 20, 21, 23, 24, 25, 26, 33, 35, 38, 39, 43, 58, 59, 64, 72, 78, 83, 88, 91, 99, 109, 113, 120, 122, 126, 127, 144, 148, 150, 159, 161, 163, 166, 168, 170, 171, 172, 174, 179
Autumn of Terror: Jack the Ripper, His Crimes and Times 83
the Avenger 102, 103–104, 116, 175
Avery, Steven 142

Bad Women: The Ripper Retold 146
Bain, Gracie 159
Barlow, Detective 107–108
Barnardo, Thomas 33
Barnett, Joseph 10, 11, 22, 33, 110, 165
Barrett, Michael 70–72
Báthory, Elizabeth 113
Batman 116
Beadle, William (author) 78
Beadle, William (murderer) 154
"Beadle Narrative" *see* "A Narrative of the Life of William Beadle"
Begg, Paul 35, 81, 82, 83, 106, 119, 122
Behavioral Analysis Unit (BAU) 17, 18, 48–49, 50, 53, 55, 56, 113, 173

Behavioral Science Unit (BSU) *see* Behavioral Analysis Unit (BAU)
Bennett, John 35, 81, 82, 83, 106, 119, 122
Berg, Alan 130
Berkowitz, David 48, 65
Bernardo, Paul 178
Berner Street 125
Bianchi, Kenneth 64
Bill of Rights 139
Bloch, Robert 112–114, 161
bloodhounds 30, 34, 46
Bond, Dr. Thomas 15, 44, 49, 54
Booth, Charles 3
Booth, William 3, 121
Brady, Ian 178
Brewer, J.F. 101
Bruzzi, Stella 98, 148
Die Büchse der Pandora 129–130, 132
"Buffalo Bill" 55
Bugliosi, Vincent 49, 152–153
Bulling, Tom 37
Bundy, Ted 49, 50, 92, 99, 106, 113, 117, 175
Buono, Angelo 64
Burgess, Ann 48–49, 173, 175

C-SPAN 94
Campbell, Eddie 109–111
the Canonical Five 1, 2, 4, 5–11, 12, 14, 26, 33, 37, 43, 46, 51, 59, 70, 71, 75, 80, 81, 83, 84, 86, 89, 91, 97, 98, 105, 106, 108, 112, 114, 119, 123, 151, 157, 162, 166
Capote, Truman 49
Carmody, John 112–113, 114
casebook.org 144, 145, 146, 149, 172
The Cases That Haunt Us 15
Centastage Performance Group 133
Central News Agency 10, 35, 36, 37
Chapman, Annie 5, 7–8, 28, 44, 62, 64, 72, 83, 97, 99, 105, 106, 110, 124, 126, 164, 167

195

Index

Chapman, John 7, 8
Chicago 112, 113
City of London *see* London
Clarence: Was He Jack the Ripper? 61
Cleveland Street scandal 42
Coles, Francis 14, 42
The Complete History of Jack the Ripper 84
The Complete Jack the Ripper 77, 83
Conan Doyle, Sir Arthur 104, 105, 124
Connelly, Mary Ann 12, 13
Conversations With a Killer: The Ted Bundy Tapes 99
Conway, Thomas 9
Cornwell, Patricia 5, 47, 63, 67, 68, 69–70, 71, 75, 78, 80, 81, 85–86, 95, 96, 100, 167
Court TV 94
Crawford, Jack 49, 173
criminal profiling *see* profiling
Crippin, Dr. Hawley Harvey 42
Crook, Ann Elizabeth 107, 111
Cross, Charles Allen 6
CSI 68, 93, 119, 140, 164, 169
the CSI effect 141, 169
Cullen, Tom 83, 84
The Curse Upon Mitre Square 101

Dahmer, Jeffrey 52, 61, 64, 67, 173
Daily Telegraph 25
The Dark Histories Podcast 146
Days of My Years 43–44
"Dear Boss" letter 35–36, 37, 38, 162
The Deliberate Stranger 50, 175
Depp, Johnny 110
Dew, Walter 42–43, 45
The Diary of Jack the Ripper 71
Dickens, Charles 147
Disney Channel 175
DNA 47, 54, 63, 67, 68, 69, 70, 75, 85, 86, 170
Doctor, Tory 133
"Dr. Stanley" 58–59, 60, 61, 65, 73, 74, 110
dos Santos, Silvio Jose 130
doss house 3, 4, 32, 37
Double Event 10, 36, 59, 125
Douglas, John 15, 48, 49, 53–56, 173, 175
Druitt, Montague John 43, 44, 56, 64, 65, 109
Dutfield's Yard 9

East End 1, 2–5, 6, 11, 19, 21, 23, 25, 26, 27, 28, 29, 30, 31, 32, 33, 34, 35, 40, 52, 59, 63, 66, 67, 72, 73, 74, 75, 77, 101, 106, 110, 117, 119, 120, 121, 122, 123, 124, 132, 136, 151, 162, 163, 165, 171
Eddowes, Catherine 2, 4, 5, 8, 9–10, 13, 15, 36, 37, 40, 47, 48, 59, 65, 68, 73, 85, 99, 105, 106, 125, 128, 131, 151, 167
Edwards, Russell 47, 67–69, 70, 71, 75, 85
Efron, Zac 175
Egger, Steven 17, 26
1888 (Jack the Ripper: A Factual Account) 133
Engel, Erich 130
English National Opera 133
Erdgeist 129–130
Evans, Stuart 68
execution sermons 49, 135–139, 140, 154, 169, 170
Extremely Wicked, Shockingly Evil and Vile 175

Facebook 141
The Fallen: A Tale of Jack the Ripper 133
"fallen women" 4, 127
Fay, Fairy 11–12, 123
FBI 13, 15, 17, 18, 24, 38, 39, 48, 49, 50–52, 53–56, 65, 66, 67, 69, 101, 113, 150, 164, 166, 173, 174, 175, 178
Feminist Jack the Ripper Tour 124
Fifty Shades 117
fingerprinting 46, 47, 127, 170
The Five: The Untold Lives of the Women Killed by Jack the Ripper 80, 84, 124, 134, 151, 152
Foster, Jodie 49, 55
Fox, Emilia 96
France 11, 43, 48, 156
Freemasons 62, 63, 65, 80, 87, 102, 107, 107–111
From Hell (film) 62, 110–111, 113, 116
From Hell (graphic novel) 62, 109–110, 113
"From Hell" letter 36
Fuller, Jean Overton 63, 88

Gacy, John Wayne 52, 64, 67
gay panic 67
George Yard 12
Glenn, Scott 55
Goddard, Calvin 48
Goldberg, Joe 117
Gorman, Joseph 62, 63, 108; *see also* Sickert, Joseph "Hobo"
"Gotham by Gaslight" (comic) 116
Gotham by Gaslight (film) 117
Graham, Heather 110

Graham, Will 104
Grey, Christian 117
Gull, Sir William 62, 63, 107, 109, 111, 113

Hanbury Street 7, 124, 126
Harkness, Margaret 101
Harmon, Mark 50, 175
Harrison, Michael 61, 62, 64
Harrison, Shirley 71, 86
Hays Code 104
Hayward, Claire 128
Hazelwood, Roy 53
Hearst, William Randolph 21
Heinrich, Edward Oscar 48
Helter Skelter 49, 152, 154
Hindley, Myra 178
History Channel 96
History's Greatest Mysteries 100
Hitchcock, Alfred 46, 103–104, 116, 175
HIV/AIDS 52, 66, 174
Hollis, Sir Guy 112–113
Holmes, H.H. 95–96, 100
Holmes, Sherlock 44, 48, 102, 104–107, 116, 164
Holmolka, Karla 178
Holt, Dr. William 132
homosexual 42, 61, 64–66, 75
homosexual overkill 52, 61, 64, 75
Hopkins, Anthony 55
House, Robert 53
Howells, Martin 79, 89
Hughes Brothers 110, 116
Hutchinson, George 15
Hvem Var Jack the Ripper? 58

In Cold Blood 49
In Darkest London 101
Instagram 141
International Working Men's Education Club 9
Ipswich 138

Jack—the Musical: The Ripper Pursued 133
Jack the Ripper (BBC, 1973) 107
Jack the Ripper: A Bibliography and Review of the Literature 77
Jack the Ripper: A New Theory 46, 59–61
Jack the Ripper and the Case for Scotland Yard's Prime Suspect 53, 68
Jack the Ripper: CSI: Whitechapel 119, 126
Jack the Ripper in Fact and Fiction 26, 83

Jack the Ripper Museum 128
Jack the Ripper; or, When London Walked in Terror 59–60
Jack the Ripper: Revealed 64–65
Jack the Ripper Suspects: The Definitive Guide and Encyclopedia 16
Jack the Ripper: The American Collection 71
Jack the Ripper: The Case Reopened 97
Jack the Ripper: The Final Solution 62, 74, 77, 108
Jack the Ripper: The Forgotten Victims 81, 106
Jack the Ripper: The Hand of a Woman 60, 72
Jack the Ripper: The Musical 133
Jack the Ripper: The Whitechapel Musical 133
Jack the Ripper: The Women of Whitechapel 133, 134
Jackie the Ripper 146
James, E.L. 117
Jan, Katrina 117
Jekyll and Hyde 29
Jennings, Thomas 170
Jew 3, 26, 28, 43, 44, 66, 67, 83, 122, 163, 174, 178
Jones, Elwin 107

Kaczynski, Ted 36
Kelly, Alexander 77
Kelly, John 4, 9–10, 131
Kelly, Mary Jane 5, 10–11, 13, 15, 22, 26, 33, 42, 43, 46, 47, 56, 57, 58–59, 61, 62, 63, 64–65, 72, 73, 74, 75, 83, 88, 99, 106, 107, 108, 109–110, 114, 119, 123, 131, 156, 165, 167, 168
Kemper, Ed 48
Kent, Clark 50
Kepnes, Caroline 117
Ketch, Jack 103
Kidney, Michael 8–9
King Edward VIII 64
Knight, Stephen 62–63, 64, 74, 75, 77, 108, 109
Koenig, Sarah 143, 147–150, 153, 154, 155, 156–157, 158, 160
Kosminski, Aaron 26, 43, 44, 47, 53, 68, 127
Krawczyk-Żywko, Lucyna 128, 129

Lambeth Workhouse 6
Landsteiner, Karl 47
Larkins, Edward Knight 82
Larson, Erik 42

Index

Leather Apron 7, 26, 28; *see also* Pizer, John
Lecter, Hannibal 104
Lee, Hae Min 147, 148, 156
Lees, Robert James 109–110
less-dead 26, 27
Lestrade, Inspector 107
letters to the editor 18, 23, 27, 29–35, 37, 38, 41, 120, 128, 132, 144, 145, 148, 162, 164, 171
The Lighter Side of My Official Life 44–45
Lipski, Israel 67
Littlechild Letter 70, 146
Llewellyn, Dr. Rees Ralph 6
Lloyd, John 107
Locard, Edmond 48
the Lodger (character) 102, 103, 110, 112, 175
The Lodger (film, 1932) 103, 104
The Lodger (novel, 1913) 46, 102
"The Lodger" (short story, 1911) 102
The Lodger: A Story of the London Fog 46, 103–104, 116, 175
"lodger" theory 28–29
London 1, 2, 11, 22, 25, 27, 29, 31, 35, 40, 55, 97, 102, 112, 113, 114, 120, 122, 125, 129, 130, 162, 163, 164
London, Jack 121
London Dungeon 132
London Hospital 3, 12
Look Up London 124
Louhelainen, Dr. Jari 68, 69, 70
Lowndes, Marie Belloc 46, 102, 103, 175
Lulu 129–131, 132–133
Lusk, George 36, 40
Lynch, Ross 175

Macnaghten, Sir Melville 43–44, 45, 46
Macnaghten Memoranda 43–44, 68, 146
Madame Tussaud's 126, 127, 128, 132–133
Madame Tussaud's Chamber of Horrors 126
Making a Murderer 94, 99, 100, 142, 144, 150, 153, 158, 171
male gaze 98
Manson, Charles 117, 152–153
Manson Family 49, 153
Marsh, Laura 96, 99
Maryland Supreme Court 147
Matters, Leonard 46, 58–59, 80
Maybrick, Florence 73, 178
Maybrick, James 70–72, 74, 86, 178
Maybrick, Michael 86

McCormick, Donald 31
McKenzie, Alice 13, 42
Menges, Jonathan 145
#MeToo 124
Metropolitan Police 14, 18, 36, 41, 44, 164, 171
Metropolitan Police Files 70
midwife 47, 60–61, 65, 74, 82
Miller, Florence Fenwick 31, 40, 162
Miller's Court 10, 75, 119
Mindhunter 48
Miranda Warning 139
Mitre Square 9, 10, 47, 68, 101, 105, 125, 131
Monk, Adrian 164
Monster 52
Moore, Alan 109–111
Morris, John 60, 72
motive 11, 16, 17, 24, 25, 28, 29, 30, 34, 37, 39, 58, 60, 61, 64, 65, 66, 72, 73, 74, 75, 82, 93, 101, 105, 110, 120, 133, 139, 140, 166, 168, 169, 173, 174, 176, 177
Mudgett, Herman Webster *see* Holmes, H. H.
Mudgett, Jeff 95–96, 100
Murder and Madness: The Secret Life of Jack the Ripper 65
Murder by Decree 107
Murdle 162
Muusmann, Carl 58
My Friend Dahmer 175
Mylett, Rose 13, 42
The Mystery of Jack the Ripper 46, 58–59
MythBusters 93

"A Narrative of the Life of William Beadle" 154, 176
National Library of Wales 72
NBC's *Hannibal* 104
NCIS 164
Netflix 48, 99
Netley, John 107, 109
New York 30, 115, 117
The New Yorker 49
newspapers 2, 5, 6, 10, 13, 18, 20, 21, 22–40, 42, 45, 46, 48, 49, 52, 57, 58, 59, 83, 103, 104, 107, 109, 116, 120, 121, 123, 124, 128, 131, 140, 141, 144, 145, 148, 161, 162, 163, 166, 168–173, 176
Ng, Charles 64
Nichols, Mary Ann "Polly" 5, 6–7, 8, 11, 13, 33, 40, 62, 99, 106, 110, 123, 167
Nichols, William 6–7, 8, 33, 40
Nilsen, Dennis 52
Novello, Ivor 103–104, 175

Odell, Robin 26, 30, 74, 77, 79, 80, 81, 83, 84, 89
Olshaker, Mark 48
Ostrog, Michael 43, 44
Othering 26, 27, 39, 52, 57, 66, 75, 80, 122, 127, 137, 142, 163, 166, 167, 174, 175

Pall Mall Gazette 24
Paul, Adolf 102
philanthropists 33, 34
Phillips, Dr. George Bagster 8
Pinchin Street 14
"Pinchin Street torso" 13–14
Pizer, John 7, 26, 28
Plummer, Christopher 107
podcasts 20, 80, 84, 99, 100, 140, 142, 144, 145, 146, 147–160, 172
Poirot, Hercule 164
Police Act of 1890 164
Portrait of a Killer: Jack the Ripper— Case Closed 63, 80
Potter, Beatrix 121
Prince Albert 65
Prince Albert Victor 16, 42, 61, 62, 63, 64, 65, 66, 107, 110, 111
Prince Eddy *see* Prince Albert Victor
Prince Jack 61–62
the *Princess Alice* 8, 11, 156
Psycho 113, 116
psychological profiling *see* profiling
profiling 15, 18, 24, 38, 39, 49–50, 52, 55, 173
prostitute 5, 12, 26, 54, 88, 89, 123, 130, 151, 166; *see also* sex work, selling sex
Puritan execution sermons 49; *see also* execution sermons
Puritans 135, 136, 169

Queen Victoria 62, 64, 74, 108

Random House 49
The Real Jack the Ripper: The Secret Life of Prisoner 1167 87
Reddit 149, 155, 171; *see also* subreddit
Ressler, Robert 48, 173, 175
revenge 59, 60, 74, 82, 177
Richardson, J. Hall 25
Ripper File 62, 107, 108
Ripper letters 16, 35–38, 40, 47, 53, 56, 63, 67, 68, 78, 85
Ripper Museum 2, 128
Ripper Street 117
Ripper: The Secret Life of Walter Sickert 63
Ripper Tours 2
Ripperana 77

Ripperature: Building the Myth 159
Rippercast 145, 146
Ripperologist 77
Ripperologists 19, 63, 69, 77–90, 101, 146, 152, 164
The Ripper's Victims in Print: The Rhetoric of Portrayals Since 1929 124, 151
Robinson, Arthur J. 32
Robinson, Bruce 85–86, 151
Rodgers, Esther 137–139, 141, 142
the Royal Conspiracy 61, 64, 111
Rubenhold, Hallie 8, 80, 81, 84, 89, 124, 134, 146, 151–152
Rule, Ann 49–50, 92, 106
Rumbelow, Donald 77, 83
Ryder, Stephen P. 144

Salvation Army 3, 121
San Francisco 114
Scarpetta, Kay 63
Schmid, David 127
Scotland Yard 10, 36, 45
selling sex 4, 10, 12, 33, 74, 152, 165, 168
Seltzer, Mark 16, 17
Serial 20, 143, 147–150, 153, 154, 155, 156–157, 158, 159, 171, 172
serial killer 13, 17, 18, 24, 29, 38, 39, 48, 49, 50–53, 55, 56, 58, 60, 64, 65, 66, 67, 69, 71, 73, 75, 81, 87, 95, 102, 104, 105, 109, 111, 114, 117, 122, 135, 146, 150, 161, 165, 166, 173, 174, 175, 176, 177, 178
sex work 3, 4, 5, 6, 7, 8, 12, 25, 26, 27, 31, 51, 58, 59, 60, 73, 74, 75, 80, 82, 84, 89, 91, 108, 110, 111, 124, 127, 129, 130, 131, 132, 133, 151, 165, 166, 167, 168, 177
Sheldon, Neal Stubbings 81
Shipman, Harold 73
Sickert, Joseph "Hobo" 107–108
Sickert, Walter 47, 63, 67, 86, 95, 96, 100, 107
Sickert and the Ripper Crimes: 1888 Ripper Murders and the Artist Walter Richard Sickert 63
The Silence of the Lambs (film) 49, 150, 165, 173
The Silence of the Lambs (novel) 39
Sixth Amendment 139
Skinner, Keith 79, 89
slumming 2, 19, 29, 119, 120–122, 123, 131, 151
Smith, Emma Elizabeth 12, 123
Spiering, Frank 61–62
The Staircase 145
Star Trek: The Original Series 113–114
Starling, Clarice 173
Steele, Anastasia 117

Stephen, James Kenneth 61, 64, 65, 66
Stephenson, Leslie John 114–116
Stevenson, John Leslie *see* Stephenson, Leslie John
Stewart, William 45–46, 47, 59–61, 80
Stowell, Thomas E.A. 61, 63
The Stranger Beside Me 50, 92, 106
Stride, Elizabeth 5, 8–9, 11, 14, 15, 33, 40, 62, 80, 83, 99, 110, 125, 156, 166. 167
Stride, John Thomas 8
A Study in Scarlet 104
A Study in Terror 105, 106
subreddit 98, 100, 148, 156
Sugden, Philip 78, 79, 81, 84
Swanson, Donald 44, 45
Swanson, James 44
Swanson Marginalia 44, 70
Sweden 8
Syed, Adnan 145–150, 153, 154, 155, 156–157

Tabram, Martha 12, 13, 112, 123
Tchkersoff, Olga 60, 61, 65, 74
Thematic Aptitude Test 16
Theron, Charlize 52
They All Love Jack: Busting the Ripper 85
This American Life 148
This Is Spinal Tap 133
Thunderstruck 42
TikTok 141
Time After Time 114–116, 117
The Times 25, 28, 29, 30
TourScanner 124
Tower of London 125
trial reports 49, 141, 170, 176
true crime 1, 16, 17, 19, 20, 34, 49, 50, 55, 56, 77, 79, 87, 88, 89, 92, 93, 94, 96, 97, 98, 99, 100, 101, 106, 107, 109, 111, 124, 129, 134, 135, 140, 142, 143, 144, 146, 147, 148, 149, 150, 152, 153, 154, 155, 156, 157, 158, 159, 167, 168, 171, 172, 176, 177
Tully, James 87
Turner, Cora 42
Twitter 141

Uhlenhuth test 46
Unabomber Manifesto 36
Uncle Jack: The True Identity of Jack the Ripper—Britain's Most Notorious Murderer 72
University of Arkansas 159
University of Birmingham 117

Unsolved Mysteries 150
Uppskäraren 102

The Victims of Jack the Ripper 81
Vronsky, Peter 49

walking tours 119, 122–126, 161, 163, 166
Warren, Sir Charles 30, 35
Watkins, PC Edward 9, 48
Watson, John 105, 107
Watt (BBC,1973) 107–108
wax museums 19, 126–129
waxworks 19, 126–129
Wedekind, Frank 129–130, 132
Wells, H. G. 114–116
West, Fred 178
West, Rosemary 178
West End 125
Whitechapel 2, 3, 12, 13, 16, 21, 22, 23, 24, 25, 27, 28, 32, 39, 42, 46, 47, 54, 59, 72, 74, 86, 96, 104, 106, 112, 114, 119, 122, 123, 124, 125, 126, 131, 132, 160, 162, 163, 165
Whitechapel 117
Whitechapel Society 145
Whitechapel Vigilance Committee 36, 105
"Whitehall Mystery" 14
Wild, Dr. Robert 71
Wilding, John 64–65, 66, 75
Wilkins, PC 15
Williams, Mary Elizabeth Anne Hughes "Lizzie" 72–73, 74, 178
Williams, Sir John 72–73, 178
Williams, Paul 15–16
Williams, Tony 72–73
Willis, Martin 104–105
Wilson, Colin 62, 77
Wilson, David 97
Wilson, VJ 133
"Wolf in the Fold" 113–114, 115
Woodhall, Edwin T. 59–60, 80, 82
workhouse 3, 4, 6, 8, 12, 123
wrongful conviction 99, 155, 171
Wuornos, Aileen 52

X 141
xenophobia 37, 163

"Yours Truly, Jack the Ripper" 112–113, 114, 115
YouTube 141

Zoom 119, 124

www.ingramcontent.com/pod-product-compliance
Lightning Source LLC
Chambersburg PA
CBHW032044300426
44117CB00009B/1186